**Jackson School Publications
in International Studies**

Jackson School Publications
in International Studies

Senator Henry M. Jackson was convinced that the study of the history, cultures, political systems, and languages of the world's major regions was an essential prerequisite for wise decision making in international relations. In recognition of his deep commitment to higher education and advanced scholarship, this series of publications has been established through the generous support of the Henry M. Jackson Foundation, in cooperation with the Henry M. Jackson School of International Studies and the University of Washington Press.

Days of Defeat and Victory

Yegor Gaidar

TRANSLATED BY JANE ANN MILLER

FOREWORD BY MICHAEL McFAUL

UNIVERSITY OF WASHINGTON PRESS

Seattle and London

The translation of this book
was supported by a generous grant from the
Henry M. Jackson Foundation.

Originally published by Vagrius Publishers, Moscow, in 1996

Library of Congress Cataloging-in-Publication Data
Gaidar, E. T. (Egor Timurovich)
[Dniporazhenii i pobed. English]
Days of defeat and victory / Yegor Gaidar ; translated by Jane Ann Miller ;
foreword by Michael McFaul.
p. cm. — (Jackson School publications in international studies)
Includes index.
ISBN 0-295-97823-6 (alk. paper)
1. Gaædar, E. T. (Egor Timurovich)   2. Politicians—Russia (Federation)—
Biography.   3. Russia (Federation)—Politics and government—1991.
4. Russia (Federation)—Economic policy—1991.   I. Title.   II. Series.
DK510.766G35 A3 1999
947.086′092—dc21
[B]   99-052020

But you are not obliged to tell
Your victories from defeats.

Boris Pasternak

Contents

Foreword

Michael McFaul

August 1991 was a momentous month in the history of Russia—filled with both joy and fear. For three days, conservative forces from the Soviet government attempted to roll back the political and economic changes initiated by Mikhail Gorbachev. While Gorbachev was on vacation in the Crimea, the State Committee for the Emergency Situation (GKChP) announced on August 19 that they had assumed responsibility for governing the country. Gorbachev, they claimed, was ill and would return to head this Emergency Committee after his recovery. In making the announcement, the Committee justified their actions as a defensive

---

Michael McFaul is an assistant professor of political science and a Hoover fellow at Stanford University, and a senior associate at the Carnegie Endowment for International Peace. His books include *Russia's 1996 Presidential Election: The End of Polarized Politics* (1997) and *Privatization, Conversion, and Enterprise Reform in Russia* (1995).

response to "extremist forces" and "political adventurers" who aimed to destroy the Soviet state and economy. To enforce their emergency measures, they sent tanks to occupy strategic positions in Moscow.

Throughout most of Russian and Soviet history, the exercise of force by the state has ended tragically for those in support of change, reform, or progress. This time, however, the reformers struck back. Russian president Boris Yeltsin and his allies, in an umbrella organization of democratic forces called Democratic Russia, spearheaded the resistance to the palace coup attempt. Yeltsin's strategy was simple. As the elected president of Russia, he called on Russian citizens—civilian and military alike—to obey his decrees and not those of the Emergency Committee. As in 1917, two independent governments each claimed sovereign authority over the same territory.

Yeltsin's appeal served to mobilize popular resistance to the coup attempt on the streets of Moscow. Hundreds of supporters assembled outside the White House only a few hours after receiving news of the coup. By the following day, Democratic Russia had organized two massive demonstrations at which tens of thousands of Muscovites defied Red Army regiments to defend their democratically elected leaders and institutions.

The Soviet putsch quickly unraveled. The organizers of the Emergency Committee had grossly overestimated their power and underestimated the fortitude of Russia's democratic forces. For more than a year before the August 1991 coup attempt, politics in Russia had been polarized between those determined to preserve the Soviet ancien régime and those seeking to destroy it. Several times during this period, moments of compromise between the two camps led many to hope that a negotiated transition was possible. Suddenly, one day in August, members of the conservative camp in this bipolar political environment moved suddenly to regain their former hegemony over the Soviet system. Three days later, their attempt collapsed.

The outcome of the August 1991 putsch dramatically and fundamentally changed the course of Soviet and Russian history. Even for a country blessed and cursed with a history of pivotal turning points, this

moment ranks as one of the most important. For the first time since the
Bolsheviks seized power in 1917, Soviet authorities had moved to quell
societal opposition in Russia and failed. However fleeting in time and lo-
calized in place, this successful defiance of Soviet authorities altered the
balance of power between the ancien régime and its challengers in favor
of the latter.

The moment was euphoric. For many Russian citizens, perhaps no
time is remembered with greater fondness than the initial days after that
failed August coup.[1] On the third day of resistance, when victory was already at hand, a chant of "for yourself" (*za sebya*) erupted among the
defenders of the White House. This moment was as much a triumph for
the individual Russian citizen as it was a political victory for Yeltsin and
the democratic leaders who organized the resistance. As Gaidar writes in
this book, he remembers being proud of his people for the first time ever,
and compares the August euphoria to Russia's last popular victory over
tyranny in February 1917. Others thought that the August moment offered Russia an opportunity to become a "normal" country at last. Even
Gorbachev belatedly recognized that there "occurred a cardinal break
with the totalitarian system and a decisive move in favor of the democratic forces" after August 1991.[2]

In the heady days immediately following the failed coup, Russia's reformers took advantage of their windfall political power to arrest coup
plotters, storm the Communist Party headquarters, and tear down the
statue of Felix Dzerzhinsky, the hated founder of the modern-day KGB.
But what to do next? As in all revolutions, destruction of the ancien
régime came first; construction of new political, economic, and social orders in the vacuum created by the Soviet collapse would be much more
difficult. Although August 1991 may have signaled the end of both Communist rule and the Soviet state, it remained unclear what kind of political regime, economic system, or society should or could fill the void. Even
the borders of the state were uncertain. Especially for those in power, euphoria surrounding the closing of the Soviet past was quickly overshad-
owed by the uncertainty of Russia's future.

In August 1991, Russian leaders faced three extraordinary challenges simultaneously—how to dismantle an empire, how to build a market economy, and how to consolidate a democratic polity. The most urgent item on the victors' agenda was to delineate the very boundaries of the state. Russia was not a sovereign state, as it had no sovereign borders, no sovereign currency, no sovereign army, and weak, ill-defined governmental institutions. Even after the December 1991 agreement to dissolve the Soviet Union and create the Commonwealth of Independent States, Russia's political, territorial, and psychological locations were still uncertain. Throughout the former Soviet Union, tens of millions of ethnic Russians became ex-patriots overnight at the same time that ethnic minorities within the Russian Federation pushed for their own independence.

The task of market reform was equally daunting. By August 1991, the failure of the Soviet command system and Gorbachev's attempts to reform it had become apparent as shortages for basic goods haunted all cities, inflation soared, trade stopped, and production declined. Before August 1991, Yeltsin and his allies could blame these economic ills on the Soviet government. Suddenly, Russia's revolutionary challengers were given both the opportunity and the burden of pursuing economic transformation.

At the same time, Russia's leaders had to create a new political system. On this front some progress had already been made within the Russian Republic before August 1991 with the free and fair elections of Russian parliamentarians in the spring of 1990, Yeltsin's election as president in June 1991, and the expansion of individual liberties under Gorbachev's political liberalization. Yet many of the rules of the game of Russia's new polity were still ambiguous, uncodified, and therefore subject to constant manipulation, especially since no new Russian constitution had been ratified. The division of power between the executive branch and the legislature and the balance of rights and responsibilities between the federal and regional governments were especially vague.

In tackling this triple transition, Russia's leaders had few *relevant* institutions to carry over from the Soviet system. In many transitions to democracy in Latin America, Southern Europe, and East Central Europe, past democratic institutions, suspended during authoritarian rule, were reactivated—a process much more efficient than creating new institutions from scratch.[3] Russian leaders had no such democratic institutions to resurrect. Likewise, even the most radical economic reform programs undertaken in the West—including Roosevelt's New Deal in the 1930s—took place in countries with experience in markets, private property, and the rule of law. In contrast to the transitions from communism in Eastern Europe, even the memory of capitalist institutions had been extinguished within the collective mind-set of Russian citizens after a century of the command economy.

But the legacy from the Soviet era was even worse than a clean slate. Russian leaders had to tackle the problems of empire, economic reform, and political change with many of the practices and institutions of the Soviet system still in place. Economic transactions based on authority rather than markets, a gigantic military-industrial complex, massive state corruption and a large second economy, no rule of law, and poor work habits were just some of the inheritances that impeded market reform. Moreover, the shadow of the past extended far into the post-Soviet era because Russia's revolutionaries ultimately refrained from using violence to achieve their goals of political, economic, and state transformation.[4] This strategic decision allowed many Soviet institutions as well as the organizations created and privileged by these institutions to linger. Yeltsin and Russia's revolutionaries, therefore, did not enjoy a tabula rasa in designing new market and democratic institutions in 1991. The Soviet regime as a whole imploded in 1991, but constituent elements of the old system remained in place.

Russian reformers also had to deal with the ambiguous balance of power between political actors who favored reform and those who opposed it. In contrast to several East European countries, consensus did not exist in Russia in 1991 about the need for market and democratic reform. On the contrary, Russian elites and society were divided and polarized.

In August 1991, those political forces that favored preservation of the old Soviet political and economic order appeared weak and disorganized. They soon recovered from this embarrassing moment, however, and organized within the Russian Congress of People's Deputies, in regional governments (both in local soviets and in executive offices), and on the streets to demonstrate their power. On the other side of the barricade, those in favor of reform looked invincible immediately following the coup attempt. But this anti-Communist coalition quickly fell apart after the Soviet Union collapsed.

Given the magnitude of change needed and the existing impediments to achieving it, ideas and leadership for beginning the construction phase of Russia's revolution were scarce in the fall of 1991. Only weeks after staring down the coup attempt, Yeltsin retreated to a summer home in the Crimea for three weeks, allegedly unable to deal with the responsibilities of arresting a collapsing state and economy. As fall turned to winter, many feared the worst—starvation, anarchy, and civil war.

Economic reform was most salient. Because Soviet collapse had developed a momentum of its own, political reforms could be delayed, but the economy needed immediate attention. Soviet gold and hard currency reserves were depleted, the budget deficit had ballooned to 20 percent of GDP, money was abundant but goods were scarce, production had stopped, and trade had all but halted.[5] Experts predicted starvation throughout Russia, prompting Western governments to ship in emergency food supplies.

Given these conditions, a consensus quickly crystallized regarding the necessity of radical economic reform. Within the Russian government, no one in the fall of 1991 cautioned against going "too fast." Such dissent emerged only later. Russian parliamentary leaders also advocated rapid and comprehensive economic reform measures. Even Ruslan Khasbulatov, the new chairman of the Russian Congress, advocated radical economic reform. Speaking immediately after the August coup attempt, he reconfirmed his belief in market reforms, warning that it was too early for euphoria, since radical economic reforms had yet to be implemented. He called for creation of an economic system resembling those in "civilized countries" and argued that "the freer the economy is from the influence of the state, then the lesser the bureaucracy is in society."[6]

The urgency regarding the economy was recognized by all. How to respond to the economic crisis engendered more debate. Yeltsin understood that the failed August coup created a window of opportunity for radical reform, emphasizing that "it would be a strategic mistake now if Russia did not find its architect of economic reform."[7] Yeltsin also knew that he himself was not qualified to draft and execute a comprehensive economic reform program.

Throughout the fall of 1991, several candidates and economic teams were discussed, ranging from Yeltsin's conservative former colleagues from Sverdlovsk, such as Yury Skokov and Oleg Lobov, to more liberal and younger economists such as Grigory Yavlinsky and Yegor Gaidar. Khasbulatov and Vice President Aleksandr Rutskoi also aspired to serve as Yeltsin's first post-Communist prime minister. Of all these candidates, Yavlinsky was the most famous and respected. Yeltsin, however, ultimately rejected him and his strategy for several reasons. Regarding policy questions, Yavlinsky advocated maintaining a single economic space, or ruble zone, throughout the former Soviet Union. Yeltsin, while initially supportive of this idea, believed that it was impractical after the dissolution of the USSR. More generally, Yavlinsky was firmly identified with the "500 Days" plan, a project that had seemed radical in the fall of 1990 but appeared dated in the fall of 1991. As Yeltsin recalled in his memoirs, he thought that returning to the "500 Days" plan would be an unwise move politically.[8] Yavlinsky's cooperation with Gorbachev in the spring of 1991 under the rubric of the Grand Bargain—a plan to provide Western aid to the Soviet Union—did not help his reputation with those in the Russian government. Finally, Yavlinsky, it was believed, had no team.

Enter Gaidar. Instead of Yavlinsky, Yeltsin ultimately selected thirty-five-year-old Yegor Gaidar and his team of young economists to head his first post-Soviet government and initiate radical economic reform. Gaidar was an unexpected choice. Before this appointment, he had never held a serious political office. In academic circles he was a well-respected economist who had distinguished himself as economics editor of the journal *Kommunist*, and then in 1990 had begun to reach a wider audience as economics editor at *Pravda*. In the fall of 1991, however, he was not a political figure at all, let alone one at the national level.

Nor did Yeltsin know him personally. The Russian president met Gaidar through his closest adviser at the time, Gennady Burbulis. Burbulis subsequently served as the intermediary between Yeltsin and Gaidar's young reformist government. Leaders of Democratic Russia also lobbied Yeltsin to select Gaidar and urged against Yavlinsky even though Gaidar had not been an active member of the Democratic Russia movement.

In his memoirs, Yeltsin recalls that he admired Gaidar's confidence, candor, and ability to speak plainly. And Gaidar's plan to move swiftly coincided with Yeltsin's approach to economic reform.[9] Though uneducated in the ways of economic policy making, Yeltsin at the time firmly believed that radical change was necessary, and Gaidar promised radical and swift change. Yeltsin also recognized that Gaidar had a coherent and unified team that could execute a reform agenda more effectively than could one individual.[10]

The rest is history and the subject of this book. First as deputy prime minister and later as acting prime minister, Gaidar initiated the most ambitious economic reform program ever attempted in modern times. And he and his government pursued this reform using peaceful methods. His goal was to liberalize prices and trade, achieve macroeconomic stabilization, and privatize property—all within a minimum time frame, earning his plan the unfortunate label "shock therapy."[11]

Gaidar's strategy for economic reform was fiercely debated in both Russia and the West. One major debate centered on the speed of reform—some arguing that Gaidar went too fast, others claiming his pace was too slow. Another debate erupted regarding the sequence of reforms. Should privatization precede liberalization? Should monopolies be broken up before privatization was attempted? No consensus emerged on these questions of timing in either Russia or the West. The politics of economic reform constituted a third major issue of debate, with some analysts arguing that the first post-Soviet Russian government did not pay adequate attention to building a wide societal coalition for economic reform, and others arguing that this government failed to pursue political reforms that might have facilitated the economic reform process.

In this book, Gaidar does not provide definitive answers to those debates, but he does reconstruct honestly and self-critically his thinking and actions concerning these issues during his time in office. In vivid detail, he also highlights the constraints on his decision making, which are often forgotten by those debating the issues safely ensconced in an ivory tower and free of the burdens imposed by reality. In particular, this book explores the difficulties of pursuing economic reform in the context of a collapsing state, an ill-defined political system, an organized opposition to market reforms, and lingering institutional legacies from the Soviet era.

Many in Russia and the West have labeled Gaidar's economic program a total failure. In the West, Gaidar's critics have speculated that "shock therapy" was not suited for the Soviet and Russian condition. In Russia, the attacks against Gaidar have been even more fierce, sometimes blaming him for everything bad that has occurred in the last decade. Even several years after his ouster as acting prime minister, Russians still blamed him for events and developments over which he had no control.

In retrospect, the intensity of these attacks and the degree of responsibility assigned to Gaidar seem out of proportion to the amount of time he had any direct influence over economic policy in Russia. As opposition to Gaidar's reforms grew soon after price liberalization in January 1992, Yeltsin quickly lost faith in his young reformist government. In the spring of 1992, he diluted the team by naming three industrialists as deputy prime ministers. This new "coalition" government no longer shared the same vision of economic reform articulated by Gaidar. Policies emanating from the Russian government became increasingly incoherent. By the end of 1992, Yeltsin acquiesced to the anti-Gaidar coalition in the Russian Congress of People's Deputies and removed

Gaidar as prime minister. Given this coalition government and its short period in office, one might argue that Gaidar's reforms cannot be considered to have failed, because they were never really implemented.

This line of defense, however, is also an oversimplification. As documented throughout this book, Gaidar did make decisions as the architect of Russian economic reform that served to undermine his own agenda. Unlike most of the Soviet and Russian leaders who have published memoirs about this momentous period, Gaidar candidly admits his mistakes. Both his admirers and enemies acknowledge his penchant for speaking honestly and bluntly, and this book remains true to that reputation. To date, there is not a more revealing account of the first years of Russian reform than what is found here.

When Gaidar joined the Yeltsin government, he initially assumed the role of an economic technocrat, advising the politicians about what economic policies should be adopted. To the surprise of many, however, he quickly became a political figure as well, and maintained that profile well after leaving office. Although he was not a leader in Russia's democratic movement before the Soviet collapse, he quickly emerged as one of Russia's leading liberal forces after his removal from office in December 1992. He founded his own political party, Russia's Democratic Choice, which has attempted to represent the voice of Russian liberalism in its darkest hours. In the 1993 parliamentary elections, Gaidar's electoral bloc won only 15 percent of the popular vote. In 1995, Russia's Democratic Choice won less than 4 percent of the popular vote, leading many to conclude that liberalism in Russia was dead and Gaidar's political career in Russia was finished.

These conclusions are premature. Russia is midstream in a political, economic, and social revolution of which the final outcome is still uncertain. How this revolution ends will determine liberalism's fate in Russia and Gaidar's place in history. If the revolution turns sour and Russia rejects markets and democracy, then Russia's contemporary liberals will be remembered as inept leaders and naive idealists. If Russia eventually consolidates a democratic polity and market economy, then Gaidar will be remembered as the father of Russia's market economy, and Russian liberals will earn their place in history as those who started the process of creating a new political and economic system in Russia after the collapse of Soviet communism.

To comprehend either scenario requires a firm understanding of what Gaidar tried to do, what he succeeded in accomplishing, and what he fell short of achieving both in and out of government. There is no better place to begin to acquire such an understanding than this book.

Preface

I began writing this book at the end of January 1996. The Communists had just triumphed in the elections; Yeltsin, who seemed to have completely lost touch with the voters, had seen his ratings drop almost to zero. The possibility that a Zyuganov victory could be averted was faint at best.[1]

I had no illusions about what might await me should the Communists win. All I had to do was skim through any newspaper sympathetic to their cause, and my name was on every enemies list, short or long. I was convinced that this time around the Communist experiment wouldn't last long, but that they would soon manage to ruin the economy, which meant that they would need some enemies of the people to blame for that ruin. I had firmly resolved that, come what may, I wouldn't leave the country. I would not afford the Communists that satisfaction. And I began writing a book. Because later, when everything fell apart, the country would again find itself in that chaotic limbo between a market that couldn't function and commands that couldn't be executed—the same limbo as in 1991. And it would again be necessary to create a base for sustainable development in Russia, grounded in free markets and private property. When that time came, my experience of both victory and defeat would prove useful.

Probably, had I known then just what turn events would actually take in the months ahead, I would have written something else, or perhaps nothing at all. It's a little odd, isn't it, to be composing your memoirs at the age of forty? Now, in the summer of 1996, after Yeltsin's victory in the elections, after rereading my old manuscript, I've decided to go ahead and publish. Working on it has persuaded me of just how many myths have taken root and sprouted over the last five very dramatic years of Russian history—in the press, in the minds of the public, in schoolbooks.

I know those years firsthand, and better than most. And so I have a right, I think, to share my view of what took place. In my previous book, *The State and Evolution* (1994), I tried to investigate the relationship between socialism and Russia's economic history, the reasons for socialism's decline and fall. This time I decided to concentrate on the tumultuous events of the early 1990s.

In my view, what we witnessed then was a revolution—one comparable, in terms of its influence on the historical process, to the French Revolution, the 1917 Russian Revolution, and the Chinese Revolution of 1949. The country saw its economic and political foundations collapse, its socioeconomic structure and its ruling ideology radically change.

The word "revolution" has a romantic ring to it. But a revolution is always a tragedy for a country, for millions of people; it involves enormous sacrifice, and both social and psychological overload. A revolution is by definition a harsh sentence visited upon the elite of the ancien régime, the price extracted for the latter's inability to introduce reforms in time for development to take an evolutionary path. Now, when I leaf through historical accounts of the great revolutions of the past, I'm struck by the obvious parallels to events here in Russia. The unfolding economic crisis in France at the end of the 1780s, for all the obvious differences in relative levels of economic development, is strikingly reminiscent of the collapse of Soviet finance. Having lived through the food supply crisis of the winter of 1991–92, I now have a far better idea of what went on in Russian cities between 1917 and 1921.

One common error made in discussing recent Russian history is a tendency to confuse the key issues being resolved at each of its stages. Without pretending to absolute infallibility, of course, I would like to offer my opinion on how those stages might be viewed.

1985 to 1991: Intensification of the socialist crisis. The chief question is whether the Communist elite will manage to cope with the crisis, move development onto an evolutionary track, and prevent an explosion of social unrest.

August 1991 to October 1993: The revolutionary fall of the old regime and the struggle to stabilize the institutions of the new. The chief question is whether it will be possible to avert a food crisis and a full-scale civil war, to shape the working political institutions of a civil society.

October 1993 to July 1996: Stabilization of the postrevolutionary regime. The chief question is whether it will be possible to stop the unavoidable and powerful counterreform wave set in motion by the hardships of recent years and prevent the breakup of newly formed market and democratic institutions.

July 1996 and after: Restored economic growth grounded in free markets and private property. The chief question is, what sort of capitalism will we end up with—a corrupt, bureaucratic capitalism, whose glaring social inequities give rise to waves of social and political instability, or a civilized capitalism subject to social controls? This choice, it seems to me, will be the pivotal one in Russian politics over the next few years.

Of course the stages I have indicated here are not all that rigid or easily separable. Yet I think it important to single out the key issues; otherwise, the logic of what has transpired is hard to see.

This book does not claim to be either a political-economic analysis of postsocialist change or a study of reform strategies applied in various countries and the results thereof. In it I would merely like to relate how a young scholar from a family of the Moscow intelligentsia was drawn by the whim of fate into the whirlwind of recent Russian history, and how he saw those events. I hope that this will help others understand what my colleagues, my cohorts, and I thought, as well as what we feared, as we planned and implemented the strategy and tactics of Russian market reform.

Days of Defeat
and Victory

Chapter 1

Childhood

If I'm not mistaken, the first question I was asked at the Supreme Soviet of the RSFSR just after my appointment as deputy prime minister of the Russian government sounded something like this: "Well, everybody knows about your grandpa. But just what are *you* planning to do?" Later I had to listen to endless Communist reproaches for my supposed denial of everything my grandfather Arkady Petrovich Gaidar had gone to war for, died for, everything my father, Timur Gaidar, had fought for. I can't help but concede that the history of the country has indeed been oddly intertwined with our family history. For me, Arkady Gaidar had always seemed to exist in two different incarnations. One of these was an inseparable part of sacred Communist lore: there was the Arkady Gaidar detachment, the Arkady Gaidar *druzhina*, the Arkady Gaidar Young Pioneer Camp. At age seventeen Arkady Gaidar commanded a regiment—*Timur and His Team*.[1]

Then there was the other Arkady Gaidar, the one I knew from stories told by my father and my grandmother, and from the books I loved. The

3

first was a sort of Communist saint, a knight without fear, without re-proach, without doubt. The second was a talented and unhappy man, whose life was forever marked by the tragedy of revolution and civil war. This son of an Arzamas schoolteacher was thirteen years old when the tsarist regime in Russia collapsed, and cruel and troubled times set in.[2]

In a divided Russia, the logic of life and heritage propelled him toward the Reds. He firmly believed that the Communist idea meant a bright future for all humankind. At fourteen he went off to war; at fourteen he was wounded for the first time. Six years later, shell-shocked and gravely ill, he was discharged from the Red Army with the rank of regimental commander.

It all sounds very romantic, commanding a regiment at age seventeen. But one has to remember what civil war is. What a terrible fate and what an enormous burden lay behind all the "romance"; how many of your compatriots you yourself killed, and how many were killed by your or-der, albeit in the name of a cause that you thought just. My father would recall how my grandfather always refused to talk about the Civil War. Sometimes, if people really insisted, he might sing an army song from those days. A late diary entry reads, "I dream about the people I killed when I was young, in the war." With such a childhood and such a youth, you might well turn into a misanthrope. But this man, instead, began writing amazingly bright and sunny books.

It sometimes seems to me that, indeed, adult responsibility came upon him too soon. He simply never got much chance to play. Perhaps the book of his I love best is *School*. And when recently I visited his na-tive Arzamas for the first time, I came to love and understand him all the more. I can't be objective about my grandfather's books. In *The Military Secret* I see his relationship with my father, and in *The Blue Cup* I recog-nize my grandmother's lively but rather difficult personality. Of all his books, perhaps the one I'm least fond of is *Timur and His Team*. Timur, after all, is such a painfully good little Communist.

I think that my grandfather, right up to his death in 1941, continued to believe in the same Communist idea for which he had gone to war at age fourteen. But with the passage of time it had become harder and harder for him to find that idea in the images of the real Communist world that surrounded him. My father says that the greatest tragedy of all for my grandfather was the arrest of Tukhachevsky and Blyukher, military leaders he had served under during the Civil War.[3] He could not believe that they were traitors, nor could he believe that the accusations against them were false. He came up with all sorts of fantastic ways to explain it to himself. One remarkable thing is that neither in his prose, nor in his journalistic work, nor in his radio broadcasts did he ever mention Stalin by name. I don't know whether this was deliberate or not. What *was* clear was that Stalin didn't fit into that bright picture of the world that Arkady Gaidar was ready to fight for.

My grandfather's sense of his world was shot through with premonitions of another terrible war soon to come. And so he considered it his duty as a writer to prepare young readers for the grave trials ahead. It would be a fierce fight; they would need all their strength in the struggle against the enemy. It was no time to be wallowing in one's own doubts, serious though they might be. Yet the closer that war came, the more yawning was the gap between what he believed and what he saw in front of him.

My father says that the war was in some sense an escape for my grandfather. It did away with any inner, psychological ambivalence; it divided the world precisely and definitively into friends and mortal enemies; it demanded clear solutions, personal courage, and a readiness to die for the cause you believed in—a readiness unclouded by any doubt over whether or not that cause was just.

My grandfather was killed in October 1941, in a skirmish between his partisan detachment and German National Socialists, the standard Russian term for whom has always been "the Fascists." I cannot fathom how the current heirs to fascism think they can claim any right to Arkady Gaidar's moral legacy. Nor, quite honestly, can I picture my grandfather in postwar Russia, with its oppressive atmosphere of patriotism on parade, its growing anti-Semitism, its pogroms against music and literature.

My father, Timur Gaidar, had a singular sort of childhood; it was simultaneously interesting and rather sad. On the one hand, he had his famous, talented, endlessly creative father, the prewar Moscow intelligentsia, friends, aquaintances from Koktebel. Among the family's closest friends were the Shilov brothers, the sons of General Shilov and Yelena Sergeevna Bulgakova. The warmth he felt at Mikhail Bulgakov and Yelena Sergeevna's house was, I think, always my father's ideal of what a home should be.[4] On the other hand, there was his parents' early divorce, then his stepfather's arrest, then his mother's.

When the war started, my father was fourteen. Like other teenagers he tried to enlist for the front. Instead came work at a defense plant, then at sixteen the naval academy, then submarine service in the Baltic. This was when the still very young and naive Lieutenant Timur Gaidar wrote a letter to the Party's theoretical journal *Bolshevik*, requesting an explanation of why there were some discrepancies between recent statements by Stalin and Marxist fundamentals. Apparently the letter fell into the hands of someone fairly honest and courageous, or perhaps the name helped. At any rate, fortunately for the young lieutenant, nothing came of it.

By 1952, Timur Gaidar was attending classes in journalism at the Military-Political Academy, and there he met Ariadna Bazhova, a history instructor at the University of the Urals, and daughter of the famous writer Pavel Petrovich Bazhov.[5] On the night before their wedding he professed to her that although he considered Stalin a traitor to Leninist ideals, he nonetheless believed this sacred cause would win out in the end. Picturing how difficult her life would be from now on, Mama cried, but the straitlaced Komsomol girl went ahead and married the senior lieutenant and, as far as I know, never regretted it.

Pavel Petrovich Bazhov's life, his character, were more or less the polar opposite of Arkady Petrovich Gaidar's. If our family inherited from the Gaidar side a taste for adventure, what it got from Pavel Petrovich was tranquil good sense, steadiness. This miner's boy from the Urals had once upon a time approached his schoolteacher and asked for something to read. The teacher gave him the first volume of Pushkin's collected

works and said that when he'd memorized it he could come and get volume two. After Pavel Bazhov had memorized Pushkin's entire collected
works, the teacher decided that the boy had a good head on his shoulders
and deserved a patron. Later came the theological seminary, teaching,
and a long-running passion for collecting the folklore of the Urals.

During the civil war, Bazhov, like Arkady Petrovich, fought on the
side of the Reds. Afterward came family life, seven children, teaching,
journalism. In 1938 he was expelled from the Party and summoned by
the local NKVD. My grandmother, Valentina Alexandrovna, packed a
small suitcase, and my grandfather set out for that all-too-familiar Sverdlovsk address. However, by that time the trail of repressions had led back
to the NKVD itself, and the terrible system had begun to break down.
After hours of sitting in the waiting room, Pavel Petrovich still hadn't had
his audience. Fortunately, he didn't go looking for any higher-ups to explain to him why he'd been brought in but never questioned; instead he
walked out the door, went home to 11 Chapaev Street, and didn't go out
again for a year. His sizable family lived on the teacher's salary brought
home by my grandmother's sister, Natalya Alexandrova, and meanwhile
my grandfather tended the vegetable garden and conjured over his
"baby"—the enormous catalogue of folklore he had compiled during
decades and decades of work.

A little more than a year after all this took place, he read my grandmother and my mother his first stories. The wave of repressions had by
then begun to subside, my grandfather's Party membership was restored,
and soon he became the author of that famous collection of tales *The
Malachite Box*.

A kaleidoscope of my first childhood memories: Cuba, of course, looms
largest. I arrived there in 1962, on the eve of the Cuban missile crisis. I
was six years old. My father was working as a correspondent for *Pravda*,
and had been there during the events at Playa Girón;[6] later he brought
me and mama to join him. My memories of revolutionary Cuba are still
amazingly vivid. Side by side with a still functioning, still intact Ameri-

can tourist culture you saw an unfeigned revolutionary spirit among the victors, and heavily attended demonstrations. There was singing, celebration.

My windows in the Hotel Riomar looked out directly on the Gulf of Mexico; below there was a swimming pool, and beside it an artillery battery. The building that housed diplomats and specialists from Eastern Europe was shelled periodically. Our battery would return fire. From my window I could see one slogan in yellow neon: "The motherland—or death!" And one in blue: "We will be victorious!" Our maid would put her machine gun down in one corner, then pick up her mop.

Offshore, directly opposite, there was always an American reconnaissance vessel. At the height of the missile crisis you could see a haze of smoke in the distance—the American Seventh Fleet. We had guests, friends of my father's, Soviet military officers from the groups stationed there. Sometimes they would take me with them to the barracks and let me climb around on the tanks and armored personnel carriers. Raúl Castro and Ernesto Che Guevara both came to visit. My father took his pistol and went target shooting with Che Guevara.

Leftists from all over the world were terribly interested in Cuba and its fledgling revolution. There were quite a few journalists from socialist countries posted to Havana. The Czechoslovak Telegraph Agency was represented by a good friend of my father's, Jaroslav Bouček. They often argued—I didn't understand what about. But I was great friends with his children Petr and Jaroslav, who were about my age.

I remember one trip with Brian Pollitt, a British economist and son of one of the founders of the British Communist Party, and his wife Penny, in their Land Rover. We were in the northern part of Oriente, one of the wildest parts of the island, when the powerful vehicle ground to a halt, mired in swampy ground. There had been fighting in the region. My father and Brian took a pistol and went for help. They left me the other pistol, to protect the women—my mother and Penny. This was pure family tradition, and I'm convinced that my grandfather, too, would have jumped at this opportunity to give a lesson in bravery. About two

. . . what it got from Pavel Petrovich was tranquil good sense, steadiness."

"If our family inherited from Gaidar a taste for adventure . . .

"We probably have the happiest family I've ever seen."

August 1986. "A discussion of ideologically dangerous issues at the Zmeinaya Gorka seminar. Anatoly Chubais is at my side . . .

. . . just as he would be years later."

1992. "A meeting of Commonwealth of Independent States heads-of-state. The President of Russia is thinking seriously about reforms."

Washington, 1992. With President George Bush at the White House.

Speaking to the Seventh Congress of People's Deputies. "If this is a socially oriented market economy, then pardon me, but Ludwig Erhard must be turning in his grave."

"I want the deputies to understand that we're not about to change our chosen course."

December 1992. Yegor Gaidar and his team. The last photo in the prime minister's office.

March 1993. "Rally in support of Boris Yeltsin. My father and I are in the ranks."

Official reception during Moscow visit by President Bill Clinton.

Launching Russia's Democratic Choice party.

June 1994. The party's first convention.

A quiet moment at the Duma.

hours later they returned; they'd found a village. The villagers brought their oxen and towed the Land Rover out, and that night we slept in a hut under tight-woven gauze nets; the mosquitoes were terrible. I remember it all.

In general, in my family, cowardice, even the hint of cowardice, was considered the deadliest sin of all. For example, when we went swimming and my father dove off the high board, he suggested I do the same. I was hardly thrilled with the suggestion. I jumped anyway and landed in a painful belly flop, but pretended to be enjoying it all immensely.

It was there, in Cuba, that I made my first acquaintance with economic issues. Havana had a supply problem, although at home in the hotel we at least had our traditional powdered eggs for breakfast. Thank God, my grandma had sent a whole crate of them over with an Aeroflot crew. You couldn't get fruit in stores unless you had ration coupons. A hundred miles outside Havana, fruit lay rotting in heaps. You couldn't go get it and bring it in to sell, because that was something called "speculating." I didn't understand why it worked that way, and nobody could explain it to me.

Time passed, and I saw my father getting more and more irritated in his conversations with Cuban friends; he kept talking about something called NEP. When we got home to the hotel he complained about the idea of "exporting revolution." But this, too, was beyond me. I was firmly convinced that the Soviet Union was a bulwark of peace and justice—it was first in outer space, first in aid to all peoples struggling against imperialism. My country was the best country in the world, the future belonged to the USSR, we stood for a just cause, and in this difficult struggle we, and it, would finally prevail. A simple, happy, romantic world. The main thing was to be brave, to fight on. Victory was only a matter of time.

We returned to Moscow in the fall of 1964. We kept an open house; it was always full of guests, my father's friends—writers, poets, journalists, soldiers. Yaroslav Smelyakov, Daniil Granin, Yury Levitansky, David Samoilov, Yegor Yakovlev, Grigory Pozhenyan, Yakov Akim, and Len Karpinsky often dropped in. They let me sit in on grown-up conversations, but only as long as I didn't interrupt. There were heated arguments about industry self-financing, about markets, market socialism, about the necessity of economic reforms and political freedoms.

In 1966, Mama and Papa and I left for Yugoslavia. *Pravda* was sending my father there as a correspondent. Yugoslavia in the mid-1960s was a remarkably interesting place—the only country in the world with a socialist market economy. In 1965 the political regime was essentially democratized, and now economic reforms were under way, and worker control was being introduced. What struck you there was the unheard of (by Soviet standards, anyway) abundance of goods, the frankness of social debate, the public discussion of issues on a scale that would be unthinkable at home. Belgrade was small, but a remarkably cosy and interesting city. In my Soviet school there were kids from Poland, Hungary, Czechoslovakia, Bulgaria, East Germany, Cuba, and Mongolia. It was a truly international children's club, where we all took a great deal of interest in one another and in what was going on in our respective countries. Here, for the first time, I began to pay attention to the economic news, to sort out the problems the Yugoslav reforms were encountering.

Yugoslavia is also a chess-playing country, and chess became a big part of my life. I had begun playing at six, and living there gave me the opportunity to meet some of the leading players of the time. Spassky, Petrosyan, Smyslov, Bronstein, Taimanov, and Tal all visited our house. I got to watch them play speed chess. Suetin and Taimanov even indulged *me*, a little boy, in a game or two. I joined a junior chess team sponsored by a Yugoslav company called "Rad." My passion for chess lasted right up to my second year at the university, when I realized that the game was distracting me from a more serious passion—economics.

There's a phenomenon called "juvenile hypermemory," which means an unusually highly developed memory in children. My grandfather Pavel Petrovich had something of the sort, and now I see it in my younger son. He remembers anything and everything, it doesn't matter—numbers out of the telephone book, the multiplication tables, grain-yield statistics that just happen to be on my desk. Apparently I used to do the same thing. At some point I noticed how easy it was for me to remember the contents of some Yugoslav statistical yearbook I'd just been leafing through, or the contents of a textbook I'd happened upon. It was a terribly convenient talent to have in school and in college. When this ability begins to fade—around age twenty—you feel as if you've lost an arm or a leg, as if the operating memory in your computer has suddenly crashed.

My father, who like his father before him was rather careless about his finances, always felt burdened by having to do accounts or keep books. When he noticed how easily everything involving figures seemed to be for me, he saddled me, a ten-year-old boy, with the job of composing the monthly financial report for the newsdesk. It's quite possible that this, too, influenced my choice of profession, at least to some extent.

At the time, though, I was crazy about the sea, and was convinced that my future was in the navy, that I would live a naval officer's life. Nothing, thought I, could possibly be more interesting than that.

During summer vacation I was usually shipped off to stay either with my grandmother Valentina Alexandrovna at Pavel Petrovich's house in Sverdlovsk, or with my other grandmother, Lia Lazarevna, who rented a dacha outside Zvenigorod, in the village of Dunino. It was a beautiful place. No wonder Mikhail Mikhailovich Prishvin, someone who knew and appreciated *Podmoskovye*, chose this particular village to live in. Our little house was right next to his.[7]

The Bazhov house in Sverdlovsk had a cosy air, and it was obvious that a large and happy family lived there. That family is scattered now, leaving only two of its members behind, my grandma and my beloved elder brother Nikita, whom I used to supply with contraband—that is, Cuban cigars. I've changed apartments countless times in my life since then, but that wooden building on Chapaev Street, and the garden my grandfather planted around it, may feel the most like home.

Dunino was a happy place—it was noisy, full of children, good friends who were to stay friends for years. It was there I met my first love—Masha, of the huge mysterious eyes. The Strugatsky brothers were incredibly popular in those days.[8] Masha, who was Arkady Natanovich Strugatsky's daughter, was embarrassed by all their celebrity and hid the fact that she was related to them. Later, three years into our friendship, I was genuinely amazed to discover that one of my favorite writers was actually her father. My passionate feelings, however, interested her not in the least. If I interested her at all, it was only as a sort of phenomenon—someone you could hit with a question about, say, the 1965 rice harvest, or steel production in Luxembourg in 1967, and get the right answer.

Years later, we were reacquainted—each of us with other lives, not particularly successful marriages, children, behind us. Masha and I were married, and of all the families I've seen in my life, ours might be the happiest. It's only lately that Masha sometimes laments that when she married Pavel Petrovich Bazhov's steady and reliable grandson, she wasn't expecting any Arkady Gaidar style escapades.

Arkady Natanovich Strugatsky and I later became friends. I think that he took to me not so much as Masha's husband, but simply as an interesting person; the original approach to the economic situation in one of my articles had appealed to him. He himself always struck me as a paradoxical combination of political naïveté and intuition far in advance of what seemed humanly possible, with an ability to forecast situations well into the future. In the 1970s a legend circulated among Strugatsky fans that the two brothers were really extraterrestrials sent down to infiltrate earth civilization. I have to say that spending time with Arkady Natanovich didn't completely disabuse me of that idea. But I'm getting a little ahead of myself.

Back then the Strugatskys really were something more that simply writers to me. There was *Monday Starts on Saturday*, *It's Hard Being a God*, *The Inhabited Island*, and so many others. These books in many ways shaped my world, my standards of behavior, my goals in life. It might seem funny, but I really do remember quite exactly that after reading the concluding section of *The Inhabited Island*, I firmly resolved to sort out economics and the causes of inflation. The Traveler says to Maksim, "Do you understand that there's inflation in this country? Do you even understand what inflation is?" I didn't want to be a dunce; I wanted to figure it all out. That was when, for the first time, I began to search out books on economics.

The summer of 1968 I spent in Dunino, and followed the newspaper stories about developments in Czechoslovakia. On the morning of August 21, I heard something about a letter from an unnamed group of Czech leaders, and about the "international aid" being provided to Czechoslovakia by Warsaw Pact troops. The blatant falsehood of the official version, the wrongness of what was going on, was so obvious, even to a small boy. What sort of nonsense was this? West German troops preparing for an invasion of Czechoslovakia? And what sort of truth has to be brought in with tanks and troop carriers?

The cozy, familiar world of my childhood—where everything was so right and clear, where we had a fine and noble idea, a beautiful country, clear-cut goals—began to crack and crumble. My childhood was suddenly over.

Chapter 2

Getting My Bearings

- My acquaintance with Marxism
- A present of Adam Smith
- Forbidden literature
- Who is to blame? And what is to be done?
- Moscow State University
- In the labyrinth of Soviet economics
- "Market socialism"?
- The Institute for Systems Research
- No easy recipes
- Only radical reform!

The fall of 1968. Yugoslavia again. Belgrade is gloomy. Serbia has traditionally been kind to Russians, who are liked here perhaps more than anywhere else in the world, except for Montenegro. But now, after Prague, the mood is wary. People are apprehensive that Yugoslavia will be next in line for invasion.

I try to sort out exactly what happened, the reasons behind the collapse of that cozy bright world, the just and right idea. I throw myself into reading. And here I discover Marxism in its original form. For many of my contemporaries their first acquaintance with Marxism was a boring process—school social studies classes, banal, threadbare quotes, amazingly dreary courses in historical and dialectical materialism, rote memorization.

But I happened to discover Marxism in a different way, on my own, independently, following a conscious desire to sort out what was happening around me. I remember what an enormous event it was for me, reading all this: *The Communist Manifesto, Anti-Dühring, The Origin of the Family, Private Property and the State*, and especially volume after volume of Plekhanov. My piecemeal knowledge of history, ranging from Mommsen to Klyuchevsky, suddenly took on an inner coherence, formed itself into a single, logical, convincing picture of world development.

What in Yugoslavia was considered permissible reading went far beyond Soviet limits. As I dug into Bernstein, Garaudy, Šik, I gradually took the route most natural for a young Marxist enthusiast trying to apply this methodology to socialist realities.[1] Bureaucracy, rising above the rest of society like a new class, the roots of its might in the acquisition of state property; the conflict between nationalized, bureaucratic property and the need to develop forces of production; the lack of any incentive to work, to innovate—all this took shape as *the* crucial economic contradiction in bureaucratic socialism.

Milovan Djilas's *The New Class*, which I had just read, fit nicely into this world view in the making, and led to a realization of the need to put an end to bureaucracy's monopoly on property. And also of the need to move from bureaucratic state socialism to a market socialism based on worker control, broad-based rights for employees, market mechanisms, and competition. But inasmuch as bureaucracy is hardly likely to relinquish its property willingly, a difficult struggle lay ahead. The struggle would not be easy, but it would end in success: bureaucratic socialism was inefficient; it obviously limited people's initiative, independence, and freedom, and consequently limited the growth of forces of production. Just as Marx said.

But what seemed logical in theory looked different in practice. I was lucky that I happened to be where I was, because Yugoslavia was the testing ground for worker control and market socialism. As I tried to sort out the ups and downs of the economic reform, I realized how hopelessly limited my own knowledge of economics was. I tried to correct that. My elder brother Nikita gave me a book that was to remain a favorite for decades, a two-volume set of Adam Smith published in paperback in 1938. Here I found a different picture of the world—this one liberal, but equally coherent.

I managed to get my hands on a textbook published in a small edition in 1963, a basic university course in economics very popular at the time in America, and perhaps all over the world—Paul Samuelson's *Economics*. Its pragmatic analysis and presentation of the laws of market mechanisms were persuasive. And although I remained an orthodox Marxist in my understanding of how societies develop, in other areas doubts began to creep in: Is the microeconomic base of *Das Kapital* really all that sound? Or the labor theory of value? They seem awfully archaic, even compared with the oversimplified world of Samuelson's textbook.

In Moscow, luck was with me. I enrolled in School 152, the best school I've ever attended. An unusually liberal and pleasant atmosphere reigned. Literature there was taught by Irina Danilovna Voinovich, my favorite teacher, and wife of the wonderful writer Vladimir Voinovich. She made the boring and official literature curriculum spring to life. Cutting the amount of time devoted to Gorky's *Mother* or Trenyov's *Lyubov Yarovaya* to a minimum, Irina Danilovna initiated us into Russian poetry's Silver Age, discussed the prose of Mikhail Bulgakov, and led debates on the works of Solzhenitsyn.[2] Our class was full of interesting people. My best friends were Vitya Vasiliev and Yura Zapol. A close-knit, friendly group, we each had our own strengths. Vitya, who would later become a world-renowned mathematician, showed me how to crack puzzlers at math Olympics. Yura, who during the reforms would become one of Russia's leading advertising entrepreneurs, amazed me with his ability to play chess "blind."

Together we argued over those traditional Russian questions—who is to blame? what is to be done? We were in total agreement in our assessment of life under Brezhnev, of the idiocy of what was going on. The question was whether anything could be changed, and if so, how? Public appeals, posters, propaganda, assassinating Brezhnev and Andropov? There were no very convincing answers. Gradually we came to understand that Soviet society, for all its obvious imperfections, for all the hypocrisy of its ideology and its readily apparent economic stupidities, was an exceedingly stable system that no mere pinpricks would ever budge.

In 1973, I enrolled in the Economics Department of Moscow State

University. Student life was both easy and hard. The core of the curriculum, its foundation, was orthodox Marxism. By graduation the prize student had to know the three volumes of *Das Kapital* backwards and forwards, and had to be adept at juggling quotes. This of course did not save you from having to know dozens of other works by Marx, Engels, and Lenin, or major Party documents. The whole idea was to train specialists who could masterfully substantiate the constantly changing Party decisions by referring to the authority of the founders of Marxism-Leninism. Classes were easy for me, because I knew the basic works well. Quotations popped out of my mouth as easily as "two-times-two."

Yet a certain feeling of discomfort, of dissatisfaction began to grow in me: the art of sophistry, the play of theses, ideological "flexibility" gave me no sense that the discipline I was studying had real ground under its feet. The university library was my salvation: it opened up enormous opportunities for self-education—Ricardo, Mill, Böhm-Bawerk, Jevons, Marshall, Pigou, Keynes, Schumpeter, Galbraith, Friedman, and many more. Getting to know these primary sources was not particularly encouraged, but neither was it prohibited.

Along with the feeling of satisfaction brought by new knowledge, a rather more complicated feeling gradually emerged, a realization that my old, seemingly solid convictions were collapsing, that the framework of my youthful world view was cracking at the joints. At precisely this point the flaw in *Das Kapital*'s entire construct became clear; it became clear that what makes Marxism interesting is its overall logic, the logic of the sociohistorical process, rather than any specific economic considerations. In the former regard, Marx's works are still quite convincing.

Another thing, though, was harder to accept. As you begin to get a more detailed understanding of the internal support structure of market socialism, you understand that none of it really works. How can you force an enterprise operating in a framework of worker control to create new jobs? How can you guarantee that redistribution of capital will benefit rapidly growing sectors of the economy? How can you resolve the question of wage differences within business and manufacturing concerns? These problems, on top of the Yugoslav realities that I already

knew and continued to follow, made it obvious that the Yugoslav economy was leading the country into high unemployment and accelerating
inflation. And that it was hardly a model for building a bright and happy
future.

So I found myself in an intellectual cul-de-sac. State socialism creates
an economic base for the absolute power of bureaucracy; market socialism continues to demonstrate its own obvious inefficiency. I gradually
came to the conclusion that there is no ready theoretical answer to any
of these questions. Which meant I had to dig deeper, to figure out how a
socialist economy works in practice, to study the economics of enterprises and the real mechanisms by which they interact with partners, employees, and the government.

But I lacked practical knowledge, although in terms of real life I already had a good deal of it. I married early. And probably because I had
kept the household budget from an early age, I wouldn't let myself take
money from my parents. So we lived a modest student life. My friends
Arkady Vilitenko, Sergei Bogdanov, Ruben Saakyan, Sasha Pagonin, and
I earned some money unloading freight cars. Later I began translating for
INION.[3] One day, after a seminar, Vitaly Isaevich Koshkin, then a docent
and later a professor of industrial economics, called me over and offered
to be my scholarly adviser; he suggested that I specialize in industrial
economics, and immediately wrote me into the state contract that his department was fulfilling for the Ministry of Electrical Engineering. The
department would give me the opportunity to work with real economic
data, and besides, the money would certainly come in handy. I happily
accepted the offer.

Vitaly Isaevich was my thesis adviser and later my dissertation adviser.
He and I collaborated on a number of articles and several books. His irrepressible energy sometimes gets in the way of his scholarly work, and
he has one trait not all teachers have—he finds his students interesting
and likes working with them. He knows how to track down the smart
ones, and how to draw them into his circle of scholarly interests. In 1992,
he would found and head "The Privatization School." Despite our dis-

agreements on some specific economic issues, we've remained fast friends.

And so, I ended up specializing in industrial economics. My thesis was titled "Indicators for Evaluating Activity in Self-financing Enterprises (Based on a Study of the Electrical Engineering Industry)."

In graduate school I continued to work on similar topics. I was increasingly persuaded that hierarchical economies, which discard the market in favor of a system of bureaucratic links, operate by a specific set of rules bearing little resemblance to the platitudes of socialist political economy, or, for that matter, to the exceedingly simplistic command-economy models followed by Western students of Soviet economics.

In 1980, I defended my dissertation—an early defense, since I already knew what I planned to do next. My father's good friend, the economics professor Valentin Terekhov, with whom I had argued a good deal about economic reform issues, had long been recruiting me to come work with him at the International Institute for Management Study and Research, created jointly with Czechoslovakia, East Germany, Poland, Hungary, Bulgaria, and Cuba. He was deputy director. This was perfect—after all, my area of specialization was the comparative study of economic mechanisms.

I received my work-assignment application from the institute. And here, perhaps for the first time in my life, my name became a stumbling block. The assignment required formal approval by the State Committee on Science and Technology. If it had been a matter of hiring some Ivanov or Sidorov, the whole thing would have been a formality; junior researchers were hardly the committee's major concern. But here you had a Gaidar. And if it's a Gaidar, somebody must be pulling strings. And if that's the case, why not pull them the usual way, through friends in high places, a phone call or two? Granted, I wasn't threatened with unemployment; I had a number of other offers, from the Academy of Sciences' Economics Institute for one, but none of them presented a good match with what I was determined to study.

Then again, every cloud has its silver lining. With the help, again, of

Valentin Fyodorovich Terekhov, I joined the All-Union Institute for Systems Research, which was also planning an extensive analysis of economic reforms within the socialist bloc. And so I became part of a group whose work was to represent a very important stage in my life. This institute had been created in 1977 by Djerman Gvishiani, deputy chairman of the State Committee on Science and Technology; he also became the institute's first director. The idea was to set up a Soviet analogue to the Rand Corporation, bringing together talented economists, mathematicians, systems analysts, philosophers, and organizational experts to conduct serious theoretical studies and to propose solutions for complex nationwide problems. The presence of Djerman Gvishiani, Kosygin's son-in-law, guaranteed that within both the formal and informal hierarchies of Soviet society of the time, the institute would be well connected, and therefore enjoy relative ideological autonomy.[4]

While Moscow University's Department of Economics, where I had both studied and worked, was under the supervision of the agency headed by Politburo gray eminence Mikhail Suslov, and was therefore subject to the most stringent of ideological controls, here at the institute the dominant influence was exerted by people who actually ran the economy, who dealt with real economic processes, who were constantly forced to confront the difficult-to-resolve problems of a socialist economy. And therefore we had a good deal more freedom of thought.

A telling example: at that time a campaign was under way at the university to fire Stanislav Shatalin, who chaired the subdepartment of mathematical methods of analysis, because of the "ideological unreliability" of his lectures and his taste for the "vulgar economic theories" of the West. At our institute he was directing the leading economics section with great success; his work brought together research involving living standards, the structure of the Soviet economy, and long-term forecasting.

The institute's lab was headed by Professor Vadim Pavlyuchenko. Assuming at first that I had pulled some strings to get there, he didn't quite trust me. Later, after reading my first memorandum on repressed inflation in Poland, he began looking at me through different eyes. And ever after, until his death in a car accident in 1984, we remained close friends and cohorts.

I have very fond memories of my work at the institute. Over time, we turned into an interesting group. Our laboratory included Vladimir Gerasimovich, Oleg Ananin, Pyotr Aven, Vyacheslav Shironin, and Marina Odintsova. Our basic area of research involved patterns of development of the socialist economic mechanism and comparative analysis of economic reforms in socialist nations.

At the institute there was none of the "doublethink" usually found in economics departments—that is, the strict delineation between what could be discussed openly and what could be thought, but under no circumstances mentioned aloud, in the official context of a scholarly seminar. Here you didn't have to cross your fingers behind your back when you talked; you could discuss the thorniest of theoretical problems without worrying about the ideological "purity" of your remarks.

This same atmosphere reigned at our sister institution, the Central Economics and Mathematics Institute. The first time I attended one such seminar (this one led by Nikolai Petrakov, whose works I had known for some time), I had the feeling that any minute we would all be dragged off to jail. But it was precisely this sort of de-ideologized, open discussion, where we could ask the hard questions, that revealed the scope of the problems that socialist economies were encountering.

I'll try to explain, briefly, how things looked to me at the time. Mass seizure of agricultural resources and merciless exploitation of a peasantry enserfed and herded into collective farms had provided the government with enormous investment capital and the ability to create, in very short order, an industrial structure that in many ways duplicated already obsolescent capitalist models.

As a result the economy became hostage to the village. As soon as the large-scale agricultural sector resources were exhausted, a crisis in socialist economic growth set in. This had become particularly evident in the early 1960s, when the proportion of the population living in rural areas dropped below 50 percent. The immediate crisis in farm production forced an investment in agriculture, while long-term agrarian problems opened the door to the first major purchases of grain, which later were to put the country at the mercy of grain imports. In this situation, some inevitable and very painful side effects of socialist industrialization made themselves felt—the bureaucratization of economic life, structural inflexibility, the inability to reallocate resources to benefit the more dynamic sectors of the economy. Enterprises and whole industries that had taken shape through forced industrialization continued to operate and even grow, regardless of how well or poorly they worked. Essentially, they were like a car stuck in the mud: the wheels spin, but nothing else moves.

More and more structural flaws in the socialist economy gradually began to reveal themselves. There was no mechanism for either generating or selecting effective innovations; there were no real incentives to work hard, or improve the quality of either the product or the scientific and technical process. Resources were largely concentrated in the defense sector, which proved to be the only place where true competition with a potential rival even existed. It became more and more evident that socialist industrialization's effect on economic development is something like that of drug use in sports: it lets you force the pace of growth over the short run, but at the cost of destroying the self-regulating function of the body itself.

The crisis in socialist capital accumulations, brought on by the exhaustion of resources in a rural Russia now bled dry, was temporarily staved off by the discovery of rich oil and gas deposits in western Siberia. These deposits created an illusion of prosperity and stability during the Brezhnev years, and allowed the postponement of decisions on radical reorganization of the socioeconomic structure. But in the early 1980s it became obvious that this lifeboat, too, was sinking. The richest oil and gas fields entered into a phase of declining yields and required new and greater capital investment. The fuel and energy sector was receiving a growing share of structural investments, but it was not clear just where the money to pay for that growth would come from. With the ravaged social structure of the villages, capital investments ran through rural Russia like water through a sieve; the return on investment in the agricultural sector was minimal, and in some areas there was no return at all. An adequate supply of food to Moscow, Leningrad, and the closed cities[5] was just barely maintained, primarily by importing food products.

Machine construction was lagging further and further behind world quality standards, making up only 3 percent of exports for convertible currency. The transportation base was wearing out. Oil refining and other branches of the chemical industry were on a level far below that of the rest of the world, and Soviet metallurgy technology was growing increasingly antiquated. Long-term forecasts spoke of an inevitable decline in the pace of economic growth and suggested that it would in the near future drop to zero, or even into negative figures.

It was becoming obvious that unless market mechanisms were engaged, it would be impossible to solve fundamental problems within the Soviet economy: without profound market reforms, the economic crisis would intensify, and—be it sooner or be it later—would inevitably become acute. It was equally obvious that switching to a consistent, market-oriented development track was impossible for political reasons. So how were we to break out of the vicious cycle?

I become convinced that there were no simple solutions. Apparently, the only sensible path was to begin to create the preconditions for making a gradual, evolutionary turn onto a Western style path of economic development, and to do so before the socialist economy entered its final, self-destructive phase. In other words, the minimal goal was to get out of the socialist experiment with the least possible damage, and to nudge the authorities in the direction of market-oriented liberal reforms enacted within the framework of the existing system, but simultaneously aimed at creating the conditions for radical transformation.

Market reforms in China were certainly one possible model, but the point of economic development at which they were begun was one that we had already passed in the late 1950s. Easing onto that same road at the beginning of the 1980s was impossible. The economic sclerosis was too far advanced. And that meant that our reform process would be sub-

stantially more complicated than China's. Hungary, whose orderly reforms were gradually laying the groundwork for market development,
also seemed interesting. But would the Soviet political elite be flexible
enough to take that route? Or would its rigidity, its conservatism, pave
the way to economic ruin, to a catastrophic collapse of the regime, to a
full-scale anti-Communist revolution inside an empire brimming with
nuclear weapons?

These were the issues that seemed most crucial to me by the time that
life forced me to look, in practice rather than theory, at real alternatives
to the current economic policy of the Soviet state.

Chapter 3

Options and Forecasts

- The reporting commission
- The war on taboos
- *Kommunist* gets agitated
- An anonymous phone call
- The Chevron story
- Mikhail Gorbachev
- That odd Boris Yeltsin
- 500 days
- Grigory Yavlinsky
- The Institute for Economic Policy
- Forecasts of impending disaster

By the end of the 1970s and beginning of the 1980s it was becoming clear to the Soviet political elite that something had to be done about the way the system was managed; it was also becoming clear that it was impossible to do anything meaningful. A second attempt at the Kosygin reforms, so long in the making, was articulated in the June 1979 Resolution of the Central Committee and the Soviet of Ministers, "On Improving the Economic Mechanism," after which the whole thing quietly expired without having had any real impact on how the bureaucratic economy functioned.[1]

At the time of Brezhnev's death in 1982 the portfolio of proposed management-system innovations was virtually empty. The only substantial thing left in it was administrative price reform. But every time the Party leadership approached such a reform, the fear of an avalanche of public dissatisfaction stopped them in their tracks. At the same time, the collapse of the gerontocratic Politburo, and the series of funerals which had been popularly dubbed the "hearse races," had created a singular sort of political vacuum requiring new ideas.

The younger generation of Party and economic leadership, headed by Mikhail Gorbachev, wanted to better understand just what was happening with the economy. One step in that direction was the creation of the Politburo Commission on Improvement of the Management System. Its formal head was Nikolai Tikhonov, the decrepit chairman of the Soviet of Ministers, but the real driving force behind it was Nikolai Ryzhkov, who enjoyed a reputation as one of the most dynamic and energetic figures in the economic *nomenklatura*, and who had recently been named Party Secretary for the Economy. Two groups were attached to the Commission: a working group that included key deputies from Gosplan, the Ministry of Finance, the Ministry of Labor, the State Committee on Science and Technology, the State Committee on Prices, the State Committee on Statistics; and a research section that brought together the heads of leading economics institutes. The director of our institute, Academician Djerman Gvishiani, was chosen to head the latter.

A number of representatives of the more conservative wing of both the economic bureaucracy and Party leadership viewed all this as just a way to let off steam, to create the appearance of furious activity. But the leaders of the younger generation saw it as a way to gather in available intellectual potential, to craft documents that could be put to use at the point supreme power came into their hands and they had considerably more room to maneuver. Much later, Gorbachev was often to recall the scores of documents drafted and ready for the moment when he would be named General Secretary. The work of the Politburo Commission on Improvement of the Management System in fact was one of the means used to create that package.

A key question in any bureaucratic organization, be it a committee or a commission, is who will actually do the work. There are a colossal number of bosses, dignitaries, and academicians, but they generally don't get behind the plow—their job is to give orders. And since it was Gvishiani who was assigned to supervise the research section, the actual work went to the institute departments headed by Boris Milner and Stanislav Shatalin and, above all, to our lab.

A Politburo directive was in those days something like an "open sesame" for any and all doors. And so getting real information on the state of the economy and the processes occurring in it became much more possible than before. It was as if we ourselves had joined the ruling elite, albeit in the capacity of a research and service staff.

I well remember my first acquaintance with the management traditions and practices of the late socialist era. In early 1985, I traveled to Minsk with a group of officials sent by the Central Committee and the Soviet of Ministers to review the progress of a so-called large-scale economic experiment at Belorussia's Ministry of Light Industry. The commission began its workday at 8:00 A.M. At breakfast, representatives of the Party Central Committee and of the Belorussian Soviet of Ministers took turns offering toasts, and the good times would go on until supper, when of course it would have been a sin not to have a drink or two before bedtime. Then again, I have to admit that my Belorussian hosts were gracious about providing me the data I needed on the experiment: *We understand, the boy's a scholar. He has to have something to put in his report.*

Along with all these antics (which were somehow almost interesting), some extremely important work was being done. Perhaps the most substantial document to come out of the Commission's research section was "A Blueprint for Improving Economic Mechanisms at the Enterprise Level," an assignment given us by Ryzhkov. This rather long 120-page document charted the main lines of economic reform for the entire USSR. Our lab worked on it, but so did a group of young economists recruited from Leningrad; the group included Anatoly Chubais, Sergei Vasiliev, Sergei Ignatiev, Yury Yarmagaev, and others. For them, being recruited to work on Politburo Commission business was a sort of special dispensation, keeping them safe from any political "unpleasantness"; Leningrad was, at the time, a well-known bastion of ideological correctness.

This document spoke of rather cautious economic reforms, the most important prerequisite for which was a tightening of fiscal and monetary policy. It proposed abandoning planning directives, introducing incentives tied to profits, maintaining strict and normative wage and salary controls, gradually freeing prices as individual markets were stabilized, undertaking cautious measures aimed at relaxing restrictions on foreign economic activity, and creating both private and cooperative economic sectors to stand alongside the government sector.

As a basis for our proposals we took the practical experience of the Hungarian reform of 1968 and its subsequent modifications—adapted, of course, to Soviet conditions. We did take into account that this model was by no means ideal, but we thought it important to make the first cautious moves in the direction of markets, to set some benchmarks for nonstate economy—preconditions for subsequent evolution of the system and a "soft" exit from socialism.

The most serious discussions within the group were sparked by the question of reform tactics. Stabilization measures (in the language of those days this was called "improving domestic economic equilibrium") were, in our opinion, first on the agenda. The memory of Polish attempts at reform in the 1970s, when financial destabilization rapidly undermined newly introduced market mechanisms, was just too fresh.

Socialism, from a market economics standpoint, is the most highly developed of all systems for regulating repressed inflation. Precisely for this reason we assumed that, if we wanted to effect at least a somewhat orderly exit from socialism, the emphasis should be on financial stability, something which socialism in its stable form was, as a rule, capable of maintaining. Concrete evidence of this could be found in the relatively successful market changes involved in Yugoslav reforms in the 1950s, Hungarian reforms in the 1960s, and Chinese reforms in the 1970s and 1980s. In all cases the road to success lay in maintaining stringent controls over crucial monetary and financial parameters.

But back to our Commission. The combination of high-level ideological protection and an authoritative leadership disinclined to interfere allowed us a certain amount of freedom in our workups; we were able to apply ideas and terms which, had they been seen in print at the time, would have immediately set off ideological witch-hunts, shut down the publishing house responsible, and caused major staff reshuffling. The Central Economics and Mathematics Institute had already gone through an ideological keelhauling and major reorganization for far less.

I should note here that the Commission's work reflected a rather broad consensus in liberal scholary and scientific circles. Our blueprint received almost unanimous support in discussions among the academic elite. Perhaps the only one to criticize it as excessively radical was N. Kapustin, director of the heavily ideologized Academy of Sciences' Institute of Economics.

However, a major disappointment was in store for us during discussions of our blueprint at the upper levels of Party and government. Responses presented to the working group by representatives of various agencies were reminiscent of old-style ideological tongue-lashings. If we accept this proposal, fumed one Central Committee representative, we'll be forced to admit that we're on the slippery slope to commodity-money relations, and how can we stand for such a thing? Gvishiani returned from his talks with Ryzhkov to confirm that the country's political leadership was not ready for such radical change. Which meant we were to give up our fruitless daydreaming and concentrate on developing an economic experiment on a more mundane level.

I left the institute in a foul mood, stopped in to visit my father (who was in a military hospital at the time), told him the latest news, and went home in the rain. When I turned on the television, they were broadcasting Gorbachev's address on scientific and technological progress. In large part here were *our* words, *our* proposals, reports written by *us*, a demonstrable readiness to throw off dogma and ideological limitations. Perhaps not everything being said was entirely accurate, but the range of ideological concessions was clearly increasing. There was hope that perhaps we could break through all those layers of bureaucracy, and get to the top, and explain what the real state of affairs and the real alternatives were, and how a new economic policy might take shape.

The early Gorbachev era, in general, was a time of both hope and doubt. And in both the Soviet Union and the West it was anybody's and everybody's guess: were there serious changes in the offing, or was this just another campaign in a long line of campaigns—a lot of talk, the ideological door opens a crack, and then anyone who carelessly takes the opportunity to get a little fresh air gets put away. Here's a typical example of intelligentsia "folk-art" of the time:

> Now we've got the glasnost era.
> Believe me comrade, it will pass,
> And the KGB will surely
> Take names and kick ass.

At the institute we were constantly arguing about that very thing: how serious in fact were the new leadership's intentions? Most of my friends and acquaintances, my cohorts, tended to be skeptical. The bureaucracy was powerful, and it was conservative. It could talk and talk, and then everything would settle back into the old patterns. Where do you see any real change? Of course they want to fool the West, dupe it one more time, maybe finagle some new concessions, get more access to Western technology, but that's as far as it goes. They're not about to agree to the sort of profound changes that could shake the very foundations of their total control of the economy. Why cut off the branch you're sitting on?

I took a different stance, although I was clearly in the minority. It seemed to me that the very fact that our economic system was so antiquated, that it lagged so far behind the West, should itself stimulate radical change, at least on the part of the more dynamic and enterprising of the younger leaders. And besides, in all honesty, I simply found Gorbachev likable; he seemed sincere in his desire to make changes, aware of just how ephemeral the current prosperity, based on oil revenues, really was. Yes, I of course noticed that his assessment of events was not always accurate. At the same time, set against the antiquated leadership of previous generations, he looked engagingly dynamic, willing to communicate, open. And what was most important, he had actually done something. Books that had lain buried for decades were being published.

People were eager to buy new issues of thick journals—this, after the dreary apathy of the late seventies and early eighties.

Arkady Strugatsky, and his brother Boris, had a whole pile of unpublished works—unpublished in Russia, at any rate. Some of them were published abroad, and others had circulated as manuscripts. I persuaded him that now they could be published. And indeed the dam *had* broken. *The Ugly Swans, Snail on a Slope, Tale of a Troika, The Doomed City, Lame Fate* all came out. There was no longer any need to fight to get something in print. Journals and publishing houses wrangled over dusty manuscripts. Not only works of fiction were in demand, but works on law and economics as well.

Much of what was being published during glasnost was genuinely good, and interesting, and well written. But it was almost as if Sleeping Beauty had nodded off somewhere in the sixties and awakened in the mid-eighties. The range of ideas, and the concepts of society, simply repeated what had been said twenty years back. You can't step into the same river twice. What was true and interesting then had little to do with present reality. This was particularly obvious in popular works on economics. What had been the dominant economic model was now outdated, and looked naive. And it *was* naive. Still, the main thing was that the ban was being lifted, and that in itself was encouraging.

We tried to get Gorbachev's ear. We wrote memoranda on key economic policy questions and passed them along to him through Academicians Stanislav Shatalin and Aleksandr Anchishkin. Later, some traces of our proposals turned up in his speeches. But the more time that passed, the stronger became our feeling that there was a dangerous breach between Gorbachev's good intentions and his actual economic policy.

By the time Gorbachev came to power, there were already serious distortions in the monetary and financial sphere; however, the growth rate of the money supply remained stable and low, and the budget was traditionally in surplus with fiscal residuals taken into account. Gorbachev declared his readiness to remove the major ideological barriers to setting market mechanisms in motion. Words like "reform" and "market" were

legalized. A resolution on stimulating cooperative and individual economic activity was in the works. At the same time, economic policy decisions undermining the very foundations of financial stability were
being made. The very dangerous anti-alcohol campaign and the attempt
to abruptly increase the growth of capital investment came on the heels
of a decline in oil revenues and a reduction in imports of consumer
goods. The state budget suffered several major blows at one time.

The support structures of the relatively stable socialist monetary system were already buckling and rapidly beginning to collapse. Everything
was moving in a direction opposite to the one we had advocated in all
our proposals and reports, the one I had advocated in recent books and
articles. Instead of an orderly preparation to start up the market mechanism, we were heading into a serious financial crisis that was drastically
increasing inflationary tendencies in the economy. At the same time, the
mechanisms that would allow us to regulate repressed inflation were being dismantled. For the experts it was all quite clear; they saw our economic policy taking on a dangerous resemblance to that of Poland on the
eve of the crisis of 1979–81, which had led to a declaration of martial law.

At the end of August 1986, a group of young economists attended a
seminar at Zmeinaya Gorka, outside of Leningrad. Those attending included, besides me, Anatoly Chubais, Sergei Vasiliev, Pyotr Aven, Sergei
Ignatiev, Vyacheslav Shironin, Oleg Ananin, Konstantin Kagalovsky,
Georgy Trofimov, Yury Yarmagaev—all told, roughly thirty "market"
economists. An even smaller circle gathered to discuss the most dangerous ideological issues, such as ways to create a capital market or to safeguard property rights.

We all acutely felt our new freedom, our new room to pursue scholarly research and real study of the processes occurring in the economy.
We could do away with the euphemisms and the elliptical references; we
could describe economic processes in the terms used in the economic literature of the rest of the world. Everyone agreed on the necessity of reforms that would prepare the Soviet economy for a gradual restoration
of market mechanisms and private-property relations. But we realized
that this would not be a simple matter. After finishing our work for the

day, we lit our campfires, sang songs, told jokes. At the final seminar, "skit night," I presented two possible scenarios for the crisis to come. The first was called "The Crest of the Wave," and it designated just who was going to play what part in reforming the economy. I should point out that I was right on the mark in casting Chubais in a key role. The second was called "Going Under," and it stipulated the length of our prison sentences and the size of the ration packets we each would receive. Overall, though, the mood was cheerful.

Throughout 1986 and 1987, there was an intense struggle to do away with ideological taboos, to open up new topics of debate, to introduce once-banned terms into open and general usage. The censors overseeing scholarly economics journals and publishing houses were tearing their hair; they no longer knew what could be said and what couldn't.

Surprisingly, one of the most powerful battering-rams now knocking down ideological walls was the journal *Kommunist*, itself a former bastion of orthodoxy. Ivan Frolov, an old friend of Gorbachev's, was put in charge. He reshuffled the editorial board and invited well-known economist Otto Latsis, who had long been out of favor, to become deputy editor-in-chief. After his appointment, Latsis spoke at our institute and shared his views on the prospects for economic development; he didn't rule out the possibility of fierce ideological battles to come. Later he phoned and asked me to stop by his office.

Evidently he wanted to commission an article. I was pleased, because I realized that notes and articles in professional publications could not, by themselves, put right the dangerous series of errors already destabilizing the economy, the monetary and financial system, and already leading to shortages in the consumer market. The impression was that the government simply did not understand what was happening, or wasn't aware of the consequences of those poorly thought-out decisions. Given these circumstances, the chance to speak out on such strategic questions on the pages of an influential publication like *Kommunist* was a great stroke of luck.

I wasn't wrong. Latsis indeed wanted to commission an article, the essence of which was to be a critique of both the "acceleration" strategy and its practical implementation. And then he suddenly suggested that I take over the journal's economics section. The idea seemed both risky and intriguing. On the one hand, how could I be a journalist? My usual genre was articles published in 500 or so copies, narrowly professional in focus, and hard for anyone uninitiated in the finer points of economics to decipher. Besides, I was planning a new book, and work on it would take time. And, in general, I'm more at home in a library than anywhere else; I've never craved constant contact with other people. I'd already earned a certain professional reputation, and probably would soon become the youngest full doctor of economics in the country. Why get out of the familiar groove? Why embark on some dubious escapade?

On the other hand I felt a passionate desire to use this unprecedented opportunity to grapple with fundamental issues of ideology, economics, politics. It was obvious that the platform provided by *Kommunist*, a leading theoretical publication, could be a powerful weapon indeed. After vacillating for several days, I accepted Latsis's offer—and have never regretted it—although I do realize that on that day I no doubt closed the door on a tranquil academic life, at least for some years ahead.

Kommunist in 1987–89 was an interesting phenomenon. Some of its contributors would later find themselves in the ranks of the national socialist or the Communist factions of the State Duma, while others would end up enacting liberal reforms. It had its seasoned, time-tested Party apparatchiks, its former dissidents, plus a younger group recruited from academe.

Igor Dedkov, one of Russia's most authoritative literary critics, joined the journal at almost the same time I did. A young journalist named Sergei Kolesnikov was unexpectedly named deputy editor. Subsequently he would serve as Viktor Chernomyrdin's adviser and press secretary.

I brought in some of my own colleagues—Viktor Yaroshenko, Aleksei Ulyukaev, Nikolai Golovnin—all of whom I would later work with a good deal. The atmosphere at the journal was one of intense internal debate over fundamental issues of ideology and politics; it was a mirror image of conflicts on upper levels of the Party between the orthodox types surrounding Yegor Ligachev and the liberals grouped around Aleksandr

Yakovlev. The journal was leaning more and more toward the latter. The weekly editorial meetings that took place around the editor-in-chief's enormous green table were both interesting and intellectually satisfying.

In order to appreciate both the opportunities and the risks of running the economics section of a Communist Party theoretical journal, one should first understand a little about the Central Committee's mechanisms of ideological control. Traditionally the person named to such a job would have a good deal of solid Party experience behind him, in which the sapper principle ruled—that is, one mistake is all you get. An executive position at a Party journal carried the right to choose, to make decisions; and a department head was not obliged to consult with the Central Committee about what could or could not be published. He was his own censor. But this also laid an enormous personal responsibility on his shoulders, one fraught with unpleasant possibilities. One mistake could cost him his career.

Precisely for this reason, *Kommunist* editors, tightly woven into the fabric of the Party hierarchy as they were, tended to be extremely cautious. But this wasn't the case with me, and I hadn't joined the staff to be looking over my shoulder at every turn. I couldn't have cared less about keeping my editorial chair, or about my future Party career. I was interested in the job exclusively because it gave me the chance to advance my own opinions regardless of any leftover ideological taboos. And so I immediately began introducing into common usage heretofore forbidden concepts, information, data; the fact that such things had never been openly published had long paralyzed whole schools of economic thought.

Terms it was once unthinkable to apply to socialism began appearing on the pages of *Kommunist*: inflation, unemployment, poverty, social stratification, budget deficit. So did the very first realistic assessments of military expenditures. And, most important, an educated discussion of what was happening to the country's economy. We tried to explain to the ruling elite how ruinous its chosen course was. This was the essence of the general economic articles and yearly overviews I began publishing in *Kommunist*. I tried to show the danger in attempting to force economic growth through increased capital formation, and the ruinous tendencies of the financial distortions now taking shape—distortions that would lead to a collapse of the consumer market. I tried to show the danger of a rapidly growing foreign debt.

Periodically phone calls would come in from Party headquarters on Old Square: *What do you think you're doing? Is this issue really subject to public debate?* Parrying remarks like this was not all that hard, as a rule. I responded with a question of my own: *You mean you don't know?* And the official, who in fact did *not* know what the latest Party goal was, would get flustered and leave me in peace.

There were, of course, some serious run-ins as well. The first one happened almost immediately after my arrival at the journal and involved the famous Pechora gold-mining collective, headed by Vadim Tumanov, an interesting and colorful man with a complex and checkered history. Gold-mining collectives had survived as little islands of market economy in the sea of socialism. Academician Abel Aganbegyan had often used them in his lectures to illustrate alternative ways to operate a business. I suspect that it was no accident that in this battle over choice of strategy, the first strike was launched at the miners—as a lesson to everyone else.

The prosecutor's review revealed nothing criminal. Nonetheless a series of condemnatory articles in *Socialist Industry*, the Central Committee newspaper, seemed to seal the Pechora collective's fate. After familiarizing ourselves with all the documents related to the case, we sent out our own experts. They mounted an investigation and concluded that the allegations against Pechora were not worth the paper they were printed on, and that this was a pure case of political pressure. We published all the pertinent materials. For the first time in decades you had a Party journal polemicizing with a Party newspaper! At the request of Yegor Ligachev, Gorbachev himself made a call to our new editor, Nail Bikkenin, and raked him over the coals. But eventually all the noise died down; we were able to stop the wheel of repression from rolling any further. I introduced Vadim Tumanov to the government's deputy chairman for construction N. Batalin, and he found road construction work for Tumanov and his collective in Karelia.

The second incident was much larger in scope and involved a grandiose plan to build several oil and gas complexes in western Siberia; the price tag was around $40 billion. Before telling that story, I would like to briefly share some of my own experience with the birth of such projects. At the Academy of Sciences my colleagues and I had more than once found ourselves caught up in disputes over our assessments of massive and totally unworkable projects promoted by lobbyists from this or that ministry. The most sensational of these were two projects involving the rerouting of Siberian rivers into Central Asia and northern rivers into the Volga basin. Neither of them was economically justifiable in any way. In both cases we were able to mobilize the support of experts and the public at large, and put a stop to these grandiose schemes.

Personal acquaintance with the mechanics of lobbying for these sorts of projects had given me a highly interesting practical lesson in how the bureaucratic economic system worked. And therefore I was no longer surprised when, for example, the initial justification for this or that construction project might be a sharp drop in the water level of the Caspian Sea, and then later it might be an equally abrupt rise. I now understood that arguments of this sort meant nothing, but that for their creators the important thing was getting the resources for a particular project and filtering those resources through the proper departmental or agency structure. At the editorial offices of *Kommunist*, we often got into debates over fundamental issues such as these, including the senseless Turukhan Hydroelectric Station project, which, if built, would have nowhere to send the energy it produced; or the plan for the Katun Hydroelectric Station, which was absolutely unjustifiable in terms of either efficiency or economic return.

This was probably why one day I received an anonymous phone call from someone in the state apparatus, who, genuinely concerned about efficient use of government resources, asked me to look into a certain unprecedented resolution currently in the works, the result of which would be the construction of five enormous oil, gas, and chemical complexes in western Siberia.

The project went far beyond anything I had previously encountered.

It would have required sums double or triple those spent on the still unfinished Baikal-Amur Mainline Railway. Now, in the face of a clearly out-of-control foreign debt, in the midst of a serious financial crisis, this was a dubious venture indeed. I had touched briefly on the project in my review of the Russian economy for 1989, and had immediately received an angry rebuke from the powerful lobby backing the project. Six USSR ministries, led by then Minister of the Oil and Gas Industry Viktor Chernomyrdin, had signed a letter to the Central Committee requesting disciplinary action against this upstart candidate in economics who was showing such lack of regard for the Party's decision to develop western Siberia. They sent a copy to *Kommunist*, apparently so that proper conclusions could be drawn there as well. The text was framed in the best traditions of Party terminology, with colorful invective and frequent references to Party resolutions replacing any economic arguments or considerations.

Well, why not? We published the letter, along with our own detailed commentary. I analyzed the arguments, pointed out examples of previously failed projects (albeit ones less grand), and published data on all the unused imported equipment scattered around the country. Once upon a time such a scheme would have been impossible for us to stop. As my friends used to say, if $40 billion needs to spill over somewhere, there's no power on earth that can hold it back. But the system was clearly wearing out, Gorbachev's democratization process had already begun, and the whole story caused quite a reaction at the First Congress of People's Deputies. As a result, the original version of the plan was put to rest, and only a few of its more well-thought-out provisions were implemented. In my later working relationship with Chernomyrdin this episode never came up.

There is perhaps one more interesting story involving lobbying for major investment projects. It happened somewhat later, after I became head of the Institute for Economic Policy. In the spring of 1991 a plan for developing the Tengis oil fields in Kazakhstan arrived at the Ministry of Economics' analysis office. One of the partners in the project was to be the big American corporation Chevron—one of the Seven Sisters of oil.

My economist colleagues familiarized themselves with the documents and, recalling the last "project of the century," asked me to head up the review group. I was warned at the outset that there was pressure from above to ensure that the review committee recommendations would be positive.

In terms of reserves, the Tengis oil fields might be compared to the famous Samotlor fields that had allowed the USSR to keep the heavy and unwieldy Brezhnev economic battleship afloat for fifteen long years. The fields had been explored, and the oil was of good quality, although high in sulfur content. The yearly yield might be as much as 30 million tons, and could be sustained at that level for a long time. Unlike Samotlor, Tengis was relatively close to transportation lines. Tengis, in the late 1980s, was considered the Soviet Union's trump card in the game for the future.

I understood that I had come in rather late in the action. The agreement, reached during negotiations between American and Soviet delegations, had already been discussed at a meeting between U.S. and Soviet presidents. They had tentatively approved it, and signed all the appropriate papers. The project had been given the green light. Technically, formal approval required a review. But . . .

A Western corporation, any Western corporation, is a predator. Otherwise other corporations would tear it to shreds in a minute. On the other hand, it's hardly some villain out of comic opera. Life has simply taught it to play by harsh rules, business rules. And when suddenly on the other side of the bargaining table you have, instead of your usual rival predator, someone barely qualified to be there, someone who also has personal interests that—to put it mildly—don't necessarily correspond to those of the country that person represents, the results can be quite astounding.

I'm not accusing the Chevron experts who drafted the contract of any particular sins. In looking out for corporate profits, they were merely being professional. And for that very reason the agreement they had worked out was truly fantastic. A multitude of legal loopholes and twists built into the text gave Chevron substantial unilateral advantages.

Once I had looked at the draft, I realized that I couldn't back away, I couldn't refuse to do the review. I needed to act quickly, keeping in mind that, review or no review, the agreement might be signed tomorrow—if not today. Both Soviet and American supporters of the project were pressuring Gorbachev to sign.

The first thing I did was send a letter to Gorbachev through Oleg Ozherelev, the President's economic adviser, in which I cited the most evident absurdities in the draft agreement. I urged him not to hurry, but instead allow the matter to be investigated in more detail. Gorbachev's positive response to the note gave us our chance to do a detailed analysis. Our work on the project documents we had received confirmed our worst fears. It was becoming increasingly obvious that if the project were to be approved under the terms offered, Chevron would end up owning one of the world's richest oil fields without taking on any clear-cut obligations in relation to our country.

Here are a few excerpts from the review's conclusion:

—In the case of Tengis, the USSR has taken upon itself virtually all the risks involved in exploration and prospecting, and has also made major industrial expenditures, thus providing its partner in the joint venture with a field that is already explored and already beginning to yield both oil and profits.

—The Soviet side has provided this joint venture, one-half the property of which belongs to Chevron, exclusive rights for exploration, development, and exploitation of hydrocarbon deposits across the entire territory, which encompasses the Tengis and Korolevsky fields. Upon signing of this contract, Chevron becomes owner of half of all wells, pipelines, and installations purchased by the Soviet Union over the last several years for development of the Tengis fields.

—As concerns any obligations incumbent upon Chevron, which has acquired a monopoly on development of an enormous oil field, such obligations simply do not exist in the contract as presented. The project does not specify any obligations regarding either the relative scope or the time frame of investments in further development to be made by the joint-venture partner. All the calculations and proposals presented are framed in tentative and conditional terms. Those parts of the draft agreement which are devoted to such issues contain much wording about the need for further negotiations, further study and assessment. Only one thing is certain: Chevron has no interest whatsoever in investing in comprehensive processing of raw materials, but is clearly focused on exporting Soviet crude oil.

Even the tiny royalties to which the Soviet side had humbly agreed (7.5 percent of total oil output as long as the contract remained in force) had not yet been approved by the American company. The sole exception, perhaps, was the promise of prompt payment of regular Soviet taxes. But even this was more or less nullified by Article 13.2 of the draft agreement, which gave the managing committee of Tengis–Chevron Oil the right to create tax-free financial funds to be spent at the committee's discretion.

I don't want to bore the reader with a list of all the provisions in the agreement that gave the American side unilateral advantages; there were quite a few. Our conclusion came down to this: the draft agreement as proposed would hand Chevron unheard-of advantages, to the detriment of the Soviet Union in general and Kazakhstan in particular.

The project supporters were alarmed. They tried to frighten Gorbachev by claiming that a review of the agreement could not only damage Soviet-American relations but could complicate dealings with business interests in other Western countries and result in serious political losses.

We conducted a series of negotiations in Moscow. The American team was led by D. Giffin, president of the American-Russian consortium built around the Tengis project. It was all very obvious, and at the same time extremely amusing. On one side were the Americans and our own Ministry of Oil Production, headed by Valery Churilov; on the other side were members of the review committee—scholars, economists, geologists, ecologists. It was an odd exchange. We asked specific questions about the absence of any legal guarantees protecting the interests of the Soviet side, about arbitrary assumptions in monetary flow calculations, about anomalies in the cost accounting mechanisms. What we got in response were arguments about the remarkable international significance of the project and the high-level political support that it enjoyed.

After the meeting in Moscow we got a call from Gorbachev's staff; he and George Bush had agreed that members of the review committee should fly to San Francisco to negotiate with Chevron executives. The intent was clear enough; the aim was not so much to discuss our fundamental objections as to convince us of their futility.

I called Vladimir Shcherbakov, first deputy chairman of the USSR Cabinet of Ministers, and Minister of the Economy. We were old acquaintances, going back to his days at the KAMAZ auto plant. I told him that I was willing to negotiate with the Americans, but first I considered it very important to take a hard line, and second, to bring in international legal consulting firms who dealt regularly with such contracts. There were far too many legal fine points here, and we might make a serious mistake and do harm to the USSR's national interests. He gave his assent in principle, and I left for the United States.

At the airport in New York I turned down the infinitely hospitable Americans' offer to fly me on to San Francisco immediately, paid my respects, and took a day in New York to consult. Once a nondisclosure statement was signed, I showed the draft agreement to friends in a large New York law firm. Their assessment coincided with mine; in its present form the agreement indisputably gave Chevron undeniable unilateral advantages.

On the following day, the negotiations with Chevron executives began. Richard H. Matzek, president of Chevron Overseas Company, headed the American negotiating team, and I headed the Soviet. At first the Americans' attitude was rather patronizing and indulgent: *We know the score, our Soviet colleagues are just trying to split hairs, but we'll explain the whole thing to them.* However, as negotiations progressed, the mood gradually began to change.

Once we had enumerated all the provisions of the draft agreement that would have allowed Chevron, should it so choose, to avoid paying a single kopeck in corporate taxes, and to refuse to put a single cent into investments, all the while retaining its full legal rights, we got the sense that the Americans were frankly uncomfortable, for they could hardly look us in the eye. Justifications came thick and fast: *Well, you do understand that we're honorable people, we'll pay our taxes, and of course we plan to fulfill all our investment obligations.*

The outcome was a document stipulating that Chevron would assent to a fundamental review of the terms of the agreement, one that would take Soviet interests into account. We agreed that negotiations would continue. And I was persuaded once again that no one would defend our national interests for us. We had to do it ourselves. I think, too, that the whole episode served as a lesson to our country's leadership as well.

This is perhaps the moment to say something about the architect of perestroika, and about my feelings toward him. From the very start I had been more enthusiastic about Gorbachev than were many of my friends and cohorts. When he began to back up all the talk about glasnost with actions, and when definite shifts took place in both foreign and domestic policy, I made up my mind to support him. And I did support him much longer that many of those who fell under his spell overnight and then just as quickly disowned him. I understood how heavy the burden borne by Russian reformers could be, and images of Speransky, Witte, and Stolypin, whose fate was hardly to be envied, constantly came to mind.[2]

Often, at the various conferences led by Gorbachev, I took note of both his strengths and his weaknesses. His strengths consisted of an ability to form and direct a consensus, and to suggest original solutions that were a revelation to those assembled, but at the same time seemed to flow from the opinions they themselves had just expressed, of their own will. But this was also Gorbachev's weakness, for that sum total of many wills, often conflicting ones, tended to be expressed in half-measures at a time when the situation demanded decisive and unequivocal solutions. This flaw presented itself most acutely in his constantly vacillating economic policy. On the one hand, mechanisms that would lead to the collapse of the old bureaucratic system of management had been set in motion; on the other hand, that process was not yet buttressed by new and fully operative market mechanisms.

In 1988, against a backdrop of deepening budget and fiscal problems, we began the so-called transfer of enterprises to total self-financing, which gave industrial managers greater independence and increased their freedom to maneuver. Norms were set for profit distribution, but not based on after-tax profits. At the same time, the notion that enterprises were responsible for the financial consequences of their economic activity was never introduced. The result was that unsystematic, piecemeal changes in the hierarchical economy spurred an increase in economic distortions. Growth rates for nominal income began to spin out of control. Unbacked money was continually being dumped into the consumer market, setting off waves of panic buying among consumers, and reducing the number of goods available on the open market. An ever greater part of the population was ending up on ration coupons.

Meanwhile the leadership remained certain that important and progressive economic decisions had been made, and that in spite of minor difficulties, smooth sailing was ahead. It was not until the summer of 1988, after a trip to Krasnoyarsk, that Gorbachev's own certainty of this began to falter. As he talked with people about perestroika, he suddenly realized that no one was optimistic about what was happening. They were posing him a stark and angry question: *What happened to all the goods that were on the shelves until just recently?* On his return to Moscow, he scheduled several conferences in a row, obviously in an attempt to understand what was wrong, where the mistake was, why the reforms were not producing the expected results.

In the fall of 1988, while working on one of Ryzhkov's assignments, I was looking through some government documents and found a classified version of the budget proposed for 1989. It was absolutely suicidal. With the deficit continuing to grow uncontrollably, it was compensated for by an expansion in the money supply. Meanwhile the government was passively observing the whole financially ruinous process, seemingly unaware that what was happening was fraught with the potential for social tumult, cataclysm, and the possible downfall of the regime itself. It was France on the eve of the revolution, Russia in early 1917, China just before the fall of the Kuomintang.

At this very moment, perhaps, I came to the realization that the Soviet Union was indeed faced with the threat of revolutionary upheaval. Revolution in a country brimming with nuclear weapons would be an enormous risk for the entire world. But however flawed the Communist regime might have been, my whole liberal essence cried out against such a radical break with the past. It was our task to ensure that the exit from socialism was a smooth one, with the least possible conflict and danger. The trouble was that neither the political leadership nor the public could imagine the extent of the real danger or the consequences of the economic decisions now being made.

Having despaired of getting through to the Party leadership on the pages of *Kommunist*, Latsis and I wrote a short memorandum to Gorbachev. We tried to give him the gist of what was happening, to explain the direct connection between the collapse of consumer markets and financial distortions. We offered an assortment of solutions that might help bring the situation under control, including substantial reductions in military spending, limits on centralized capital investments, a move to increase the percentage of the most profitable imported consumer goods—all measures that would allow us to substantially reduce the size of the budget deficit and bring the growth rate of the money supply under control.

We were not overly hopeful of success. We had already written quite a few such reports, and we wrote this one probably just to keep our consciences clear. We sent it through Ivan Frolov, who was by that time one of Gorbachev's aides, and we threw in an assortment of materials that had been published in *Kommunist* which went into great detail in revealing the dynamics of the financial—and the overall—economic crisis. To our surprise, the report made an impression on Gorbachev. In some ways it probably reflected much of his own thinking. In any case, he read it in full at the next meeting of the Politburo, led a painstaking discussion of it, and then issued specific directives to his government.

But our attached recommendations looked far too radical to him—they weren't his style at all. True, small changes in economic and financial policy were made, but none of them on a scale corresponding to the magnitude of the impending crisis. The potentially ruinous policy stayed in force.

In 1989 and 1990, I frequently met with Gorbachev—in large, small, and quite private meetings; I worked with him on a variety of documents. My original assessment of his personality seemed more valid than ever. There was no doubt that he was a genuine reformer, that he wanted to change both his country and the socialist system, to do away with its ugliest sides. In introducing the changes he did, he of course couldn't foresee how complex these problems would be, or what titanic forces of opposition would be launched against even the most timid of attempts to alter the framework of the totalitarian Soviet empire. When he collided with these powerful and unmanageable processes, he seemed to lose his bearings, his orientation. He had let the genie of political liberalization out of the bottle but could neither control it nor stuff it back in. Nor could he decide what he truly wanted. And herein lay Gorbachev's most serious weakness—his inability to make the necessary, if risky, decisions and then follow through with them.

At that time the whole world was discussing our problems, trying to sort out the exact nature of Gorbachev's strategy. My own impression was that there was no strategy at all, that Gorbachev was taking small tactical steps, encountering new problems, then taking more small steps without really knowing where any of them might lead. It was no surprise that the liberal intelligentsia's "Gorbymania" of 1989 and 1990 faded quickly. Nonetheless, I felt a profound liking for him, this man who had taken upon himself the Russian reformer's burden—a burden that perhaps was too heavy for him.

In the summer of 1990, I declined Grigory Yavlinsky's offer of a post in the government of the Russian Republic, if for no other reason than that I didn't want to abandon Gorbachev at a difficult time. It took his abrupt shift in direction that fall—his refusal to cooperate with the governing bodies of the Russian Republic, his choice to cast his lot with conservative factions in the Party elite and the military and security agencies, the bloody events in Vilnius—before I realized that the tale of Gorbachev-the-reformer was ended.[3] Meanwhile, for the liberal intelligentsia, the political split had long since become bipolar. If not Gorbachev, then Yeltsin.

My feelings toward Yeltsin were also mixed. He, too, hailed from Sverdlovsk, where he had served as first secretary of the Sverdlovsk regional Party committee. Our family had always maintained close ties with the city. We knew how our friends and acquaintances felt about local political leaders. They had liked Yeltsin, felt a certain regard for him. They said that he was one of the leaders who actually did care about his work, who was capable of carrying on a normal conversation with people. They were chagrined when he was moved from Sverdlovsk to Moscow. Among people who dealt with him in Moscow, reactions were largely positive. Yes, there had been problems with personnel—he did not know who to bring in—but at least he was trying to do something, to straighten things out.

His speech at the Central Committee plenum in the fall of 1987, his subsequent recantation at the Moscow city conference, and his speech during the summer of 1988 at the Nineteenth Party Conference all made for a fairly complicated picture.[4] His strength and his political potential, his ability to grasp what was really bothering people, were easy to see. Much less evident was just where that political potential might be channeled. And anything relating to the economy seemed particularly vague.

Gradually it became clear that Yeltsin had a weapon of his own in reserve—admittedly somewhat dulled by the passage of time—for use against the decrepit socialist regime. This was an aggressive social populism. When through that little door of glasnost opened by Gorbachev there suddenly came a flood of information about Party and government privilege, when the real scale of social inequity became visible for all to see (all those Kremlin special requisitions, special departments in GUM,[5] special medical clinics, resorts, state dachas), radical opponents of the Communist regime used their criticism of privilege as the most powerful sort of propaganda, the sort that went to the very deepest historical roots of human social consciousness, of people's notions of justice. The call to "take it all and divide it all up," which the Bolsheviks had used so effectively in their own struggle for power, was now turned against the Party itself.

Yeltsin, who traveled by streetcar and went to the neighborhood polyclinic for his checkups, rode to the top on a wave of popular affection, after which he could get away with a few unsuccessful appearances in America and mysterious river plunges. Nothing could stop the growth of his popularity, and any blunders were generally written off as some "plot" by the elite to bring down the people's protector.[6]

When the Moscow elections ended with Yeltsin's steamroller (90 percent) victory over an opponent supported by the Party apparatus, it became obvious to everyone that we had a genuine political leader on our hands. But just what was this leader going to do with the powerful support the people had accorded him?

Those who wanted, as I did, profound but nonetheless gradual and orderly reforms put our hopes in a strategic alliance between Gorbachev the tsar-reformer and Yeltsin the man-of-the-people. Of course neither their impersonal rhetoric in relation to one another nor Gorbachev's rather awkward maneuvers aimed at preventing Yeltsin from being elected Chairman of the Supreme Soviet of the Russian Republic worked to promote such a tandem, but neither did they rule one out. An alliance of this sort became a real possibility in the summer of 1990, when Yeltsin and Gorbachev came to an agreement on the development and implementation of the economic reform known as the "500 Days." It seemed that together they would be able to halt the socioeconomic freefall, and steer the changes into more or less orderly paths.

I had first met Grigory Yavlinsky, initiator of the above-mentioned program, in the fall of 1988. I had been asked to help prepare a report, to be presented by Chairman of the Soviet of Ministers Nikolai Ryzhkov, on long-term prospects for development of the Soviet economy. Our working group was based at the Soviet of Ministers' health spa, "The Pines." The group included several acquaintances of mine, including Yakov Urinson, who headed Gosplan's computer center, Vladimir Mashitz, who worked at the Central Economics and Mathematics Institute, and Tatyana Ivanovna Koryagina, a professor from Gosplan's economic research institute.

Tatyana Ivanovna, who had arrived before us, had already found a table in the dining hall and invited Grigory Alekseevich and me to join her. At the time, he headed the Social Development Board at the State Committee on Labor and Social Issues and was said to be a rising star, especially given the paucity of talent in Ryzhkov's government.

I was responsible for those sections of the group's report that had to do with financial policy and economic reform, and Yavlinsky for those having to do with social development issues. During the month or so that we worked together, we got to know each other well, had some good times, and talked about all sorts of things. The work was not easy. Our views on real long-term (and short-term, for that matter) prospects for the Soviet economy differed greatly from those held by the leadership.

I tried to teach Nikolai Ivanovich Ryzhkov at least a bit about the basics of economics and finance—with, I must admit, remarkably little success. Vladimir Savakov, one of Ryzhkov's closest advisers and the supervisor of our group, would regularly deliver our texts to the higher-ups and, as a rule, come back upset and disappointed. They were unhappy, they could not understand how the collapse of the consumer market could possibly have anything to do with the state budget, nor could they fathom any number of other economic subtleties.

What they wanted from Yavlinsky was an exact and precise accounting of the tumultuous gains made in the Soviet standard of living over the last decade; they wanted information on how many Soviet eggs would be laid per capita in the year 2000. He fought them off as best he could, tried to make them see the comedy in egg projections—but in vain. His jokes fell flat.

My general sense of Yavlinsky, formed over several months of working with him, was fairly clear-cut. He was undeniably talented, colorful, madly ambitious, and secretly bothered by the obvious gaps in his economics background—of which, to his credit, he was quite aware. Later, in Moscow, we often spoke on the phone or met in person. Grigory Alekseevich would more and more often complain that trying to break through the Soviet of Ministers' bureaucracy was utterly hopeless, and asked me to somehow get him a meeting with Gorbachev.

Yavlinsky's rise began in the fall of 1989, after his teacher Leonid Ivanovich Abalkin took a government post. Abalkin invited Yavlinsky to head a combined section of the Commission on Economic Reform. The Congress of People's Deputies had directed the government to draft an economic recovery program. Much of this work was assigned to Abalkin's commission, and at the implementation level to Yavlinsky and my old acquaintance, Professor Yevgeny Yasin, who had been tapped to head another section of the commission. And here begins the gripping tale of the creation of roughly ten programs which, right up until the summer of 1991, were being developed by experts and were widely discussed and accepted at the highest levels. Yet they had virtually no impact on the real economic processes at work, processes subject to the entirely different and entirely real logic of a collapsing bureaucratic economy—a logic never foreseen in any of these programs.

The documents are interesting in their own right, and when compared they show a growing realization of the need for a massive privatization program; they also show that the architects of these programs, in an effort to combine economic necessity with political capacity, built utterly unrealistic estimates into their forecasts. I had a hand in either the writing or the reviewing of many of them. An economic historian would have a fascinating time studying them all.

The clear exception among these documents was undoubtedly the "500 Days," although its impact was political rather than economic. Yavlinsky had shown me an outline of it back in March 1990. In terms of content, it held nothing particularly new. For the most part it reiterated the logic of previous program documents, and included stabilization measures as a base that would precede freeing of prices, structural reforms, and privatization. But the program featured one brilliant stroke of public relations—the decision to break it down day by day. Of course this had nothing to do with economics, and it's quite impossible to take a process involving massive social and economic reforms and break it down into daily increments, especially when the economy is falling apart. But the program fit the political demands of the day amazingly well; it promised a disoriented Russian populace a simple recipe for free-market happiness. And at such a low cost!

That the fall of socialism should not be seen as synonymous with the appearance of an already developed and effective market economy, that the birthmarks of socialism would take decades to fade away, that an enormous amount of difficult work lay ahead before even the prerequisites of a normally functioning market could be created—all these notions were far beyond any economic views dominant in the public mind.

On a political level, this day-by-day, short-term program for building a developed market economy in the Soviet Union was exactly what Yeltsin and that part of the elite who followed him needed. Whether the program was realistic or unrealistic from an economic standpoint meant nothing. Even a false idea that has taken hold of the masses becomes a material force.

Both in the summer of 1990 and later, Yavlinsky and I, and co-creators Yevgeny Yasin, Vladimir Mashitz, and Boris Fyodorov, discussed how we felt about the program. There is no doubt that most of them had no illusions about it being anything other than utopian. But politically "500 Days" was indeed useful at that juncture in that it allowed for a rapprochement between Gorbachev and Yeltsin. It created a base for a possible alliance between the two, a possible common course of action—and consequently a way to prevent a destructive legislative war. This is what in the end impelled me to support the program publicly, and to express only mild doubts about how realistic many of its basic parameters were.

But alas, Yavlinsky's program was not fated to fulfill its political purpose either. After vacillating for a long time, under heavy pressure from military and security interests and the conservative wing of the apparatus, Gorbachev refused to come to terms with Yeltsin and refused to support "500 Days." From that moment on we could forget about any sort of meaningful economic policy. Between Russia and the crumbling Soviet Union a fierce struggle for power began.

It became clear to any unbiased observer that the country was approaching economic collapse. This had been obvious to the creators of "500 Days," who wrote in their preamble that in the case of a refusal by the leadership of the Soviet Union and Russia to undertake joint action in enacting market reforms, the process of disintegration in the economic system would continue and scores of autarkies would spring up in regional and ethnic enclaves. Exchange of goods and products would take the form of barter, and the result would be a choice of either hyperinflation or direct confiscation of funds from enterprises and the populace. The decline in production would become even more precipitous, and many major enterprises would shut down for lack of component parts and supplies. The acute shortage of consumer goods and production materials would be compensated for by imports, but the country would probably be denied new loans. A deterioration of major urban centers would set in, and marketability of the richest agricultural regions would drop. The consumer market would be squeezed out by planned distribution and the black market. The economic crisis would be aggravated by the lack of any unified program of action. Each republic, and then each territory (right down to district level), would try to find its own way out of the crisis, which would be ruinous for an integrated, supermonopolized economic system. The political consequences would be the ultimate disintegration of the Soviet Union, and nationalist conflict in ethnically diverse regions. Flouting the law would become common practice throughout society.

Now this scenario was becoming inevitable. The only question was how to proceed when this precisely drawn picture of impending catastrophe did indeed become reality. Would there be any way to limit the economic and political hardship? How could one even begin trying to influence authorities on both Union and republic levels to use every opportunity to avert disaster or at least minimize the damage? Many people were waiting for the very popular Yavlinsky to provide an answer to these questions. But he submitted his resignation, in spite of Russian Republic leaders' pleas and attempts to persuade him to remain in government and continue his work on the preparation of market reforms. It was a time-tested and certain political move. Of course, staying in government would have allowed him to accomplish a good deal toward laying the groundwork for privatization, developing market legislation, legal safeguards for private property, and much else. But all this would have gone on against a backdrop of growing economic crisis, the responsibility for which would inevitably be laid at the doorstep of those in charge. The contrast with the sweet little fairy tale of "500 Days" would be too glaring. The political cost too great.

On the day of his resignation Yavlinsky dropped in at the government dacha in Volynskoe, where Yevgeny Yasin, Stanislav Shatalin, Nikolai Petrov, Abel Aganbegyan, and I were working. Ivan Silaev, the Russian prime minister, called Yasin and asked if he would agree to take Yavlinsky's place. Yavlinsky tried to dissuade Yasin, but in any case the latter hadn't planned on accepting. Later, Gorbachev arrived. We discussed an eclectic sort of document—a hybrid of the "500 Days" program and the government program prepared by Leonid Abalkin. We talked about various things. Gorbachev suddenly came up with the rather exotic notion of appointing Belorussian deputy Zhuravlyov (in my view, a rather emotional and unbalanced person) chairman of the Central Bank. We advised against it. On the whole we had the feeling that Gorbachev knew he was in a political cul-de-sac.

There, in Volynskoe, Aganbegyan suggested that I take charge of a newly organized research institute at the Academy of the Economy. Its proposed name was the "Economic Mechanism Institute." After some thought, I accepted. We then and there came to an agreement with Shatalin, then secretary of the Economics Section at the Academy of Sciences, that the new institute would be under the supervision of both the Academy of the Economy and the Academy of Sciences, but that it would be named the Institute for Economic Policy. We would try to bring in the most dynamic of the younger generation of economists.

I accepted the offer all the more eagerly because I had begun to feel burdened by my journalistic work. Early in 1990, at Ivan Frolov's suggestion, I had taken over the economics section of *Pravda* and had published several major pieces on economics, including what was probably my best-known newspaper publication, "Good Intentions," summarizing the lessons of Gorbachev and Ryzhkov's economic policies. However it was becoming clear that with increasingly conservative tendencies now afoot, we were hardly likely to succeed in turning *Pravda* into an organ of reform. My pieces were strikingly out of sync with what was being printed in other sections of the paper.

By that time I had already informed Frolov that I was leaving. I thought about what I would do next. I was firmly resolved to go back to scholarly work. The offer to head a new institute unburdened by the ballast of "favors," where I could pick and choose people according to their abilities alone, was very attractive. The institute was intended to be small, only about a hundred people. And I did choose practically all the staff myself. It seems to me that I was able to put together quite a good group. The deputy directors were Andrei Nechaev, who came from the Institute of Economics and Science and Technology Forecasting, and Vladimir Mashitz, from the Central Economics and Mathematics Institute, a fine statistician and an expert on economic mechanisms. From the Institute of Economics, I invited Vladimir Mau, who at the time was doing a good deal of work on the history of economic thought and was just beginning his research on contemporary political economy. From Gosplan's Institute of Economics came Sergei Sinelnikov, who dealt with the economics of natural resource use; I persuaded him to switch his specialization to tax and budget issues. Other talented economists came on board as well: Aleksandr Radygin, Yelena Zhuravskaya, Vadim Ivanov. The Leningrad branch of the institute was headed by Sergei Vasiliev. On the whole it turned out to be an amicable and hard-working group.

We all agreed that we would not write grandiose programs, we would not formulate economic policy, we would simply study it. Of course we would be more than willing to do analysis and review of normative acts, proposals, and program workups for either the Soviet or the Russian government. We would evaluate and assist, but our focus would be the study of the mechanisms by which the Russian economy operated, the processes at work within it, and short-term forecasting. These areas were all the more crucial because any real possibility that the government could influence events in the economy was becoming fainter and fainter all the time.

At the institute's first major seminar in January 1991, I gave a presentation entitled "The Economics of Instability and Prospects for the Development of the Soviet Economy." Since the fall of 1990 the Soviet economy had entered a period of both repressed and open inflation. Prices were rising rapidly, and there was still a shortage of available goods on the market. I forecast three stages: a period of combined repressed and open inflation; a period of open inflation; then stabilization. We could not pinpoint the dates for a transition from the first stage to the second, or from the second to the third. But on the other hand, it was relatively easy to estimate what the parameters of socioeconomic development would be during each of these stages; in particular, the rate of growth of the money supply, the budget deficit, the share of subsidies in the gross domestic product, real and nominal personal income, and the volume of industrial production. I drew up graphs of these parameters for the periods before and after liberalization of prices, and at the onset of stabilization.

Later events would confirm that my forecast was largely accurate.

Chapter 4

August of Ninety-one

- Thoughts of a new book
- The GKChP
- At the White House
- Gennady Burbulis
- Postvictory paralysis
- A strange country
- Barter economy
- Convulsions

At the beginning of August 1991, I took a sabbatical and, breaking away from routine institute concerns, left for Krasnovidovo, a dacha settlement just outside Moscow, to finally get down to work on a long-planned book.

In 1989 and 1990 the entire Communist empire, encompassing both the USSR and the vassal nations of Eastern Europe, entered into a stage of grave crisis and collapse. Serious economic transformations, systemic in nature, began taking place everywhere. The order of the day was radical restructuring of fundamental socioeconomic institutions. The process was not uniform: it might take on the tragic tension of Romania in 1989, or move along more peacefully, smoothly, as in Czechoslovakia or Bulgaria. But the scale of the economic problems during this transitional period exceeded even the most pessimistic of expectations.

Of course, in each case you might find specific reasons for those problems. For example, in the Soviet Union it was the reduction in oil and gas production and the drop in crude oil and gas prices worldwide, while in East Germany it was exaggerated expectations of what would come of re-unification with West Germany, and in Poland the inevitable cost of curbing hyperinflation. Nonetheless, whatever the specifics of each nation, whatever the particularities of their reforms, certain general tendencies, even patterns, emerged. These general laws and the particular difficulties of the road from a socialist economy to a normal one were what I wanted to ponder in my new book.

The previous one had been titled *Economic Reforms and Hierarchical Structures* and was devoted to an analysis of attempts to modernize the socialist economic model without destroying its foundations. Such reform attempts had been undertaken more than once, but had generally been erratic, partial, and faced with powerful bureaucratic opposition. But nowhere had they ever led to a decline in output. They had, on the contrary, spurred it at least temporarily, leading to an improvement in the consumer market and, in some countries, promoting the development of small business. Now it was an entirely different picture. The catastrophic crash of the old system of management had given rise to fundamentally new problems that differed substantially from those I had studied earlier.

On Sunday August 18, I had stayed up particularly late. It was after midnight when I finished writing the last paragraph of my introductory chapter: "In that particular stage of the economic transformation now being undergone by the USSR and Eastern Europe, the most reasonable economic policy is more often than not also the most unpopular. Implementation of such policy is possible only when government is both strong and effective. The further any given post-Communist nation has progressed in this direction, the more confidently economic policy moves onto a track that will allow that nation to lay the foundations for stable economic development. In the USSR, where any reasonable government action is now stymied by constitutional crisis and 'legislative war,' events are deviating from the professional-economic standard, and this in turn pushes the nation onto the path of 'Latin-Americanization.'"

Of course at that moment I could hardly imagine that in two months I would be taking on the responsibility of carrying out reasonable but clearly unpopular economic reform policy in Russia.

Early the next morning my wife's uncustomarily loud and uncustomarily anxious voice woke me: "Yegor! Come quick!"

"What is it? Is it Pashka?"

"It's a coup! A military coup! Gorbachev's been arrested."

On Mondays the earliest regular bus from Krasnovidovo into Moscow left at 11:00 A.M. There was a line waiting at the small watchman's booth housing the only city telephone in the settlement. I called the institute, informing them that I'd be there around 12:30, and set a meeting in my office for that time.

Masha called her father. "Tanks," she said, coming out of the booth. "My father said that there are columns of tanks moving right under his windows along Vernadsky Prospekt. Toward the center of town. . . ." Later she and the children saw me off. She waved, there were tears in her eyes, and she was obviously wondering if we'd ever see each other again. It was not clear to anyone just how big this might be.

On the way I tried to imagine the possible consequences of a coup. At that moment I had no doubt that it would lead to a change in government. Or that for several months, or even years, its architects might manage to stay afloat. But what happens then? I didn't see any "enlightened dictatorship" or "Russian Pinochet" on the horizon. As with Pinochet, blood would flow—in fact a good deal of blood. But it would all be for nothing. The conspirators hadn't a single sound idea among them on how to cope with a crumbling economy. In two, three, four years, no more, this tormented country would in any case end up taking the hard road to free markets. But the way would be a thousand times more difficult. So it would be a year, or two—say even five. In terms of history, that's a blink of the eye. But what about those living now? How many of them would make it past all that?

The bus neared Moscow, crossed the circumferential highway. Just past the suburb of Tushino all heads on the bus turned left. There was an armored personnel carrier at the bridge. I took out my folder to start drafting what I planned to say at the institute. But I didn't have any fresh paper, and had to write on the back of the chapter I had just finished the day before.

My institute staff had already gathered. I told them that I didn't have any new information, but the situation was clear: this wasn't Deng Xiaoping and his enlightened market authoritarianism—this was the GKChP.[1] If the putsch were to be successful, nothing but darkness, vileness, and blood lay ahead; but even if it failed, the existing system would disintegrate and the threat of chaos and anarchy would become all too real. In any case, if there was one person whose authority might give the country some chance of avoiding disaster, it was Boris Yeltsin. And that meant that our task was to do everything in our power to help him.

From the institute, I tracked down everyone I could reach by phone. I called Gorbachev's aide, Oleg Ozherelev. I asked him if Gorbachev was still alive, and if there was anything we could do. He was evasive, didn't have much to say. I called Sergei Krasavchenko and Aleksei Golovkov at the Russian White House. I asked them to let the government know that our institute was at their disposal.

My colleagues and I did a high-speed analysis of the economic portion of the coup leaders' program. In all honesty, our analysis came out more malicious than judicious. We distributed it to democratically oriented Russian newspapers and to Western news services.

In history, everything that happens soon takes on a certain finality. It's easy to convince oneself that things couldn't have gone otherwise. Hence the reigning current attitude that sees the coup as something operatic, doomed from the start. After familiarizing myself with the documents, with accounts by those who took part in the failed attempt, I was persuaded—and still am—that strategically they were indeed doomed to fail, but that they could have caused a great deal of bloodshed, and could have maintained themselves in power for at least some time. The greater part of the population opposed the coup, but only passively. Other republics held their breath, waiting to see what would happen in Russia. Georgian nationalist leader Zvyad Gamsakhurdia, once so belligerent, was clearly alarmed, and announced his readiness to cooperate with the

GKChP. In the Baltics, the Soviet military acted decisively enough, securing key military sites. The issue would be decided by developments in the capital cities, especially in Moscow.

As I see it, tactically, the putschists' defeat was conditioned by two factors. The first was their profound contempt for their political opponents. I know for a fact that among those favoring the use of force there was a widespread notion that all democrats were cowards by nature. All you had to do was pound your fist on the table, and they would scurry off to their burrows and hide. The fact that in Moscow and Petersburg nothing of the sort happened, and that the coup instead came up against massive protests and opposition, was a most unpleasant surprise for them. Nothing in Russian history had given anyone much reason to hope that such opposition would not be brutally crushed. The conspirators were clearly willing to do just that. It was merely a matter of detail: a question of who would take responsibility for massive bloodletting and mass repressions, who would organize and force the military to act, who would put the most reliable, proven, and resolute general into the lead tank and personally order him to crush the opposition. In short, who would succeed in overcoming the perfectly natural reluctance of military and security structures to take the fall? Nobody. Hence all the vacillations, the inconsistency, the attempts to foist off responsibility on each other, the breakdown of the military machine. All this has its own logic: the sclerosis of the socialist system had progressed very far indeed, and avoiding responsibility had, over the years, been raised to the level of an art. And this certainly didn't encourage the appearance of strong characters at the military levers of control. At the same time, there is always the element of chance; the presence of a Varennikov or a Makashov at the crucial time and place might well have radically altered the situation.[2]

In any case, when the tens of thousands of Muscovites gathered at the Russian White House on August 20, 1991, and heard the news that it was about to be stormed, they had no reason to suppose that the outcome would be anything other than a bloodbath—just as when two years earlier in Beijing, on Tiananmen Square, the corpses had to be bulldozed away. But they came anyway. They came because they did not want to be wordless little puppets, because they valued their freedom and wanted to defend it. This was perhaps the first day since August 1968 that I felt I had every right to be proud of my country and my people.

The morning of August 20, at the White House, a sea of people filled Rochdel Street and the entire space between the Comecon Building and the Hotel Mir. There was a general feeling that the putsch was doomed, that the people of Moscow were not intimidated and did not plan on giving in. However, in the latter part of the day, after I had returned to the institute, the situation again seemed uncertain. A curfew was imposed, and information filtered in about troop movements. It looked as if there would be an attack after all.

I suspended my own order on the cessation of any organized Party activity at the institute (issued in the wake of Yeltsin's decree banning Party cells) for the space of one hour. We convened an official Party meeting, with two questions on the agenda. The first proposal concerned institute employees' resignation from the Party in light of the current attempt, supported by the Communist Party of the USSR, at a government overthrow. The second concerned the liquidation of our Party organization in light of this event. One colleague said in a trembling voice that this was a very difficult decision for her and she needed to talk it over with her husband. Everyone else—people of different generations, of different backgrounds and experience—unanimously supported both proposals. And so, in very short order, the last Party meeting at the institute came to an end.

By around seven in the evening, the men from the institute were at the White House in full force. Here I met Gennady Burbulis for the first time.[3] His office was noisy; Viktor Valentinovich Ivanenko, chairman of the Russian Federation Government Security Committee, was sitting at a desk trying to reach the generals in command of local districts. Gennady Eduardovich and I lamented that we had to meet at a time like this, after hearing about each other for so long.

Later we were to meet often, especially in the fall of 1991, when the Russian leadership's post-August strategy was being developed. It was in fact Burbulis who introduced me to Yeltsin, and Burbulis who perhaps more than anyone else was involved in putting together the reform government that began its work in November 1991. Later we worked together in this government, often meeting in the President's office; and together we led his 1993 election campaign. Burbulis was campaign manager. He is an undeniably intelligent and subtle analyst; he knows how to weigh the options, take the long-term view, recruit interesting people, bring in the right specialists. He is perfectly suited to play the role of the gray eminence behind the leadership. Unfortunately, this role for which he seems to have been created is one that he dislikes intensely. He wants to be in charge, to make the important decisions himself. But he has no gift for it. I remember meetings that he chaired. They were always very satisfying intellectually, but as a rule they never led to any concrete results. It's distressing—your day is planned out minute by minute, a colossal number of problems are lined up at your door, waiting for you, and here you're having an admittedly interesting but quite inconclusive conversation.

My realization of all this came much later. At the time, our discussion focused on the topic at hand: if today doesn't end in disaster, if the situation is left hanging in the balance, what do we do to shift that balance in our favor? Who has what levers in hand? Newspapers, radio, printing houses. What will happen in the other major cities? Will the call for a general strike get any response? One scenario—that of a swift and decisive victory over the Committee—seemed as unreal as ever, and wasn't even discussed. Ivanenko was on the telephone nonstop, talking with commanders in the Moscow military district, with MVD forces, with KGB units. He was telling everyone roughly the same thing: I'm calling at Yeltsin's behest, don't get tangled up in this business, keep your men and materiel out of it.

Grigory Yavlinsky came in. We hadn't seen each other for a long time. We talked—obviously not about economics. He thought that Gorbachev was privy to the plot and secretly supported it, but I had my doubts —what good would this do him?

Burbulis came back from talking with Yeltsin. The President has asked us to track the routes that tanks might use to move on the White House. Radio operators were trying to intercept conversations between commanders of tank units and their subordinates.

Gradually, sometime after midnight, the atmosphere began to heat up. Tanks were indeed on the move. Using a government line, Burbulis dialed KGB chairman Vladimir Kryuchkov's office. It was all very strange: we were all about to be killed, and still we were making calls, talking. . . .

Tension was at its height at around 2:30 A.M., then died down. At roughly five o'clock in the morning I went outside through entryway number 8 to look for my soaking wet, chilled-to-the-bone colleagues. It was as if nothing had really happened, just a long sleepless night. But something *had* happened—an unexpected, seemingly improbable, absolutely stunning victory. Not everyone realized that yet.

"Everybody go home and get some sleep," I told my colleagues. "We'll meet at the institute at twelve. We need to think through what we should do next."

August 20 and 21 represented the total collapse of the Committee, the Communist regime, the empire. The coup leaders were arrested, there were jubilant crowds on the streets of Moscow, "Democratic Russia" activists shielded Party Central Committee members from the crowds; at KGB headquarters everyone was busy burning archives. There was Minister of the Interior Boris Pugo's suicide, and the far more mysterious suicide of Central Committee business manager Nikolai Kruchina, head of Party finances. There were sycophantic pieces in *Pravda*. Their gist: *We'll be good from now on; we'll loyally serve the new democratic government.* There was total demoralization within the Communist Party. Those who supported the coup were scared to death, fearing that the democratic forces would treat them the same way they themselves would have treated the democrats had the Committee won the day. It all reminded me of February 1917, at least as I imagine it from books and con-

temporary accounts. And this was precisely what gave me no peace. I knew all too well what came after the euphoria of the February Revolution.[4] Yes, it was wonderful that the putsch had failed, but now what?

The swift and total collapse of the Communist Party, the organization that synchronized all the little wheels of power throughout the country, the fall of the all-knowing KGB, the total bankruptcy of the ruling political elite and its ideology—might not all these events simply clear the road for chaos, anarchy, terrible economic ruin, and a new dictatorship? The danger seemed particularly grave if one bore in mind that heretofore all our economic relationships had been built not on a system of working markets but on the strength of coercion, on command.

Tomorrow all the kolkhozes and sovkhozes would stop turning in their grain, the fear of punishment would vanish, and the ruble would be worthless. What do we do next? Tomorrow it would become clear that the republics were de facto sovereign states that no longer recognized Soviet jurisdiction. But who then would control the nuclear arsenal? A multitude of urgent questions—and no answers. Despite all the fluttering Russian tricolor flags and the jubilant crowds, I was profoundly anxious about the country's future. What we had here was unquestionably a liberal, anti-Communist revolution brought on by the inflexibility and recklessness of the ruling elite. But revolution is always a terrible tragedy for any country, and revolution is what we had wanted to avoid, by steering development onto a path of orderly reform. What was once considered an abstract threat was now becoming a cruel reality.

One characteristic feature of the first two months after the putsch was a kind of sudden paralysis, a frightening passivity on the part of Russia's governing bodies. It's understandable, though. On August 21, a powerful opponent, against whom a long and arduous battle had been planned and prepared, simply disappeared. Yeltsin was like a warrior-knight in a fairy tale who had crushed the foe and burst into the enchanted castle only to find, instead of his long-suffering and beautiful princess, nothing but darkness, neglect, and piles of garbage. And now he was the one who had to deal with it all. The unexpected victory deprived the President of Russia of the advantage of being in the opposition, but gave him nothing in its place, no magic wand to stop the ever-hastening process of economic collapse. The situation merely became more complicated.

Soviet economic ministries no longer administered anything. Their employees were busy looking for work in the private sector, creating commercial firms and transferring public money and property to them. Work by Party organizations, which until August 1991 had out of sheer tradition still mediated and regulated economic ties on the republic, regional, and district levels, was now officially banned. Kraikoms, raikoms, obkoms—all those ruling committee offices were closed down, their doors sealed.[5] The military and security forces—the army, the KGB, the MVD—were demoralized.

The new Soviet administrative bodies formed after the failed coup made no serious attempts to take the situation in hand. That too is understandable: now, after the August victory, all responsibility for what was transpiring in Russia and in a considerable part of the territory of the entire former Soviet Union rested squarely on the shoulders of the Russian leadership.

In this political context there was still one chance left, or so I thought at the time, to save the USSR: Gorbachev would promptly abdicate and turn his responsibilities over to Yeltsin, president of the largest Soviet republic. Yeltsin would then legitimately assume control over Soviet governmental structures and, with his undeniable current authority as the Russian people's chosen leader, ensure the merger of these two centers of power, the struggle between which had greatly contributed to the general collapse. Hope springs eternal.

In reality, something entirely different was going on: the Russian leadership was sitting idle as the first trickle of disintegration rapidly turned into an avalanche, as interrepublic customs services were holding up all exports. Formally the Union still existed, but its soul had expired, leaving only a body that had already ceased to function. There were no death throes. It might be possible to reach various sorts of agreements with other republics, but issuing directives, demanding their execution, enforcing them? This was pure fantasy. Gorbachev telling Nazarbaev how to handle the Tengis-Chevron project? Impossible. The issue was moot.

The Soviet Union, as a real force, was gone, and it was no surprise that Soviet military weapons in the Caucasus were now up for grabs. Military and security organizations were in a state of shock. The shell of a power structure was still standing, but there was no one inside, in charge. Who was in charge? The Soviet Union? There was not a single republic left where Soviet laws had any force. All the republics had their own laws, and republican law officially took precedence over Soviet.

Yeltsin had a large reserve of popular trust, unimaginable responsibilities, and almost no levers of control. After all, up to this very moment the Russian Republic, as a government structure, had been purely decorative. Nothing in it was connected to anything else. It had no army, no KGB, no MVD, no control over other regions of the country whose local governments might pull who knows what. It effectively had no central bank. No control over the greater part of industry. No customs service. In fact, nothing at all, except the name—the Russian State.

The first economic reaction to the August putsch was just what I had expected it to be: the next week, grain deliveries to the state dropped by a factor of four. People simply weren't hauling it to the elevators. This was natural. Why should they? To get some pieces of paper that, out of habit, everyone still calls money? Oh no, better to hang onto that grain, trade it for something useful when you get a chance.

Barter had replaced money exchange, and Moscow and St. Petersburg, only yesterday showcases of the command economy, found themselves in a particularly difficult situation. The socioeconomic structure of these two major cities (the defense industry, science and scholarship, culture, administration) was hardly suited to a barter economy. Their population's traditional dependence on imports made the the very problem of supplying these two Russian capitals insoluble. No amount of arguing would convince the rest of the country to send them food supplies.

The public clearly recognized how alarming the situation had become. Autumn of 1991 was rife with expectations of catastrophe, famine, total breakdown in transport and communications systems. Primus stoves were at a premium. The most common topic of conversation was "how will we all survive?" The horrific picture of Moscow in the not-too-distant future created by Aleksandr Kabakov in his novel *The Defector* conveys this atmosphere of foreboding rather well.[6] And the responsibility for this lay on none other than Russia's first democratically elected government. It's no surprise that Communist activists, barely recovered from August's crushing blow, began rubbing their hands in vindictive glee: *Well, we'll just see how you manage. Like it or not, you'll have to call us back.*

To use a chess analogy, you might say that in the fall of 1991 the democratic forces of Russia were in a losing position. Their only chance, using the same analogy, was to force the issue, to put the game on a fast track. It was a plan that certainly didn't guarantee success, but did provide some hope of avoiding certain defeat. And, all analogies aside, there wasn't much choice: it was either constantly increasing chaos or, with no preparation whatseover, an immediate start-up of the free market mechanism—with the understanding that the parts required for it to function normally would be built in later, as we went along.

Within the rigid framework of a hierarchical economy, the leadership was free to take the profits from those who made them, and pass them along to those who could only dream of such things. You could set a price at ten times the manufacturing costs of this or that product, and in another case you might practically give something away. You could do anything—but only as long as all the economic, ideological, and political features of the system were fully integrated. We could not return to that situation. The market start-up would have to leave the realm of good intentions and become a real imperative. Otherwise we would have a disaster on our hands.

I should remind the reader that the most critical issue dividing economists at the time was the relationship beween Russian and centralized economic policy. After August, on paper, there was still a "center" and a Soviet Union; and Yavlinsky continued his work drafting an interrepublic economic agreement. For my colleagues and others of like mind, it was obvious that without a meaningful Russian economic policy such agreements would be largely unproductive. Negotiations would be difficult and unlikely to yield the desired results, and an effective economic union could not exist in the absence of a political one. Clearly there was no chance of quickly creating either.

A shared economic space requires a shared political space—this is axiomatic. The obvious example is the European Community. Before serious discussions on a unified currency system for Europe could begin, the long process of creating inter-European political institutions had to take place. And the process still had a long road to travel before the monetary system could begin functioning normally.

But the sort of unity gradually being cemented in Europe was something that in our case had collapsed overnight: previously, economic ties between Soviet republics were based on a centralized command-management system. An enterprise in the Baltics, for example, would get a government order for goods to be sent to a plant in the Urals. The factory in the Urals, in its turn, would get an assignment to produce goods for a factory in Kazakhstan. This last might be linked to hundreds of specifically designated factories scattered throughout the USSR's fifteen republics. Each of these links involved a command.

This entire nonmarket system could exist on one condition only, which was that the entire Soviet Union be linked by a chain of command among industrial managers, a system extending down through republics, regions, areas, districts, all the way to the individual plant director—controlling him, rewarding him, punishing him. Only in such a case could a shared nonmarket economic space exist.

But as soon as a situation arose in which a republic-level plant director could ignore or rescind the order of a USSR-level one, and the regional factory boss could treat the republic boss the same way, and so on down the line, the system fell apart. The catastrophic rupture of these USSR-wide ties is a consequence of destroying a totalitarian structure: when the instruments of coercion in a command economy, which is quite literally run by commands, break down, the whole directive system begins to tumble like a house of cards. What inevitably springs up to replace it is the spontaneous economy of natural exchange.

Districts, cities, regions, republics were all encountering tremendous problems in securing both materials and equipment. They could no longer, for example, get their meat by directive; but they could not yet get it for money. What is a regional official to do? Let's suppose he has nails, refrigerators, and bushings. He slaps a ban on shipping those products out of the region and says, "Whoever needs these can offer me some meat for them. Ah, so you haven't got any? In that case, passenger cars might do. We can trade *them* for the meat."

If you translate this into political terms, you might say that there is nothing like a barter system forced upon a country by economic woes to promote both separatism and isolationism. You have, in other words, the proverbial vicious cycle: the rupture of USSR-level political ties leads to the rupture of economic ones, and this latter provides fertile ground for the growth of centrifugal forces capable of destroying the integrity of the Soviet Union itself. This tendency had been developing throughout 1991, and manifested itself most clearly in autumn, when barter became a major source of economic isolationism and political separatism. Many republics declared themselves sovereign states. Local authorities began issuing quotas and licenses, pursuing their own independent monetary policy. Soviet structures nominally existed, but no longer controlled anything.

Yavlinsky's group, in preparing the draft version of an interrepublic economic union, was hoping that the negotiating teams on both sides would be mutually courteous, cooperative, and willing to make concessions. But it didn't turn out that way. Negotiations on an economic union limped along in hardly promising fashion. Even after they managed to get some signatures on general framework documents, everything ground to a halt when it came to the substantive questions: control of the money supply, the exact decision-making process within the central bank, the specifics of both designing and administering the economic union's budget, who would pay the army. And much more. It was obvious that this could go on for months without anyone agreeing on anything, all the more because behind these disagreements lay genuinely disparate interests.

Here is how the situation looked to Academician Abalkin at the time (October 1991): "At the moment the Yavlinsky Agreement is awaiting

passage. But working out the package of specific stipulations and agreements contained in it will take several months of intensive work. We
were proceeding on the assumption that if, in the course of two months,
all-out emergency measures were not taken to stabilize the country's
financial and monetary situation, we could expect a social explosion
compared with which the events of last August would look like an evening of ballroom dancing. . . . I have here a memorandum composed by
institute researcher O. Rogova; it concludes that we have about two
months before the onset of total economic collapse. Other calculations
support this same view. . . . We could keep on arguing about whether the
details of this forecast are correct. But we would still be collating our
drafts and our blueprints with no one left to read them."

In my opinion, this quote makes it clear that, for all our disagreements over economic policy, in our assessment of the situation that
had developed in late 1991 the esteemed academician and I were of
one mind.

Chapter 5
On the Eve . . .

In the fall of 1991, Gennady Burbulis, at that time state secretary of the RSFSR, suggested that I put together and head a working group to prepare proposals on the strategy and tactics of an economic policy for Russia. This was a natural extension of our conversation on the night of August 21 at the White House. During the latter part of Gorbachev's administration the unwillingness to take decisive steps or action made the creation of any programs a senseless exercise. Now vigorous action could no longer be avoided, this protracted pause had become alarming, and I considered myself duty-bound to accept his offer.

Initially the group included V. Mashitz, A. Nechaev, A. Golovkov, K. Kagalovsky, and Andrei Vavilov. Later it was to expand. For days and nights on end we closeted ourselves in a dacha in the village of Arkhangelskoe just outside of Moscow. We had to come up with a quick but thorough analysis of information on the state of the economy as a whole, and also on that of various industries and regional economies: product reserves, monetary flows, government debt both foreign and domestic.

Only then could we make any sort of reliable forecasts, draft our recommendations, and shape them into finished projects and resolutions.

Of course, much of this was already familiar ground. The Institute for Economic Policy had studied these issues at close range. But now we were presented with previously unavailable information. Moreover, analyzing economic processes academically, so to speak, is one thing; creating a program that will directly affect the lives of millions of people and radically change the whole face of the country is quite another.

At the end of 1991 there was no time to measure once, let alone twice—we had to cut, and we had to cut to the quick. I was only too aware of this, and it was a constant headache for me. The situation had placed truly tragic questions on the agenda: Could we avoid economic disaster? Would there be any goods in the stores, or, with prices skyrocketing, would people still be standing in endless queues for hours at a time, or chasing from store to store with handfuls of unredeemable ration coupons? The threat of hunger was very real.

We understood: the more complex the situation, the less tolerable any fantasizing on our part. Our analysis had to be coolheaded, our solutions well considered.

As I began to work on a reform program that would stand a serious chance of being implemented, I tried to mentally reconstruct the 1990 Sopron economic conference. That forum was in many ways unique. The day the conference began, it was announced that Yeltsin and Gorbachev had reached an understanding on joint development of a program for radical market reforms in Russia. There was suddenly hope that the word "reform" might finally acquire real substance. Several conference participants—Yevgeny Yasin, Vladimir Mashits, Leonid Grigoriev—were included in the working group created by Yeltsin and Gorbachev's joint directive.

If in the West the study of socialist economies had previously been the province of Sovietologists, whose authority in questions of economics was, to put it mildly, with rare exceptions not particularly great, the transformations now under way had turned the attention of leading economic scholars from all over the world (truly first-class economists who combined broad theoretical knowledge with a high level of both scholarly authority and practical experience in the study of liberalization and stabilization processes in many countries) to the problems of postsocialist transition.

Our Western colleagues were terribly interested in learning what was really happening in the Russian economy, and what the range of possible alternatives might be. What attracted us to the conference was the chance to test our own assessments and proposals. The result was an atmosphere—not often encountered at the usual run of scholarly and scientific conferences—of unfeigned and intense mutual interest. When sessions ended, no one wanted to leave. We tried to make use of every possible moment for joint analyses of the situation, for designing proposals. Most interesting for me, perhaps, was the discussion of Russian economic issues with Professor William Nordhaus of Yale University and Professor Rudiger Dornbusch of MIT. I had known the work of both these celebrated economists for a quite some time. Now I had the opportunity to discuss in detail a vision for the developing situation in a postsocialist world.

Rudi Dornbusch was wary at first. For some reason he thought that we were going to argue that the standard relationships between the growth of the money supply, the budget deficit, the dynamics of inflation, and the currency exchange rate were inapplicable to post-Soviet conditions. When he was persuaded that our basic hypothesis was that although this structural transformation had certain specific traits born of the government sector's once dominant role, basic macroeconomic models could in fact be adapted to post-Soviet realities, the conversation moved on to the discussion of concrete issues arising out of such a transition.

In my opinion, those who were involved in creating the "500 Days" program weren't really able to make use of the discussions at the Sopron conference. The "500 Days" plan became too politicized, too propagandistic a document. But in the fall of 1991 the results of our discussions at Sopron on key issues such as the synchronization of steps in the reforms, the opening up of the economy, and monetary policy served as important points of departure.

We had no doubts about the need to liberalize prices. But, before undertaking that step, should we first take the plunge into privatization? Arguments in favor of this sequence of events had been made often enough. It's hardly necessary to point out that an effective market requires a well-developed private sector; it cannot function normally in a state-run economy. State-run enterprises react to market stimuli feebly at best; they have little financial responsibility. Even with prices formally freed, they will continue to reproduce the same patterns of deficit distribution. But by weakening the monopoly of the state, privatization introduces elements of competition, without which there are no genuine market mechanisms.

But private property and the guarantees of inviolability that must accompany it are institutions not built in a day, or a week. Nor can they be created by government fiat. Inevitably, as soon as the issue of privatization moves from the theoretical to the practical plane, conflicting interests emerge.

The factory collective is convinced that by rights it owns the factory it works in: people have worked here forever, giving the best years of their lives. And now it's goodbye, close the door on your way out? And besides, there's that old familiar battle cry—power to the people, factories to the workers! The director of the enterprise also has a claim to stake. He runs the place, he's put his heart and soul into it. And over these last few years of perestroika he's become used to handling all this property as if it were his own. The director is convinced that this right should be guaranteed.

Local government represents the population of whatever area the plant is in: *We know our own situation better than anybody else; we know who should get what, and how to go about getting it.*

Heads of concerns and corporations think themselves the only ones capable of intelligently managing the factories that were once subordinate to their respective industrial ministries.

And finally there are the state employees, teachers, students, retirees, the military, all who have heard for so long that "we are the state and the state is us" and been told that all its wealth in fact belongs to them, the citizens.

And all of these people are right, in their own way. So how do we find a just solution, one that is both economically feasible and satisfactory to everyone concerned? We had seen this happen before. Previous to the reforms of 1861, the gentry, mindful of its past and present service to the state, sincerely believed that it had a natural and traditional right to the land, while peasants believed that the land was theirs and always had been. And the tsar's manifesto satisfied neither. Remember Nekrasov's lines?

> The great chain has broken!
> Broken and snapped:
> One end whips the master
> The other whips his man![1]

The same thing occurred after socialism—divvy up state property however you please, you can't please everyone. And therefore it was so important that we find not so much economically optimal solutions—there were none—but socially acceptable and sustainable ones.

Privatization in Russia was made all the more complex by two sets of circumstances. In the first place, an extraordinarily weak private sector emerged only at the end of perestroika and most people initially associated it with the old shadow economy; for that reason it lacked any real legitimacy. In the second place, the hope of attracting major foreign investment was, given the risky social and political situation, slight at best.

In general, most of my colleagues and I, including Anatoly Chubais, were skeptical of the idea of introducing special payment notes—later known as "vouchers"—aimed at creating a demand for privatized property. The risks connected with inevitable and massive speculation were simply too obvious. Of course we would rather have avoided all this exotic stuff by applying, to the maximum degree possible, privatization processes already worked out in mature market economies. However, coolheaded analysis forced us to concede that such a strategy in Russia would mean simply giving up on the possibility of radically reducing the amount of property owned by the state. What we gained in terms of effectiveness we would lose in terms of time; we would miss the window of opportunity when a breakthrough in restructuring property relations was still possible.

In the end, the strategy we worked out was shaped by the following fundamental tenets:

— the right of all Russian citizens to own privatized property;

— an emphasis on the creation of privatization coalitions that would serve to encourage a massive grass-roots privatization process, taking into account the interests of those social groups and political forces capable of paralyzing the whole process if they saw no place for themselves in it (work collectives, enterprise directors, regional administrations, and so on);

— broad application of universally accepted procedures and standard rules in order to limit dependence of the privatization process on individual decisions, and hence the possibility of abuse of power by the administrative apparatus;

— no attempt to restructure enterprises until the form of ownership was changed.

Russia was facing the largest and most complex privatization process in the history of humankind. A legal rather than coercive transformation of property relations that attempts to take into account the interests of every social group is a highly complex procedure indeed. Creating its legal and organizational infrastructure alone takes considerable time. Ownership has to be properly and officially recorded as such; and where, for example, would we get the notaries to do that? If it's not recorded anywhere, what kind of ownership is it?

At first glance it seemed expedient to privatize at least retail trade, service, and the restaurant industry immediately. But there was a hitch here too: if a store has no goods to sell, it's not a store. Even a half-empty, dirty, and neglected store is still a temple to the distribution of worldly goods, and its employees are the priests with authority from on high to grant or withhold, to reward or punish. This was precisely how it looked in the fall of 1991. The decision to privatize retail trade, in a starving, besieged city, would have been tantamount to requisitioning all the public food supplies set aside for just such a situation.

As a result, we had to do the only logical thing under these circumstances. The lack of time, the paralysis in the command system of economic management, the feeble state of the market infrastructure, and the absence of any legal base for its development—all this was forcing us onto the fast track to price liberalization, with no time to weigh the results of these fundamental structural reforms. Of course we would try to introduce privatization in the shortest span of time possible. But putting off liberalization of prices until we saw the results of privatization—this we would not do.

There was another question: do we liberalize prices gradually or at one fell swoop? Proponents of the gradual approach based their arguments on the possibility of controlling the process. We objected that an attempt to hold down prices on a rather wide range of essential goods would not eliminate price disproportions, and would continue to increase the subsidy burden on the budget and once again create shortages. The inescapable need to raise these fixed prices periodically would continue to set off inflationary impulses. The result would be to deepen, rather than end, the crisis—something which, by the way, subsequently did happen in Ukraine and Belarus.

Jumping ahead, I would like to note that although in Arkhangelskoe we anticipated precisely such developments as these, and made a decision to strictly delimit the list of products for which prices would be regulated, the Russian government was later forced into surplus regulation. This naturally complicated the reform process, and needlessly extended the initial and most difficult period. However, these tactical maneuvers and retreats allowed the Russian government to hold the line against the Ukrainian-Belorussian syndrome.

Finances were a particular concern. Even in the midst of this crisis in the domestic economy, the government continued to support the largest army in the world, to purchase military technology on a massive scale, to invest money in long-term construction projects. The Supreme Soviet had year after year adopted one new and costly expenditure program after another. The situation was aggravated by the ongoing battle between Russian and Soviet government agencies, which made the budget's revenue base shakier than ever. The Russian and Soviet governments in 1990 and 1991 were tripping over each other to see who could lower taxes on profits the fastest. The former, having granted local governments the authority to establish their own sales tax, had essentially lost control of a critical source of budget revenue. So at the time it was extremely important, at least in the first few months after the price liberalization, and at least until the mighty wave of inflation had subsided, to shut down the currency emission engine.

The monetary system had two fundamental and quite unpleasant problems. The first was the problem of monetary reserves (the monetary overhang). The second was monetary flow. Let's use an everyday analogy: your apartment is starting to flood, and water is pouring out of the tap. You need to shut off the tap and mop up the water. But the threads are stripped and the drain is clogged! You're looking at a major flood.

Almost from the inception of perestroika, money came streaming out of the government tap, and if the flow wasn't terribly generous, it still clearly exceeded the government's means. For lack of a drainpipe (i.e., products to buy), the money pooled in accounts in savings banks. That's the monetary overhang.

Now about the monetary flow. For a long time, the state had been spending more than it took in, allocating funds for a variety of costly projects, for arms purchases, for subsidies to unprofitable enterprises. There was an enormous budget deficit, and the holes in the budget were promptly patched by automatically taking people's savings from the savings banks and using them to finance those same rips and tears. People who had spent decades on the waiting list for a car, or had time and again begged their union committee for a television coupon, thought that they had money, but nothing had been backing that money for a long time— it had all been squandered by the state.

There was not a single socialist economy that had been successful in overcoming the deficit while still preserving, in their entirety, savings accumulated under deficit conditions, savings that were unsecured. Of course it wasn't for want of trying, but solving this problem was like trying to pull yourself out of a swamp by your own hair. Which meant you would always have that inevitable crowd of Munchausens assuring everyone that they had a solution.[2]

By the end of 1991, the budget deficit was approaching 30 percent of the gross national product. The size of the monetary overhang was impossible to determine (especially after the Pavlov "currency reform," which undermined people's faith in the ruble once and for all), but it was clearly very large.[3] Nonetheless, in preparing to free up prices, you need to determine at least the approximate scale of that initial wave of inflation linked to eliminating the surplus cash funds.

Estimates of the monetary overhang and, correspondingly, of the initial jump in prices are usually based on the hypothesis that the population's spending-and-saving behavior remains constant. We took the early 1980s, a period of relative stability, as our base. We then totaled the anomalous money accumulations from the second half of the 1980s and the early 1990s, when the percentage of forced savings shot up abruptly. The resulting figures then served as our point of departure. By that method of calculation, had liberalization been implemented in late 1990, the initial jump in prices would have come to 60 percent.

But 1991 reshuffled the deck. The Pavlov reform in January, the administrative price hike in April, the growth in nominal cash income, and people's constant, and constantly growing, anxiety, which set off rumor after rumor about new monetary reforms, all altered the picture in cardinal fashion. It was clear: we were in a situation where theory was powerless, and scientific forecasting was impossible. Estimates ranged anywhere from 200 percent to 250 percent.

If the problem of the monetary overhang consists primarily in finding someone who can get up the political courage to tell the truth, to admit that the state has squandered people's savings, the question of the monetary flow—that faucet with the stripped threads out of which worthless rubles continue to gush—is of a somewhat different order. The most important impetus for currency emission was the state's inability to conduct its business in such a way that its expenditures were always covered by revenues and market borrowings. The pretty term "seigniorage"— government revenues brought in by printing additional money—attests to the link between it and the traditional rights of the feudal seignior. This is the simplest and most effective of all existing taxes. No tax police are needed to collect it. It is automatically levied on citizens with each thump of the printing press. But it is also terribly destructive for the economy. Sooner or later it is bound to throw the nation's currency— that most important component in a delicate market mechanism—into turmoil. And sooner or later that currency retaliates, in the guise of price increases, capital flight, and the undermining of any incentive to either save or make long-term investments.

Hyperinflation is the most terrible monetary catastrophe of all. It occurs when the public has lost all faith in its own national currency, and rushes to get rid of it, buying up whatever comes to hand. This is what happens if the growth in prices begins to approach 50 percent per month. Then the state, too, suddenly realizes that its own currency issue revenues are falling drastically. And often enough it simply cranks the printing press a little harder, and the economy responds with even more accelerated activity, which essentially takes the national currency out of circulation. Only once in its history had Russia experienced hyperinflation—from December 1921 to January 1924, when the average monthly growth in prices was around 57 percent, and the maximum growth reached 213 percent.

In discussing the outlines of our upcoming reform program, we understood that one of the most serious risks involved in the inevitable liberalization of prices was the threat of an immediate burst of hyperinflation—detonated by the monetary overhang. If that were the case, prices would shoot up, but products still wouldn't appear on the shelves. The decades-old tradition of deficit economics would simply not allow weak, expiring money into economic circulation.

That was why it was necessary to shut down that particular motor for revving the budget, at least for a few months, until the first inflationary wave subsided and illusory savings were transformed into real ones.

Hence also the necessity of keeping government spending to a miserly minimum.

But while Russia was an enormous part of the Soviet Union, constituting roughly 60 percent of the latter's economy, it was not the whole USSR. At the end of August 1991 there were fourteen other central banks besides the Russian, all operating virtually independently of one another within the borders of the USSR. They could not issue cash rubles, but with one stroke of the pen, through noncash accounts, they were free to launch any amount of money into circulation, and the smaller the republic, the greater the profit from such noncash emissions. The result was increased inflation throughout the entire ruble zone.

One well-known historical example of this sort of problem occurred after the First World War, when former territories of the Austro-Hungarian Empire adopted a unified currency, a choice which led to hyperinflation disasters in both Austria and Hungary. Only Czechoslovakia, which quickly introduced its own currency into circulation, managed to escape the same fate.

Hence the pressing need to introduce a Russian national currency as quickly as possible. There was no other way to put the brakes on inflation. But this involved a highly complex technical operation. Given the intricate economic linkages between republics, to proclaim that as of tomorrow Russia's monetary system was totally severed from that of the republics would be to bring the economy to a halt, to unleash total chaos in the payments system. So we needed to prepare for the change in accounting systems, to switch the central banks of the republics over to correspondent accounts, to introduce new payment procedures. Which meant that, overall, introducing a new national currency would take at least six months of highly intensive work.

Out of this came a lengthy discussion of the possibility of carrying out the initial changes in two stages, as Poland had done. Devote six months to a price liberalization similar to the one implemented by the last Communist government under Mieczysław Rakowski, and only then take separate stabilization measures, as the first democratic government under Tadeusz Mazowiecki and Leszek Balcerowicz had done.

The Russian version would have looked something like this: unfreeze prices at the beginning of January 1992, which would allow for the introduction of those critical changes in the tax system required to maintain the necessary level of budget revenues in the face of increased inflation; continue monetization of the deficit, then wait until June to introduce a Russian currency and to begin the business of financial stabilization.

But in the end we abandoned this alternative. Unlike the last Polish Communist government, Valentin Pavlov's had made its successors no such gift. The political responsibility for inescapably controversial decisions on both liberalization of prices and financial stabilization fell on us and us alone. If prices were liberalized in January without a serious concurrent effort at stabilization, the economy would unavoidably and immediately go into hyperinflation mode.

It's easy enough to figure out that by the time the technical groundwork for introduction of both a national currency and serious stabilization measures was completed, the public base of support for such a policy would be seriously undermined. Price liberalization could not be postponed, for the old administrative system was totally paralyzed. There could be no liberalization without serious efforts at stabilization— otherwise the economy would go into hyperinflation mode, with useless money. At the same time, there was no real hope of success in a stabilization policy in the first half of 1992, before Russia could establish its own money circulation. So what were we to do?

In September and October 1991 it was quite clear: the situation mercilessly dictated that we choose the most risky and controversial scenario for launching reforms. Moreover, we could already see that their progress would be significantly affected by factors that could throw the whole program off track, factors beyond the government's control.

Once the market mechanism was engaged, the bare-bones program was to convert repressed inflation into open inflation, avert the collapse of money circulation, deal with the supply crisis in major cities, and begin structural reforms and the formation of market mechanisms.

As soon as prices were liberalized, the government would simultaneously reduce food subsidies, cut allocations for arms purchases by roughly two-thirds, drastically reduce its level of capital investment, especially in agriculture, limit social services to real budget revenues, and, at the same time, introduce an extremely high value-added tax (28 percent) in place of the random and disorganized sales tax.

These draconian measures would be sufficient, initially, to balance the budget, control hyperinflation to some degree, and spark the start-up motor of a market economy. The optimal program consisted in first accomplishing all of the above, and then guaranteeing a level of financial and monetary stability sufficient to overcome inflationary momentum, creating the preconditions for a structural overhaul of industry and agriculture, and laying the foundation for economic recovery.

There were no guarantees that even the bare minimum would be accomplished. The continued existence of the ruble zone along with the unpredictability of monetary behavior on the part of former USSR republics, which threatened to topple the monetary system, was one very dangerous attendant factor. But there were no other, gentler, options for guiding the country through the crisis and onto the road of certain development.

We worked on a variety of documents, dispatched them to Boris Yeltsin, sent our proposals, got responses. By this time the Arkhangelskoe working group included almost everyone who would later join the government: Anatoly Chubais, Viktor Danilov-Danilyants, Pyotr Aven, Boris Saltykov, Sergei Glaziev, and many more. Others already working in the government would occasionally drop by: Burbulis, Mikhail Poltoranin, Valery Makharadze, Andrei Kozyrev, Nikolai Fyodorov, Sergei Shakhrai.

Minister of Labor Aleksandr Shokhin was with us throughout, while the others came to inform us on the current situation, to look at documents, or just to talk. It was obvious that the mess in the Silaev government had come to a head, that confusion and disorder reigned.[4]

The atmosphere at Dacha no. 15 was one of growing anxiety for the country. We brought in employees of former Soviet ministries and agencies. Many of them we knew to be competent specialists, and we tried, with their help, to sort out the situation in some of the more critical areas. Currency, grain, fuel, contract agreements for 1992, relations with creditors. The picture that emerged from the information they gave us was a truly disastrous one.

Currency emissions were increasing, currency reserves were melting away, the consumer market was utterly destroyed, and virtually no contracts had been executed for the coming year. Soviet government offices were mired in impotence and helplessness. No one wanted to make any decisions, to act, to take responsibility. After the events of August, Yeltsin had left for the south, for a vacation. Rival political forces were trying to pull him over to one side or the other.

Yevgeny Saburov stopped in often. In 1991, after Yavlinsky's resignation, he had been moved into a leading role in the formation of Russian economic policy. Now he was deputy chairman of the government and also the minister of economics. I had known him, and his two deputy ministers Vladimir Lopukhin and Ivan Materov, for a long time. Saburov talked about how critical the grain situation had become. At the same time he argued for the need to first privatize, and then and only then unfreeze prices. The decision was not his to make—privatization was in the purview of Mikhail Malei, another deputy chairman of the government. So far it had gone nowhere. But because privatization was making no headway, launching any price liberalization measures was impossible. What we had was a closed circle, with everyone in it foisting the responsibility onto someone else—politically expedient, but utterly unacceptable in a crisis.

Saburov still believed in the possibility of reaching a working economic agreement with the other republics, and was the Russian government's chief negotiator. At the same time he clearly saw that the fundamental issues that had to be resolved before any economic union could function were simply skirted in the draft documents. Agreements were being signed, but with such a plethora of qualifications and provisos that they were obviously nonviable. You got the general sense that he knew a great deal, and felt the tragedy and the urgency of the situation, but at the same time was unwilling to take on the responsibility for difficult or unpopular measures, as if he hoped that everything would work itself out and we could avoid the most socially explosive solutions.

It was obvious to all those who took part in the consultations that in the coming months and years there would be frequent changes within the Russian government. There were very few people willing to shoulder the heavy burden of beginning those transformations. It was at this point, after this series of meetings, that we began discussing the question of perhaps having to take it on ourselves.

The idea that I would have to take practical charge of the reforms had come up earlier, in conversations after an international economic conference in Paris in 1991. But at the time I took it more or less as a joke, a continuation of "skit night" at Zmeinaya Gorka. In August, a few days before the putsch, Golovkov had stopped in to ask how I might feel about becoming Yeltsin's official adviser on economics; the newly elected president was beginning a structural overhaul of the executive branch. I said that the answer was extremely simple—it all depended on what Yeltsin was planning to do about the economy. If the general thrust of his intentions coincided with my beliefs, I was ready to look seriously at such an offer. Then I would need to meet with the President and discuss the whole thing.

By the morning of August 19, I had made my decision. If Yeltsin came to me with such an offer, I would definitely accept it. I believed that I could be genuinely useful in this post. Our institute was, after all, currently the leading scholarly institution dealing with the present state of the economy rather than in abstract and theoretical investigations or long-term forecasts, and was therefore capable of predicting the consequences of decisions now being made and of drafting practical recommendations on how to prepare and implement market reforms.

Our September work in Arkhangelskoe was predicated on just such a relationship with the government. It was only gradually, toward the beginning of October, that doubts began to arise about the viability of this plan. Well, fine, we can give our advice. But who is going to act on it? Who is going to pilot the plane? At first I tried to dismiss the thought. I understood perfectly well that the post of presidential economic adviser would be far easier, more pleasant, and in fact safer than that of minister of finance in a bankrupt government. It would be very nice to have the privilege of merely analyzing, advising, critiquing, tinkering. But I gradually came to the conclusion that if no one else could be found to take on the responsibility of launching these vital, difficult, and controversial radical reforms, I would have to do it myself. Yes, it would be hard, and yes, I had too little administrative experience. Even if we were successful, I would most certainly be tossed out with hardly a word of thanks. Post-socialist political and economic realities were already obvious enough to tell me that. But still, I couldn't watch the country slip over the edge of the abyss just because everyone else was busy playing hot potato with the responsibility for unpopular and controversial decisions.

My father, on his way home from vacation in the Crimea, stopped by for a visit in Arkhangelskoe. I told him how I saw the economic and political situation, what was going on, and what we proposed to do. He agreed with me that the strategy we had proposed for starting the reforms was the only realistic one. When he realized that his son might not only have to advise someone on what to do but actually be the one to sit down and do it, I saw, perhaps for the first time in my life, an expression of stark fear on his face. He understood, and so did I, that if events took such a turn, not only my life but that of our whole family would change. Life before had been calm, measured, intellectual. Life after would be uncertain and unpredictable. My father looked at me and said, "If you're sure there's no other way, do what you think is right."

I wanted to take a deep breath, the way you do just before you dive into deep water, to look around me a bit, to get my thoughts in order. After some hesitation, I decided to keep an old promise and take a brief trip to Erasmus University in Rotterdam, to give a series of lectures on post-socialist economics. On my third day there, the call from Moscow came in. I had to fly home—Yeltsin wanted to see me.

It was the end of October, and my first conversation with Boris Nikolaevich Yeltsin. Staffing questions were not discussed; the economic situation was. My general impression was that for a politician Yeltsin knew his way around economics rather well, and was on the whole aware of what was happening in the country. He understood the enormous risk involved in initiating reforms, and also understood just how suicidal passivity and a wait-and-see attitude would be. It seemed that he was willing to take political responsibility for the inevitably difficult reforms, although he knew this would hardly add to his popularity.

I began the conversation by saying that in my view the situation was grave but not hopeless, and ended with some words to the effect that he himself would, in all probability, eventually have to sack his first government, the one that would begin the reforms, and bear the responsibility for the most difficult decisions. He smiled skeptically, dismissing that with the wave of a hand as if to say "that's where you've got me wrong."

Later we met numerous times, grew close, grew apart, quarreled, made up. I have a fairly precise idea of both his strengths and his weaknesses. And he will always have my respect for the resolution he showed in that exceedingly difficult situation in the fall of 1991. He did then what Gorbachev was never able to bring himself to do.

Yeltsin is a complex and contradictory man. In my view, his greatest strength is his intuitive ability to sense the public mood, to take it into account when making the critical decisions. You would often get the feeling that he was mistaken on this or that political issue, that he didn't understand the possible consequences. Later it would turn out that you were the one who had failed to look a sufficient number of moves ahead.

On fundamental issues he trusts his own political instinct far more than he trusts his advisers. Sometimes this leads to the absolutely right decision, but other times to a serious mistake. In the latter case, as a rule, the fault lies in his moods, which tend to change often and sometimes betray him.

Another strength is his ability to listen. A persuasive personal appeal can influence him far more than the finest or most beautiful written one. But there's a danger lurking here as well: the person who has gained his trust and knows the art of persuasion also has the opportunity to abuse that trust. This has happened more than once, sometimes when extraordinarily important decisions were being made.

I often caught myself musing over the resemblance between Yeltsin and Ilya Muromets, that larger-than-life folktale hero who would valiantly rout his enemies one day and snooze away the next. Yeltsin can be very decisive and organized, but when the problem seems to be solved and the opponent defeated, he may fall into long periods of passivity and depression. Several times this sort of apathy has led to the loss of crucial and hard-won advantages. That is precisely what happened in September and October of 1991, and to an even more serious degree between October and December of 1993.

Characteristic of Yeltsin, too, is his respect for independent people, and his contempt for slavish behavior. Hence his ability to agree with arguments that he finds unpleasant—if he feels they are sound. In 1991 and 1992, I told the President "no" more often than "yes," and tried to show him why following much of the advice he was receiving, which seemed convincing enough to him, would in fact be suicidal—why he should *not* do what some governors, former ministers, and old comrades were asking him to do, and why certain staffing changes or transfers were not expedient.

I am utterly convinced that I could not have accomplished any of this had the President himself not been convinced, that autumn of 1991, that my attitude toward power was purely a functional one, that power was not my goal and that I was not particularly attached to my government job. I remember offering Boris Nikolaevich my resignation at either our second or third meeting after my appointment to office. And this is why. At the time Gavriil Popov very much wanted to leave his post as mayor of Moscow—a very uncomfortable one in that hungry winter of 1991—and had asked to be appointed Minister of Foreign Affairs and Foreign Economic Relations, a move that would combine two separate ministries. Yeltsin was ready to agree, while I was categorically opposed. The foreign affairs post was outside my purview, but my conviction that foreign economic relations had to be guided by one of the members of my team—if we indeed wanted comprehensive and integrated reforms—was absolute. Therefore I asked Boris Nikolaevich not to put the appointment through, because otherwise I could not take any responsibility for the conduct of economic policy. He acceded. Later in our relationship there would be quite a few such episodes.

Yeltsin is a direct person, sometimes too direct. He has little time for human weakness. He can humiliate. This never happened to me, but it did to others, and it was painfully embarrassing to watch both the servant trying to ingratiate himself and the master lording it over him. Boris Yeltsin's "broad Russian soul" does not always work to the benefit of government business. Let's just say that close, sincere friendship or stark confrontation both come easier to him than do more subtle or complex feelings. He works in the same way: sometimes he charges ahead when what's needed is patience, careful study of all the arguments presented, an unhurried approach. There were times when this had a damaging effect on the national interest. Leaders of foreign governments, especially postsocialist governments, knowing Boris Nikolaevich well, frequently exploited this weakness to extract lopsided and disadvantageous concessions from the Russian side. This happened particularly often at friendly negotiations with the leaders of the Commonwealth of Independent States (CIS). Several of my more difficult talks with the President had to do with this very thing, and the rather harsh and public objections I was forced to make against this or that obligation he was planning to take on. Boris Nikolaevich would be offended, and would take me off to one side and tell me that I should express my objections in private. I tried, but I couldn't restrain myself when, with a single wave of the hand, he could manage to wipe out the results of months of effort. As happened, for example, with the establishment of a Russian ruble zone.

But this was all still to come. Back then, in October 1991, our first talk struck a chord in me. It showed me that the President was taking the idea of reforms seriously, that he understood the necessity of moving quickly from planning to action and was ready to do so, that he had some idea of the direction the upcoming transformation should take, and that he was quick to grasp the essence of economic issues, even those unfamiliar to him.

Although the conversation with Yeltsin didn't touch upon staffing

questions directly, in later talks with people close to him at the time—
Burbulis, Poltoranin, Shakhrai—topics related to the formation of a
new government began to emerge more and more concretely. By that
time Yeltsin, after much conferring and many refusals by prominent
politicians to head his government, decided to head it himself. There
was considerable discussion of who would become his first deputy
and thus have de facto responsibility for the day-to-day functioning of
the Soviet of Ministers. The two most likely candidates were Mikhail
Poltoranin and Gennady Burbulis. Each stopped in at the dacha to consult with us, asking about our position on the appointment and whether
we were willing to work with them. Our position was extremely simple.
Yes, we were willing. Willing to work with either one—it was Yeltsin's
choice. But only under two conditions: first, that our program of radical
market transformation in Russia be adopted; second, that control of the
key economic ministries go to people who thought as we did. In spite of
all these conversations, there was still a feeling of unreality about what
was happening.

At the end of October, Yeltsin convened the State Soviet and delivered
an address. He outlined the basic points of the program we had prepared: Russia would begin the reforms on its own and propose that the
other republics join the effort; Russia had laid a course toward radical
market transformations and in the near future would prepare and implement liberalization of prices, begin structural and land reforms, and
initiate a privatization process; it would begin opening up foreign trade
and begin preparations to introduce a Russian ruble and guarantee its
convertibility. He asked those assembled if they agreed on the necessity
of a rapid liberalization of prices. All heads nodded in agreement.

Two days later Yeltsin presented his program to the Fifth Congress of
Russian People's Deputies. The basic planks of the speech came from our
drafts. He sketched out the general contours of the reform program and
spoke of his readiness to head the government himself, requesting additional powers that would permit him to regulate the process of creating
market relations by executive decree. He received them.

Lev Ponomaryov, Gleb Yakunin, and Bella Denisenko, leaders of

DemRossiya (the chief political force backing the President at the time), plus a few people's deputies from the democratic camp, set up a meeting with our working group.[5] We explained the gist of what we thought needed to be done.

Yeltsin, now in his capacity as head of the Soviet of Ministers, continued to consult with us about its makeup. If I'm not mistaken, on November 3 news came in from informed sources: the basic decisions had been made, Yavlinsky and his colleagues were rejoining the Russian government, and I was to be Yeltsin's economic adviser.

I wasn't entirely convinced that Grigory quite suited the role he would be called upon to play right now. I was afraid that he would find a variety of excuses to leave his post before prices were liberalized. Nonetheless, it felt as if I'd just managed to jump out of the way of a speeding train. The most difficult job had fallen to someone else; I would have the far more tranquil, familiar, and comfortable role of adviser. The next morning it turned out that the information was incorrect, that Yavlinsky had refused.

At that moment I finally realized that working within the government was unavoidable, and that I wouldn't be able to sit it out as an adviser, waiting until the roughest times were over. I, who between 1987 and 1990 had perhaps shouted loudest of all about the terrible danger of liberalizing prices when government finances were in disarray and monetary circulation was in chaos, would end up being the one to pick up the pieces.

November 5. A telephone call. The President had signed the decree: Gennady Burbulis, first deputy prime minister; Yegor Gaidar, deputy prime minister and Minister of Economics and Finance; Aleksandr Shokhin, deputy prime minister and Minister of Labor and Social Welfare. I sensed that it had to happen, but still the announcement itself came like a clap of thunder, severing the part of my life that had come before from the unknown part yet to come. I had been transformed from an advice giver to a decision maker. And now the weight of responsibility for the country, for saving a sinking economy, and hence for the lives and fates of millions of people, lay on my shoulders.

Before leaving for Arkhangelskoe, where my team was waiting for me—those future ministers and their deputies—I ran home. Masha was alarmed; our son was running a high fever and having trouble breathing. He was almost choking. She'd been told to apply cups, but the nurse hadn't come. So my first accomplishment as a minister and deputy prime minister was to help cup my one-year-old son.[6]

Chapter 6

The First Step Is
Always the Hardest

- The session at Gosplan
- Forming the government
- Portraits of ministers
- Working style
- I'm offered a bribe
- The problem of grain imports
- Negotiations with the Paris Club
- On licenses and quotas
- Belovezhskaya Pushcha

I moved into the office previously occupied by Ivan Silaev, former head of the Russian government. It was quiet, clean, and empty. There was a roomy desk. On the very edge of it sat a stack of folders with some papers inside. A bank of white telephones. They were switched off for the moment. But my thoughts were something I couldn't switch off. And they were not comforting thoughts.

In formal terms the Soviet Union still existed, but in practical ones the Soviet government did not. All the ministers had resigned. The Russian government was just now being formed and was utterly unprepared for the task thrust upon it of governing an enormous nation.

At the next session of the Supreme Soviet we were faced with rescinding the order declaring an emergency situation in Chechnya. Enforcing it had proved impossible. Yeltsin had signed the order on the urging of Vice President Aleksandr Rutskoi, who had volunteered to head the operation personally and had issued the order to send troops. The Soviet leadership had ordered the troops to stay put. Minister of Internal Affairs

Viktor Barannikov was caught in the middle. Some units were deploying, but not to where they were supposed to be, while others were going where they were supposed to go, but without any weapons. If before this episode I had any illusions left about the government having army and security forces organized and well in hand, this humiliating fiasco banished them once and for all.

Nadezhda Petrovna, my secretary at the institute and here as well, came in. She told me that the phones were connected and that everyone I had invited was here. The pause was over. The first thing we had to do was gain control of Soviet structures, force them to do their job, rely on them. Their people were experienced, knowlegeable.

I called Gosplan, informed them that I was on my way, and asked them to assemble the collegium.[1] I took both Yeltsin's decree appointing me and the RSFSR resolution appointing Andrei Nechaev as my first deputy and slipped them into my pocket; together he and I, plus a militiaman from the White House security detail—just in case—dashed over to the Gosplan offices.

It was a brash move, of course. Before August 21, any such action— let alone that the entire staff of the mighty Gosplan should be called in on the strength of a phone call from the mere deputy chairman of the Russian Republic—might well have ended with the door being slammed in our faces. But here they were. Wary, dismayed, and, in some cases, looking frightened.

I informed those assembled of the decision to bring Gosplan under Russian jurisdiction. I would be leading the parade, we would treat people well, and we would try to use all our valuable employees to the greater good of the state; Andrei Nechaev, deputy minister of economics, would remain here at Gosplan as my representative. I could sense that many of them wanted to ask just why they should comply with any of this, carry out orders from some Nechaev whom almost no one in their enormous organization had ever heard of. But no one said a word, and my announcement was received without any overt protest. And within several days Nechaev reported that Gosplan was working on a program to reduce arms production for 1992.

The next step was to combine the Soviet and Russian Ministries of Finance. I've already mentioned the "budget war" raging between them. While still at work in Arkhangelskoe, we had begun inviting in experts from the Soviet apparatus, both to consult and to help clarify the situation, and to sort out whom we could rely on once reforms were launched. One of these was Vasily Vasilievich Barchuk, who was at that time a USSR deputy minister for the budget. Even at our very first meeting he impressed me, and my colleagues as well, with his sense of responsibility and his profound knowledge of budget issues. He was taking the whole financial mess very hard, almost personally. I offered him a post as first deputy minister at Russia's Ministry of Finance, and Barchuk agreed at once, realizing that this was the way to bring the ruinous standoff to an end.

As in the past, underwriting the army would be the job of the Soviet government, as would a number of other obligatory expenditures; however, no money whatsoever was coming in from the republics. And therefore the last Soviet budget for the fourth quarter of 1991 was based purely on new currency emissions. Naturally, the army, science and scholarship, and social programs all had to be paid for; but insofar as practically all the burdens of the Soviet budget would now be shifted to Russia's shoulders, we declared quite firmly that these things could be financed only on condition that the two budgets would be combined under our very strict control.

Negotiations were difficult, with Yeltsin, Gorbachev, Barchuk, acting USSR Minister of Finance Raevsky, and Viktor Gerashchenko, chairman of the State Bank (Gosbank), taking part, but in the end our solution was adopted. From that moment on, the Soviet and Russian Republic budgets were for all practical purposes combined, a move that simply acknowledged the actual state of affairs.

That very day Barchuk and I called in Goznak chairman Leonid Alekseev and gave him his orders to begin preparations for the issue of higher denominations—200 and 500 ruble notes.[2] Once both prices and salaries were freed, there would be inevitable growth in the money supply, and we had to avoid a cash shortage. We didn't have to elaborate; he understood how vital this was and said that he would carry out the assignment. The next day he called to tell us that the appropriate directives had been issued.

The process of forming a government continued. In accepting this appointment I had proceeded on the understanding that the President had agreed to the terms I had outlined, one of which was that people from my "team"—that is, those who shared my views on how to implement reforms and lead the country out of this crisis—would be appointed to ministerial posts dealing with the economy.

The three of us—the first deputy prime minister and the two deputy ministers—would meet, discuss the roster of candidates, prepare drafts of executive decrees, and dispatch them to the President. We would meet with him, and discuss the candidates and other matters together; we argued, but as a rule, managed to find mutually acceptable solutions rather easily.

This goverment was dubbed the "reform team," but in fact its composition was rather diverse. It was made up of four different groups of people, all with substantially different backgrounds, skills, and outlooks. First, there were the experts—professional economists who came from an academic background. Besides Shokhin, Chubais, and me, this included Minister of Foreign Economic Relations Pyotr Aven, Minister of Scientific and Scholarly Affairs Boris Saltykov, Minister of Ecology Victor Danilov-Danilyants, Chairman of the Committee on Cooperation with the CIS Vladimir Mashitz, Minister of Agriculture Viktor Khlystun, and the first deputy minister of economics and finance and later Minister of Economics Andrei Nechaev.

The second group was composed of those who had been in Silaev's government: Minister of Communications Vladimir Bulgak, Minister of Transport Vitaly Yefimov, and the chairman of Roskhleboprodukt, Leonid Cheshinsky.[3]

The third group was made up of people from former Soviet ministries: Stanislav Anisimov, who had been Minister of Trade and Material Resources and had headed the last incarnation of Gossnab;[4] Gennady

Fadeev, former Minister of Transportation; Vasily Barchuk, Deputy Minister of Economics and Finance and shortly thereafter Minister of Finance.

And finally, the fourth group was composed of those ministers who had come from the political realm, former Supreme Soviet deputies like Gennady Burbulis, Ella Pamfilova, and Nikolai Fyodorov.

The question was whether these very different people would produce a plan of action and work together smoothly as a team. Some of them hadn't the slightest experience in the ways of bureaucracy. The most vivid example of this might be Pyotr Olegovich Aven, Minister of Foreign Economic Relations—an intellectual possessed of a good understanding of economics, well versed in Russian literature and poetry, a graduate of the elite Mathematics School no. 2, and later of Moscow University's Economics Department. Before his appointment to the government he had worked in the All-Union Institute of Systems Research, and later in the International Institute of Applied Systems Analysis. He had helped organize the international conferences that had given the future reformers of Eastern Europe and the CIS an opportunity to meet one another and in some cases even become friends. He had never held a government post, and the only thing he'd ever supervised was his own desk.

I have to admit that Aven turned out to be a rather indifferent organizer. He was hindered not only by lack of experience, but by nerves and frequent mood swings. All of this made him extremely vulnerable, for the job of heading a major ministry was a tempting one; any number of people were after it that spring of 1992. The question of replacing Aven came up regularly in my discussions with Yeltsin. His basic argument was always the same. "Well, Yegor Timurovich, he may be an expert in his field, but you can see for yourself he's no minister." This was true enough, but a feeling of camaraderie was not the only thing that compelled me to defend Pyotr Olegovich every time and to categorically oppose his dismissal. For me, all his shortcomings were outweighed by the fundamental fact that he understood the overall intent behind the transformations, and so I had no need to monitor the actions he was taking in preparation for introducing a convertible ruble. He might fall short here or there, not quite get the whole job done, but overall, and of this I was convinced, the strategy would stay on track. And it seems that I was right. Today I most certainly know that, of all the heads of Russian ministries, no one did more to help introduce the convertible ruble than Pyotr Aven. And that issue was one of the keys to our economic policy.

In a certain sense, Minister of Finance Barchuk was Aven's polar opposite. A highly experienced government official who had risen through the ranks from district tax inspector in Khabarovsk to the office of Minister of Finance, he knew his business, and he knew precisely how to organize the work of his ministry. I think that no one could have managed the unthinkably complex problem of consolidating the Soviet and Russian budgets, the change in the whole budgeting structure, better than he. In handing Russia's purse strings over to him, I was quite sure that he would do everything possible to prevent the money in that purse from being squandered. And yet it took him a rather long time to understand and acknowledge one simple truth grasped by any financial expert raised in a functioning market economy—that centralized nonfiscal credits from the Central Bank had just as destructive an impact on the economy as direct financing of the budget deficit. And this meant that in one critically important general economic sphere I could not entirely rely on the judgment of the finance minister. And therefore the macroeconomic side of the ministry's work demanded my constant attention and monitoring, even though there was often no time for it.

It seems to me that in our government there were only two people who combined a genuine administrative savvy with profound understanding of the essence of the transformations necessary in their relative fields—Anatoly Borisovich Chubais and Minister of Communications Vladimir Borisovich Bulgak. Bulgak, who had stayed over from the Silaev government to work with us, had a unique combination of managerial precision in organizing the system under his control and an utter lack of desire to keep it in some unchanging, rigidly managed form. This is one case in which implementing market-oriented changes in a large and highly important industry essentially became the industrial ministry's job. He was quick to grasp the new problems his ministry encountered in this radically altered situation, and it's no wonder that the communications industry was one of the first to bring in major foreign investment, and was where we first succeeded in realizing large-scale, highly effective, and remunerative projects. Only a few years earlier, the virtual impossibility of telephoning Moscow directly from abroad was a major obstacle to developing any kind of decentralized system of foreign trade. Now that problem was a thing of the past, almost as if it had never existed.

As far as Chubais is concerned, he alone, of all the former academics, possessed that same combination of administrative efficiency and precise understanding of the essential problems facing him in the conduct of economic reforms.

And me? Of course, organizing the work of the government was no easy task for me. I had never overestimated either my administrative experience (I'd never been in charge of more than a hundred people before) or my administrative talents. The chief danger for me was in the daily paper chase, the bottomless pit of in- and out-files, the obligatory protocol that could not be sidestepped. If you let yourself be pulled into all that, it's easy to become a rubber stamp that simply sanctions decisions worked out by the apparatus—easy to lose control over events, to lose the broader perspective on problems and prospects. And for that reason it was crucial to place people I could trust absolutely in key areas of economic policy.

It was obvious from the beginning that if we did not take control of the apparatus and make it work on implementing economic reforms, our government was doomed. Like our predecessors, we would be unable to move from words and programs to actions. I had tried to persuade Gennady Mikelyan, then head of the Union government office, later Minister of Labor, to agree to head the apparatus. He couldn't quite bring himself to say yes.

One should keep in mind that very few people wanted to work in the new government. Many of those I invited, summoned, and cajoled found all sorts of excuses to refuse or avoid answering at all. The first joke told about our government sums it up. It went like this: the new government is like a potato—it'll either get chewed up in winter or buried in the spring. It was only later—toward the end of spring and the beginning of summer in 1992, when it became clear that the worst was over, that there would not be any mass hunger, that the shelves were filling up again, and that the market was starting to function—that people who earlier had refused to come into the government were now happy to accept an offer to join it. But that was later. Back then, in the fall, finding someone whom you trusted, who could cope with a very difficult task, was not so simple.

I decided to appoint Aleksei Golovkov to the post of head of the government apparatus; he had taken an active part in our work in Arkhangelskoe, I had known him from the Central Economics and Mathematics Institute, and he was now working closely with Gennady Burbulis. Of course, there was an understandable risk in such an unexpected move. Aleksei had virtually no experience working within a bureaucracy. Would he be able to cope with the apparatus, force it to work the way it should? When I suggested him as a candidate, Viktor Ilyushin—whom the President had invited to the discussion—declared that he had nothing good to say about Golovkov.[5] I noted mildly that I was the one who would have to work with him, and that he was exactly the type of person I needed to ensure that the apparatus would not be fiddling around doing God knows what but in fact would be preparing the necessary normative documents. The President heaved a sigh, but agreed, and signed the decree.

I was hardly surprised when the decree somehow got lost in the bureaucratic shuffle. I had to return to the issue again and again, more insistently each time, citing the very fact of constant misplacement of a presidential decree as evidence of how impossible it was to work with the apparatus when we had no control. Finally the decree was issued. However, any and all efforts at supervision evoked furious resistance; the idea of fully integrating the apparatus into the presidential administrative structure constantly came up, and I was under heavy and insistent pressure to remove Golovkov. All this was further proof to me that his was a key position.

From the very beginning it was clear that our opportunity to influence the President in a crisis was like the *peau de chagrin*. It would inevitably shrink, and ultimately disappear. By that point the opportunity to do anything meaningful in the government would have been lost, and it would be time to leave. And what was so painful was that a good bit of that "skin of shagreen" had been wasted on our battle with the apparatus. Perhaps no other staffing issue in 1992 caused so many tense discussions with the President as this one did. Nonetheless, I'm convinced that the Golovkov decision was the right one. For all his shortcomings, Aleksei managed to recruit qualified and experienced staffers from the former USSR Soviet of Ministers, from Russian Republic structures, and succeeded in getting them to work on drafting the normative measures that would ensure enactment of reforms.

When you put your signature at the bottom of a government document, you feel as though you're walking through a mine field. Under no circumstances can you rely wholly on the apparatus. The ultimate responsibility is yours. But in assessing 1992 from today's perspective, I have to say that although mistakes were made, Aleksei managed to disarm the vast majority of "mines" before any paper reached my desk.

Subsequently, when in 1993 I again joined the government in the capacity of first deputy prime minister for economic policy, I recognized how hard it was to conduct business when the apparatus (headed at that time by Mr. Vladimir Kvasov) was, for all its appearance of civility, essentially disloyal. Any useful measure could sink like a stone, leaving only the flotsam and jetsam of excuses floating on the surface. In 1995 and 1996 Golovkov would join the staff of Our Home Is Russia,[6] and would later play an active part in Aleksandr Lebed's electoral campaign, but I nonetheless remain profoundly grateful to him for his work in the government in 1991 and 1992.

To keep from drowning in the sea of papers, and from losing sight of the general line, I created a working center for government economic reform, with Sergei Vasiliev in charge. He was an old friend and a confirmed liberal, ideologically even stricter than I. The center's chief task was to examine and evaluate documents from the various government agencies. The work done by this small office turned out to be extremely useful. I also called in the economic part of the team for regular meetings. We would gather in my office, usually after midnight, discuss the most recent statistics, the most pressing problems and disagreements, and set our priorities.

But the papers continued to flood in. In the beginning I hadn't caught on to some of the little bureaucratic tricks people used, like shoving the riskiest and most complex documents at you just when you are in a terrible hurry to get to a meeting, and telling you moreover that the matter is urgent. But on the whole, I rather quickly got the hang of working with official documents. I began to learn how to tell what amidst this flood of paper was pure formality and what required careful scrutiny.

The majority of papers presented for my review were trivial, of minor significance. But there were also important, even explosive, ones. The first conclusion I came to in government service was that no matter how tired you were, no matter how people tried to rush you or how often your aides told you that a document was fine, or harmless, you never signed anything in a hurry without reading and understanding it. You could be tripped up at the very moment you least expected it.

A characteristic example. In early autumn of 1992, I was flying to Baku to meet with the prime minister and president of Azerbaijan and sign several documents, including one on cooperation in the area of monetary policy. The documents had long since been worked out by experts and basically approved; these were final drafts, and there should be no problems with them. While the Azerbaijani leaders and I were busy discussing economic cooperation issues and ways to settle the conflict in Nagorno-Karabakh, my colleagues and members of the delegation were preparing the agreement for signing. The prime minister of Azerbaijan and I came out to sign the documents in the properly ceremonial setting. Out of longstanding habit, I skimmed through them there in front of the audience. To my immense surprise I discovered that the key provisions of the agreements proffered for me to sign were strikingly different from those we had worked on and approved, and in fact were in direct conflict with the policy we had pursued in our negotiations with other republics.

Softly, lest God forbid there be any sort of scene, I whispered this to the prime minister. My Azerbaijani colleagues were terribly embarrassed—*some sort of technical difficulties, someone brought the wrong version by mistake*—and quickly retrieved the approved text. All's well, we congratulate one another, and drink a glass of champagne. On the flight back I held a postmortem to find out how what was essentially a different document had ended up on the table. It was a lesson for the delegation. And for me as well.

Another example. This one from early October 1993, when I was deputy prime minister for the economy. In to see me walked a high-ranking apparatus official. Among the documents he brought was a report on the Committee on Precious Metals' efforts at international cooperation, and a draft resolution approving said efforts. Although my time was terribly short, I looked through the papers. There was something strange about them. It was not clear just who or what this Golden Ada, the proposed partner in cooperation, was; nor was it clear what the terms of the contract were, or just who this Prince of Botswana was. In place of the prepared directive, I substituted my own: "To Yevgeny Primakov. Please run a confidential check on the data presented here and inform the government of the results."[7] Intelligence reports told us that the company called Golden Ada looked highly suspicious, and that there was no such prince. I didn't suspect those who prepared the draft of any sort of malice aforethought. It's just that unthinking bureaucratic zeal can cause a good deal of trouble.

I subsequently learned that this was not the first Golden Ada episode: the firm had done its share of damage in Russia, tens of millions of dollars worth. Naturally, after the intelligence reports, there could be no question of approving a deal with the company. Subsequently the matter was taken up by the prosecutor's office.

Of course you can't be 100 percent mistake-proof. I remember one document I signed early in my tenure, involving work with a firm called DP. There were always colossal numbers of opportunists buzzing around the government, proposing what seemed, at first glance, attractive projects. Sometimes they had quite responsible people—who as a rule had little understanding of any of it—doing their lobbying for them. Whenever I heard that some obscure company or other was proposing a loan of five, ten, fifteen billion dollars, I was sure we were dealing with scam artists. The essence of the scam was generally quite simple: nobody, of course, was ready to provide that kind of money, but once a clever huckster got the official piece of paper with government guarantees, he could go on playing Ostap Bender in grand style for rather a long time, cutting deals and traipsing all over the globe as an "authorized representative" of the Russian, Moldovan, Kirghiz, or whichever government.[8]

With DP we had just such a case. A certain people's deputy doggedly lobbied for them, accusing the Ministry of Finance of foot-dragging and conservatism. The firm proposed a loan to the Russian government on very advantageous terms. Given the amount of pressure being exerted, I assigned Leonid Grigoriev, chairman of the Committee on Foreign Investment, to investigate the firm. To my surprise, he quickly came back with a draft resolution approving cooperation. Subsequently, in trying to sort out just how it all happened, I realized that they had simply snowed him—convincing him that I had already made the decision and all he needed to do was prepare the paperwork. In any case, I dictated an extremely cautious directive; we would be willing to accept the firm's offer if it would secure the required funds and have them transferred to Minfin's account.[9] If not—there could be no relationship. Just as I suspected, we never saw any money, but we did learn another lesson. After that, I simply gave such projects the boot without a moment's hesitation.

When I agreed to join the government, I of course knew that corruption within government bodies was already widespread in both Soviet and Russian state systems. I realized that it sprang from the fact that officials were given the opportunity to make individual decisions favoring one enterprise over another. Therefore I started out by setting up a strict system within my office; any gifts, however insignificant, had to be turned in to the protocol service. My colleagues snickered over this, especially when it was a question of obviously trivial things; but I thought that in this matter it was better to go a little overboard. Apparently my reputation, and my family name, did have some effect. Even my political opponents, who were convinced I was leading the country down the road to ruin, never accused me of dipping my hand into the government till.

One evening, after a meeting of CIS prime ministers and the state dinner that followed, a neighboring country's leader came up, took me aside, started a conversation on the need to develop mutually advantageous cooperative efforts, and then delicately mentioned possible consideration of my own personal interests. I thanked him for his eagerness to develop economic ties, and pretended that I hadn't caught the transparent hint; however, after that, I began scrutinizing any contracts involving that country with special care.

Perhaps the most difficult part of adapting to government work, especially in times of crisis, is the radical change in one's time frame. Scholars plan their time in terms of years, months, weeks. An adviser measures time by hours and days. A government leader is forced to operate in terms of seconds, or at best, minutes. Several hours to think something over, time to consult—these are almost luxuries. Half an hour for an important meeting, three minutes to call the Ministry of Finance and issue instructions, two minutes to eat lunch, and then another minute before you have to rush out of the office to get to the Supreme Soviet—that's the norm, and that's how it goes day in and day out, from early morning until late at night. A pace like that inevitably creates real obstacles to having friends or a social life. You can hardly invite a friend over for a serious talk at 2:35 in the morning, and then give him seven minutes. It's just not done. As a result, your circle of friends and acquaintances inevitably shrinks to those you see on business. There's no time even for the people closest to you. In 1992, I managed to get out to see my parents perhaps three times—each time in the wee hours of the morning when I was dead on my feet.

It was hardest of all on my mother, a historian with a doctorate in her field, specializing in Russian policy in the Balkans in the eighteenth and nineteenth centuries. She was fourteen years old when her father, Pavel Petrovich Bazhov, gained nationwide fame. Ever since then she had enjoyed an emotionally comfortable life. There were no particular problems with her own children. She had been called to attend parent-teacher meetings at my school only a few times, and at those meetings she heard mostly good things. And suddenly there was this avalanche of hostility, of hate! In late 1991 her son was being ripped apart verbally in enormous, endless, and hopeless food lines. Once, while queuing up for bread, she was amazed to hear how the Gaidars themselves were living high on the hog, how you could bet that *they* didn't have to stand in any lines. And suddenly it turned out that the old circle of friends who had for decades frequented our house were split between those who backed her son's reforms and those who categorically refused to accept them. All of this had come so abruptly, with no warning. Understanding that, I tried to carve out some free time, at least to call, to reassure her.

In my work with people's deputies I often recalled something Thomas Jefferson said. It's worth quoting in full: "The executive in our governments is not the sole, it is scarcely the principal object of my jealousy. The tyranny of the Legislatures is the most formidable dread at present, and will be for long years. That of the executive will come in its turn, but will be at a remote period." [10] That was written in 1789, when American democracy was just coming into being. The same principle holds true for the development of our own Russian democracy.

Of course, numerous worthy persons for whom I felt a tremendous respect were serving as people's deputies: Boris Zolotukhin, Mikhail Molostvov, Sergei Yushenkov, Sergei Kovalyov, Oleg Basilashvili, Georgy Zadonsky, and many, many others. Unfortunately they were not the ones insisting on meeting with me, crowding my waiting room; more often than not it was deputies who wanted to push through some commercial contract, who were obviously promoting the interests of some brash hustler looking for an export quota or a profitable loan, or maybe offering a cut in some dubious financial deal. I had to receive them, then turn them down—which hardly improved relations.

My most energetic and powerful support in the Supreme Soviet came from Pyotr Filippov, chairman of the subcommittee on privatization. He was from Petersburg—we'd known each other since 1986—and one of the most colorful personalities in Russian politics in the last decade. An economist, a jurist, a journalist, an entrepreneur, he was a man of irrepressible, feverish energy, and in his time did much to mobilize me and my Petersburg friends into active participation in politics. In the summer of 1989 he and I, along with Chubais, Vasiliev, and ten or so other economists, spent a week sailing on Lake Ladoga, talking over the economic and political future. Pyotr was a genuine tribune, a politician of the people, who had been elected people's deputy in 1990. By autumn of that year he had become one of the most highly regarded figures in the Supreme Soviet, and the author of crucial economic legislation. Immediately after the government was formed he came to see me to work out an agreement on coordinating legislative projects. By supporting us and our programs in 1991 and early 1992, he invested every bit of his parliamentary authority in our cause. Methodically, simply, loudly, he explained to the legislators the essence of what we were doing, tried to show them how necessary it was, and why there were no other solutions to be had. But the parliamentary majority couldn't stand mentors, especially those who explained unpleasant or unpopular things to them. If in 1991 Filippov's backing was enough to ensure enactment of almost any economic legislation, by spring of 1992 his influence on decision making was almost nil. Even worse—his support of a given bill was a guarantee that it would fail.

The majority of parliamentarians love to ask members of the government questions. In the first place, unlike creating legislation, it demands a minimum of intellectual effort. As everyone knows, a single idiot can ask more questions than a hundred wise men can answer. In the second place, it graphically demonstrates to voters that their representative is concerned with their interests. This was especially true between 1991 and 1993, when parliamentary debates were, by law, broadcast nationwide. During discussion of this or that issue, the oft-posed question *And shouldn't we summon some member of the government for clarification?* was greeted with cheers every time. Adjusting to this was difficult. We would, as a rule, be called on the carpet with no warning, often at a time when other important things were planned. Moreover, the issue that had excited such passionate interest might be absolutely anything, and in our view hardly the most pressing matter facing the government at the time. As I recall, my second or third appearance before the parliament in late 1991, with economic collapse imminent, was devoted to the earthshaking question of how to enforce economic sanctions imposed on Georgia by the Congress of People's Deputies in connection with the Georgia-Ossetia conflict. I wasn't yet current on the issue and didn't know the details. I didn't have time to read through the materials prepared for me until I was in the car on the way to the session. In a word, it was a fiasco. Later, with experience, I realized that it was better to insist on postponing the discussion, and that if you were going before the Supreme Soviet you needed to carve out at least half an hour of peace for yourself, to think and prepare. At first, when I was at the Supreme Soviet, the deputies would try to stretch the answering period to the maximum. But later they realized that if you ask a question related to the economy, you should probably know at least a little about the subject. Otherwise you look like a fool in front of the whole country, and in front of your constituents. Of course only the merest shreds of my "juvenile hypermemory" remained intact, but being constantly in the thick of economic developments made it easy enough to remember the context of this or that problem or statistic.

My impression is that the Communists gave up asking me too many questions when, in response to some rant on the state of medical care, I launched into an impromptu but detailed analysis of the dynamics of illness, grouped by individual disease, for the preceding year. And when the leader of the Duma's agrarian faction, Mikhail Lapshin, was publicly exposed as being totally ignorant of the difference between elevator weight and hopper weight of grain, it was clear that the opposition had disgraced itself. After that, whenever I appeared to testify, a whisper would go up throughout the Communist ranks: "Don't ask Gaidar any questions." Frankly, I counted this a small but very pleasant victory.

Besides the parliamentarians' intellectual curiosity, there was one other thing that made planning one's time or organizing one's work extremely difficult. That thing was protocol. When you see some government official on television inspecting an honor guard, or signing some papers, or raising a glass of champagne at a banquet, you might think he has a fairly cushy job. That may be true enough when the machinery of government is calmly and steadily chugging ahead. But in 1991 and 1992, when there was so much to do, we begrudged every minute wasted. Every time I suddenly had to go somewhere to greet someone, to see someone off—always, of course, at the most inconvenient times—I felt a helpless sort of rage. The important questions don't get discussed at banquets, or at parades. At the same time, *not* observing protocol was absolutely out of the question.

I realized rather quickly which administrative tasks I was good at and which I was not. The greater part of my work consisted of making decisions when agencies could not agree. Someone had to take the responsibility, hear out the various arguments, and then say, *This is the way it will be*, or else the merry-go-round of interagency coordination and consent would have circled endlessly, round and round. Probably because I had a fairly clear view of the strategic problems facing us, the meetings I conducted generally ended with some concrete decision. I won't deny that the solutions were perhaps not always the optimal ones, but given the situation that had developed by the end of 1991, a not-quite-optimal solution was better than none at all. I was not good at the "bosses' bark," something that many people in administrative structures, thanks to bad old Soviet habit, were used to hearing. I seemed genetically incapable of shouting at my subordinates, and became convinced that it was simply better not to work with anyone who deserved being shouted at.

Perhaps our greatest achievement in the winter of 1991, while setting up the government, was the emergence and growth of a sense of shared purpose and, for all our personal differences, a unified team. Probably the chief reason for this was the truly ominous situation. Everyone realized that we had taken on a tremendous burden of responsibility. This created, in those first crucial and dangerous months, a genuine and unfeigned camaraderie that made coordinating our efforts far easier. I realized that this wouldn't last forever, that when the crisis began to abate, the laws of bureaucracy would, alas, come into play. But in that winter of 1991–92, we genuinely felt ourselves to be a team.

Division of authority is a useful, indeed a necessary thing. But in the sort of situation in which the country now found itself, economics had invaded every part of our lives. I mentioned earlier that Gosplan had begun working on reductions in arms purchases. In discussing this issue with Ministry of Defense representatives, one of the generals, who had just heard that procurement would be cut by two-thirds, said, after a stunned pause, "But that requires a political decision!"

"Absolutely," I concurred. "You can henceforth consider government decisions political decisions. Because as far as I know, the Politburo no longer exists."[11]

You might say that any decision was a political decision at that time. Take, for example, the country's bread supply. In 1991 the grain harvest was not particularly good, but it was hardly catastrophic—perhaps 85 percent of the average harvest for the period between 1986 and 1990. But immediately after the putsch, as I've already said, grain deliveries to the state took a sharp drop. No one was willing to deliver grain to the storehouses, and there was no longer any authority that could take it by force. On December 1, the goverment had a grain reserve of 10.1 million tons, or two and a half times less than the year before. But even these scanty supplies proved extremely hard to manage. North Caucasus regions rich in grain came up with a thousand reasons not to ship it to needy Moscow, to the Urals, northwestern Russia.

Meanwhile, calculations showed that even if the average monthly consumption compared to 1990 were to drop by 20 percent (from 5.3 to 4.3 million tons), and even if the government could pull off an interregional maneuver with its reserves, there would only be enough bread to last until mid-February. It was necessary to bring in Minister of Agriculture Khlystun and chairman of the Committee on Cereal Products Cheshinsky and direct them to reduce feed grain deliveries, and, if necessary, cull livestock herds. But this alone would not solve the problem. Holding out until the next harvest and avoiding a catastrophic food shortage would be possible only if grain imports could be secured in time.

This sad and humiliating dependence on massive wholesale grain imports, a position into which the Soviet leadership thrust the country in the early 1970s, manifested itself in particularly dangerous form. Here are excerpts from government-commissioned reports on the situation in several regions, as of mid-November 1991:

> The sale of meat products, butter, vegetable oils, grains, pasta products, sugar, salt, matches, tobacco products, alcohol, [and] household, bath and other soap is effected primarily through coupons, as these goods become available.
>
> Sale of bread and bread products is restricted, sale of milk products depends on availability; both are accompanied by long lines and limited hours of store operation.
>
> *Arkhangelsk region.* Meat products, for which there is no reserve supply, are sold at 0.5 kilogram per person per month. Belorussia, Rostov, and Ulyanovsk regions have cut off meat shipments. . . . Milk sells out in less than one hour. Butter is distributed by coupon at 200 grams per person per month. The coupons are not backed by reserve supplies due to short shipments from Vologda and Smolensk region. Flour is not offered at the retail level; it is sold exclusively to bakeries. By the end of the year the shortfall in flour reserves will reach five thousand tons. Sale of bread is sporadic. Sugar is sold at one kilogram per month per person; due to short shipments from Ukrainian refineries, sugar coupons have not been redeemable since June.
>
> *Nizhegorod region.* Meat products are sold by coupon; reserves will run out in December. Milk is sold for one hour per day. Butter is sold by coupon—200 grams per person per month. Reserves are insufficient. There is no vegetable oil available because suppliers in Krasnodarsk region and Ukraine refuse to ship it, nor is it being imported. Sale of bread is sporadic; bakeries will face a grain shortage of 20 thousand tons by the end of the year.
>
> *Perm region.* For the month of December, butter coupons were distributed at 200 grams per person, but there are no reserves to back them. Smolensk, Penza, Orenburg, Tver, Lipetsk region and the Republic of Tatarstan refuse to ship any. No vegetable oil is available because suppliers

in Volgograd, Kostroma and Saratov regions, as well as in Krasnodarsk district are not shipping it. There is no sugar available for sale. Refineries in Kursk and Voronezh regions have cut their shipments. Sale of bread is sporadic and is accompanied by long lines. Flour for bread production is short by 15 thousand tons. . . .

In the vast majority of other industrialized areas the situation was roughly the same.

When a state crisis is at hand, it is time to put all those reserves saved up for a rainy day to work—first and foremost, hard currency and gold. In a normal state, such reserves are carefully husbanded, and in any case are never just thrown to the winds. The tsarist government might serve as a reminder: in February 1917, after two and a half years of debilitating war, it still had 1,300 tons of gold left to hand over to the Provisional Government.

Unfortunately, our leaders didn't show even such elementary foresight. Between 1989 and 1991 they exported more than 1,000 tons; and moreover, the pace was accelerating. The year 1990 set a sad record—478.1 tons. By the end of 1991 the gold reserves of the former USSR had fallen to an unprecedented low of 289.6 tons. They were insufficient to cover even the most pressing of financial obligations, the most immediate needs of the country.

If the paltry amount of the remaining gold made the food situation merely grave, the state of hard currency reserves and the enormous scale of foreign debt made it seem virtually hopeless.

One week after I joined the government, Vneshekonombank[12] deputy chairman Yury Poletaev issued an official statement:

USSR convertible currency accounts for the first nine months of 1991 break down as follows. Export revenues in convertible currency totaled 26.3 billion dollars U.S. A total of 15.9 billion of these dollars went to a centralized fund for repayment of foreign debt and centralized import payments, while 10.4 billion dollars U.S. went to exporters' currency funds. At the same time, payments out of centralized hard currency funds totaled 26 billion dollars U.S. The situation is further complicated by the outflow of deposits and short-term loans, which on a net basis amounted to 4.1 billion U.S. dollars at year's start.

Hence the shortfall in export revenues to centralized funds amounted to 10.6 billion dollars U.S. Government resolutions over the course of the year allowed this shortfall to be covered by a "gold swap" in the amount of 3.4 billion dollars U.S., by acquisition of new loans in the amount of 1.7 billion dollars U.S., and by use of currency funds on account at the USSR Vneshekonombank belonging to enterprises, organizations, and local governments, in the sum of 5.5 billion dollars U.S.

In connection with the deteriorating payments situation, over the course of the year the country had more than once teetered on the brink of insolvency due to insufficient convertible currency reserves—about which the government was more than once informed.

And by the end of October 1991 liquid foreign currency reserves were totally exhausted, and hence the Vneshekonombank of the USSR was forced to stop all foreign payments except for those servicing foreign debt, of which the USSR Committee on management of the economy was duly informed.

The shortfall in current export revenues for payments abroad against obligations incurred as of 1 December 1991 (even without taking into account the minimum requirements in convertible currency for import costs, including shipping) might reach more than 3.5 billion dollars U.S., and for November alone, 1.3 billion. By the end of the second ten-day period in November, liquid currency reserves are expected to be insufficient to cover the government's basic obligations and the country may be declared insolvent.

Thus the Communists crowned their very last year of rule by doing exactly what they had done seventy-four years before—they requisitioned all the Vneshekonombank foreign currency accounts belonging to enterprises, organizations, and private citizens.

So, in general, there was no bread, and no gold. And no way to pay off loans. And nowhere to get new ones. This was hardly a total surprise to me, but somehow, before joining the government, I had cherished some illusions, some hopes that maybe things weren't quite so bad as they seemed, that there were some secret, subterranean reserves somewhere. But there was nothing, nothing at all!

You know how it is when you're having a nightmare? It's terrifying, of course, but somewhere in your subconscious there's a little flicker of hope: *It's OK, all you have to do is make the effort, just wake up, and all the terrible things will disappear* . . . But then you make the damn effort, open your eyes, and the nightmare's sitting right there beside you.

All the talk about "soft" or "painless" reforms that would solve problems overnight—everything would be fine, no one would lose out—and all the reproaches that filled the pages of newspapers and even scholarly publications didn't really hurt. The detailed picture gradually revealing itself bore out the sad truth: there *were* no reserves to ease the hardships that would be caused by setting the economic mechanism in motion. Putting off liberalization of the economy until slow structural reforms could be enacted was impossible. Two or three more months of such passivity and we would have economic and political catastrophe, total collapse, and a civil war. I was convinced of it.

Even those who were generally sympathetic to the government's efforts, who worried along with us, who empathized—even they rather often reproached me for my supposed reluctance or inability to simply and clearly explain to people just what we were about. To some degree I can accept those reproaches. Part of it was my lack of experience in communicating with a lay audience. Another hindrance was the constant, unshakable fatigue, especially at the beginning, when one overload came right on top of another. My head was filled with hundreds of concerns, and eloquent speeches were the last thing on my mind. This sometimes led to rather comic moments.

In the fall of 1992, at a very tense time, I had to drop everything and at Boris Nikolaevich's personal request fly out to Yakutia. There I conducted some difficult negotiations with the leadership of the republic, appeared before their Supreme Soviet, after which I flew with the president, M. E. Nikolaev, from Yakutsk to the village of Cherepcha, about 500 kilometers to the east. Late that evening I met with the public. I talked about the work the government was doing, about prospects for development in Yakutia and in their region, about construction of a canal—a crucial local issue. After that there were lots of questions. One of the people in the crowd asked me about my religious affiliation. I answered frankly that I was an agnostic. "So is that some cult, or what?" somebody asked. I explained that it's a philosophy. The crowd was astounded, and my Moscow colleagues couldn't hide their smiles.

But still, I don't think this was the main reason. Perhaps it seemed, in late 1991 and early 1992, that we were flying a plane with only one wing, with no guarantee we'd land safely. That it was impossible to make any forecasts of inflation levels because we weren't in control of the entire ruble zone and that all our efforts could be canceled out tomorrow by an unexpected move by Kazakhstan or Ukraine? That we were consciously shutting our eyes to all this and proceeding on a path of strictest austerity in our own budget policy because we had no other choice, and that this was our only chance to pull the country out of its nosedive? I think that even if people had been told all this clearly and simply in December 1991 and January 1992, nothing could have saved us from hyperinflation and economic chaos.

Unfortunately, the impossibility of telling people the whole truth about the country's situation, about what you are doing, is something that comes with any position of real power. This is where you realize how right Kant was in saying that what you tell should always be the truth, but that does not mean that you should always tell the whole truth.

At the end of 1991, in order to avoid the worst, we had to solve two problems, at almost any price: make our money work, at least a little, by ensuring the prospect of a gradual normalization of the market situation; and reach an agreement with foreign creditors that would allow the country to survive until the next harvest.

This forced the following measures and decisions:

—Relying on the dominant role played by the Russian economy within the ruble zone, combine price liberalization with a drastic tightening of Russian budget and monetary policy, thereby compensating for the consequences of probable monetary intervention by the former republics.

—Speed up preparations for shifting the republics to correspondent accounts and for ensuring Central Bank control over monetary circulation within Russian borders, and for the introduction of a Russian national currency.

—Simultaneously attempt to reach at least temporary agreements with the republics that would limit their ability to issue currency.

The plan came with no guarantees, but it did have some hope of success. This perhaps was the toughest decision we had to make. It was extremely risky and dangerous, but no matter how you cut it, there was no other alternative.

The first few days and weeks whirled by relentlessly. The government was more or less formed. The young ministers were energetic, decisive, but only now beginning to get acquainted with their agencies, to work out their relations with their staffs, their industries, their enterprises. I was hardly an old government hand myself, but the reforms had to begin without delay. Ideas had to take shape as directives, resolutions, decrees. Operative questions required quick answers. A flood of visitors, an avalanche of telephone calls. You had the feeling you were standing in front of a fire hose, and not only had to keep your footing but also your head, and keep moving in the direction you'd chosen instead of where circumstances were pushing you. And meanwhile, day and night, the greatest anxiety was—bread.

All the strategic significance of the reforms that lay ahead could not obscure the fundamental fact that by the end of November, seven months before the next harvest, the government would have roughly a two-month supply of grain at its disposal. State food reserves—all the canned meat, butter, and sugar that were going to patch up the biggest holes in the urban food supply—were dwindling. And as hard as it might be for this great country to swallow, her ability to survive to the next harvest would depend on the generosity of neighbors near and far.

Since that time, I've had no patience for the ritual Communist lamentations at rallies and in parliament over the lost imperial greatness of a nation—a nation which they and they alone, after seventy years of their harsh control, had forced to go begging.

After familiarizing ourselves with the data on the catastrophic drop in USSR gold and foreign currency reserves, and also on the failure of Vneshekonombank, and after looking at statistics on currency outflows and gold exports for 1990 and 1991, we began to wonder if everything here was on the up-and-up. Perhaps the ruling political elite, realizing the inevitability of the fall of the Communist regime, had transferred some part of the currency reserves into Western bank accounts?

It was no secret that there had long been a mechanism for performing such operations. After researching the specifics of the many contracts in which prices on product supplied by the Soviet Union were inexplicably lowered, and wholesale prices on manufacturing components were just as inexplicably raised, it wasn't hard to figure out that all this had served as a cover for ways to finance illegal activity or aid Communist regimes in foreign countries. The only question was where the money and gold had actually gone.

At the end of December 1991, two high-ranking intelligence officials had written a letter to President Yeltsin about these issues. They suggested bringing Kroll Associates, a large international organization well known for its success in resolving similar issues, into the investigation of Soviet foreign currency reserves. Perhaps their most significant case had involved exposing Iraqi dictator Saddam Hussein's secret bank accounts. The President ordered me to meet with the letter's authors, and to make a determination. One of them I knew personally; he had served as one of Gvishiani's deputies at the institute, where he worked on classified material. After talking with the intelligence officers, I was persuaded that there was little chance we'd succeed, but that there was no harm in trying.

I arranged a meeting with Kroll executives. We met in Madrid in February 1992 while I was on an official visit to Spain. We agreed that the firm would launch an investigation, for which we would sign a short, three-month contract; we would pay them $900,000 to determine whether we had any real hope of regaining control of the financial resources taken out of Russia.

With the President's approval, I called Security Minister Barannikov and asked for his assistance. It was clear that without cooperation from law-enforcement agencies Kroll would inevitably end up just playing amateur detective. The firm went to work, and it was a good deal like prospecting. They first had to sift through a colossal amount of barren rock in order to find some small nugget of information. Bank accounts with Russian connections were traced, and certain anomalies were found in operations conducted by Russian foreign trade organizations. By May 1992 these efforts had yielded a multitude of interesting details, but nothing definite enough to give us any hope of recouping the losses in the near future. The main obstacle became clear rather quickly: despite the President's support, and my request, the Ministry of Security was extremely reluctant to cooperate. And in order to turn these hints and guesses into hard evidence, we needed a serious analysis of the anomalies we had exposed. This would involve opening a series of criminal cases and working with witnesses. Meanwhile, my conviction was growing that someone in one of the law-enforcement agencies was purposely dragging his feet. By May 1992, I finally realized that I didn't have the power to force the Ministry of Security to give the case serious attention. And therefore paying Kroll for any more work would be a senseless waste of government money. With a heavy heart, I decided not to extend the contract.

By the time the government was formed, the Soviet Union's foreign debt in convertible currency had exceeded 83 billion rubles. In addition, payments owed in convertible currency for 1992 alone had reached $29.4 billion, far exceeding the country's means. Also, the Soviets had conducted their affairs so brilliantly that they had managed to loan almost $30 billion to their former allies in the socialist camp. In other words, the Soviet Union was bankrupt.

Negotations with major creditors were begun in September 1991 by the USSR Committee for Strategic Management of the Economy, an entity formed soon after the putsch, when the Soviet government had for all practical purposes ceased to exist. The committee was chaired by Silaev, with Yavlinsky, Arkady Volsky, and Moscow mayor Yury Luzhkov as his deputies. It was a strange organization, whose leaders tried very hard to demonstrate to the public that they had no connection whatsoever with the country's leadership. At one critical juncture, Volsky took off to attend some minor conference abroad, while Luzhkov kept insisting that his sphere of responsibility was Moscow and Moscow alone. Silaev and Yavlinsky conducted the negotiations—remarkably ineptly and unsuccessfully, it must be said. The fundamental aim of the official creditors, now joined together as the Paris Club, was to ensure that newly independent republics would take over the Soviet Union's obligations, and would not permit a replay of the Bolshevik refusal to pay off the tsarist government's debts. From the very beginning it was obvious that, Russia aside, no one wanted to pay, no one could, and no one would. And therefore the entire burden of responsibility lay on Russia herself.

We joined the negotiations in November, when representatives of the Paris Club arrived in Moscow. By that time the Soviet side had accepted, in principle, the contractors' terms, including a commitment to export 100 tons of gold from the country's reserves, at which point this agreement-in-the-making began to look very much like the Bolsheviks' 1918 Treaty of Brest-Litovsk. In another words, what we had here was something like a financial Brest-Litovsk, 1991.[13]

Russia's starting position at the negotiations was hardly promising: the agreement had already been put together and approved by both the Committee for Strategic Management and the Interrepublic Economic Committee.

Negotiations were difficult, tense, and not without some sharp exchanges. Undersecretary of the Treasury David Mulford threatened that if the agreement was not signed as written, he would stop delivery of American grain. I vowed in that case to go over the heads of Western government officials and appeal to Western public opinion by explaining the consequences a disastrous food shortage in the former USSR would hold for international security.

Finally we were able to reach a compromise. We accepted the liability incurred by our predecessors and the joint responsibility of all former Union republics for Soviet debts, although we knew that Russia would be the only one to pay anything off. Our Western counterparts agreed to drop their demands that we export the remainder of the gold supply. We also managed to save our network of banks abroad from ruin and immediate bankruptcy, including the People's Bank of Moscow, Ost-West Bank, Danau, and Eurobank, which under the terms of the previous agreement were destined for liquidation. Prompt aid from Russia to these banks allowed us to avoid the serious losses entailed by the forced sale of their assets and to stay on our feet. This averted a serious blow to our merchant marine, which had been using its ships as collateral for major loans from these banks.

The most unpleasant outcome of the negotiations was the preservation of artificially high and, for 1992, obviously unrealistic obligations in servicing the debt. Russia could not fulfill those obligations in full, and this put grain imports under a cloud. Yet even minor breakdowns in grain delivery might have grave consequences. Nothing less than an uninterrupted flow of grain from abroad, up to the limits of what our ports could handle, about 3.5 million tons per month, would allow Russia to somehow make it to the next harvest.

That is why further negotiations with creditors, the responsibility for which now lay entirely on the Russian government's shoulders, remained an extremely important task. But the chief thing was that the grain ships were on their way. Daily, early in the morning and late in the evening, reports came in on those still at sea, those awaiting loading. A single delay caused alarm. Interception of our ships (such things did happen), equipment breakdowns in port, or misunderstandings over freight charges were now high-priority concerns.

Much depended on Western belief in the future of Russian reform, on whether the West would be able to look at reform in terms of sociopolitical strategy rather than bookkeeping. And the progress of the reforms themselves, as I've said before, would be heavily influenced in the coming months by actions taken by our ruble zone neighbors—hence the extreme importance of attempts to reach accord with the republics, if not about heartfelt agreement, then at least about keeping everyone's behavior civil during the divorce.

The first session of the new entity—the Interrepublic Economic Committee—conducted by its chairman Ivan Silaev, hardly made us very optimistic about our chances of resolving the issue. Although the Soviet Union still existed on paper, the republics were for all practical purposes totally independent. No one wanted to discuss coordinating budgets or monetary policies. That was now the sovereign business of each republic. The only issue that sparked genuine practical interest was how to divide up the USSR gold supply. The news that there was almost nothing left to divide met with skepticism: *You can't fool us, it's probably squirreled away somewhere, we should appoint a commission. . . .* On the majority of remaining issues, from energy prices to dividing up the Diamond Fund, a broad-based coalition formed—almost all the other republics against Russia. The general attitude was articulated most frankly by Ukrainian Prime Minister Vitold Fokin: Soviet property within the borders of the Ukraine of course belongs to Ukraine; Soviet property within Russian borders belongs to all the republics.

The only republican leader whose support I could count on in discussing general economic issues was Hrant Bagratyan, then deputy prime minister and later prime minister of Armenia, a firm believer in free markets whom I had known since a series of economic seminars in the 1980s. But Armenia itself had so many problems that all he could offer was moral support.

Our position at the negotiating table was complicated by the fact that Russia—huge, unwieldy, with no customs service of its own—was ill suited to a barter system. The more "compact" republics were nimbler; they had already learned how to sidestep the Russian federal authorities and reach direct agreements on a regional level. So what if without Central Asian cotton the Ivanovo textile plants are shutting down? Who cares if Moscow, St. Petersburg, and the Urals are stuck without sugar, when Ukraine can swap its sugar for Tyumen oil? Uzbekistan needs lumber? Get it from Krasnoyarsk in exchange for fruits and vegetables.

The reaction to Russia's announcement on economic reform was mixed. The prime ministers understood that price liberalization was unavoidable. At the same time, with the exception of Bagratyan, they wanted Russia to take all the political responsibility for enacting it. Then, when they returned home from Moscow, they could tell their unhappy citizens that they were forced by Russian dictate—reluctantly, of course —to accede to this harsh and antipopular measure.

It must be admitted that despite all our efforts, our patience and gentle insistence, the meeting led to no agreement on anything worthwhile. Perhaps it did show the other participants that there could be no discussion of dividing up property within Russian territory, and that no political blocs could undermine Russia's will to reform. But this was cold comfort. The danger that our ruble zone neighbors might exert a destructive influence on the Russian economy remained.

Financial difficulties were complicated by the fact that in 1991 and 1992, with international sanctions against Yugoslavia and the accompanying stoppage of oil exports through the Adriatic pipeline, with reduced demand for oil in the Czech Republic, Poland, Slovakia, and Hungary, and the utter confusion resulting from attempts to export oil through Baltic and Ukrainian ports, the opportunities for export of Russian fuel had dwindled considerably.

Moreover, over the last two years, against a backdrop of Soviet-Russian infighting and hostility, general governmental disorganization, blatant and now rampant corruption, the number of licenses and quotas for oil export handed out by various government agencies and bodies had far exceeded the bounds of common sense. An export quota had become a sort of "philosopher's stone" that could almost instantaneously transform increasingly worthless rubles into dollars. If at the end of 1991 the exchange rate was 170 rubles per dollar, someone with an official quota in hand might pay as little as one ruble. Thus even minus the hefty bribes officials took, the quota was, on the very day it was issued, already 10,000 percent effective. Moreover, once this truly magical piece of paper was acquired, there was no need to buy oil or export it, either one. You could simply resell your permit to people who actually did deal in oil, and your fortune was made.

We shut off this money faucet immediately, and the issuing of individual quotas to brokering organizations was halted by executive order. Quotas were now allotted to producers in proportion to their oil output. All previously issued quotas and licenses were subject to review and registration, for which an operations committee was formed, headed by Minister of Fuel and Energy Vladimir Lopukhin.

It was this executive order, signed even before reforms began, before prices were freed, that set off the first mighty wave of resentment toward the government. Representatives of highly influential factions rushed to Yeltsin's office, to Ruslan Khasbulatov's, to the microphones in the Supreme Soviet chambers, to editorial offices, to TV and radio stations. They complained, they threatened, they demanded.

They tried influencing me in a different way, a more intellectual-cultural one, so to speak. Highly respected people came to my office—academicians, writers, artists, actors. They described genuinely important and urgent problems: saving science and culture, feeding the children, aiding our fellow countrymen in what were now foreign countries. But time and again, somewhere toward the end of the conversation, like a jack-in-the-box, out popped the quota-seeker. The visitor would furtively inform me: "There's a certain company [or enterprise, or public organization, or fund, whatever] that is willing to help us solve this problem. We don't need money. We have money. We don't need oil, either. The company has that too. All the company needs is one little thing—an export quota." And then, depending on just how brazen the entrepreneur who had managed to gain the trust of this respected person was, the respected person would name a figure ranging from 100 thousand to 18 million tons.

The government stood its ground. But with some difficulty. And with some unpopular but unavoidable steps.

To remind everyone once again, in late 1991 and early 1992, the former Soviet republics could pay for goods imported from Russia, primarily oil, by simply conjuring up rubles backed by nothing at all. There was only one way to block this sort of practice while simultaneously gaining some sort of leverage against them and limiting their ability to issue money until Russia could introduce its own national currency. That way was to regulate the volume of raw fuel products flowing in their direction. To do this by normal market means was impossible, since the republics, by creating worthless rubles, could pay any duties required and then reexport the oil elsewhere, thus making an enormous profit at Russia's expense. Limits on the volume of fuel and energy resources delivered, and aggressive development of a Russian customs service, would give us some chance of protecting the Russian economy from any destructive actions taken by our ruble zone neighbors.

The President didn't share his plan for the Belovezhskaya Pushcha meeting with me.[14] He merely said that I should fly to Minsk with him, and that there would be a discussion on ways to strengthen cooperation and coordination of Russian, Ukrainian, and Belorussian policy.

By this time, after the referendum on Ukrainian independence, practically nothing remained of the Soviet Union's former power and authority, except for an increasingly dangerous vacuum in the administration of military and security structures.

That evening, just after our arrival, we invited the Belorussians and the Ukrainians to sit down and work on the meeting documents. We gathered in the little house where Sergei Shakhrai and I were staying. Our side included Burbulis, Kozyrev, Shakhrai, and myself. The Belorussians had Deputy Prime Minister Mikhail Vladimirovich Myasnikovich and Foreign Minister Pyotr Kuzmich Kravchenko. The Ukrainians came to the door, stood around for a minute, and then left, scared off by something or other. At that point Shakhrai proposed a legal mechanism for escaping this political cul-de-sac, this situation in which the Soviet Union legally existed but neither governed nor was capable of governing. That mechanism was the formula for the Belovezh agreement, the dissolution of the USSR by the three governments that had in 1922 been its founders.

The idea seemed a reasonable one; it would allow us to cut the Gordian knot of legal ambiguity and begin the business of state-building in countries that were already de facto independent. There were no objections from anyone present. Together, we began working on a draft document that outlined the idea as formulated. It was very late, around midnight, and we decided not to bother the clerical staff, so I began writing out the text myself. At four in the morning we finished. Andrei Kozyrev took the papers to the typists. The next morning the staff was in a panic. It turned out that Kozyrev couldn't bring himself to wake up the typist at four in the morning and had slipped the draft declaration under what he thought was her door. It wasn't. So when the typists did get to work on it later that morning, time was short; and hardly anyone could decipher my—I admit—remarkably awful handwriting. I had to go dictate it myself. So if anyone wants to know who is responsible for the Belovezh accords, I won't deny it—I personally wrote every word from beginning to end.

Despite all the comic mishaps, the overall atmosphere that day was one of profound anxiety. I think everyone who took part in the talks understood the inevitability of the proposed solution, as well as the enormous responsibility that those who had to sign it were taking on. Belorussia's Stanislav Shushkevich seemed to me the most agitated and emotional of all. One leitmotif rang through everything he said: *We're a small country, we'll accept any decision reached by Russia and Ukraine. But you big countries, have you really thought this through?*

When I finally brought in the typed document, Yeltsin, Ukraine's president, Leonid Kravchuk, and Shushkevich were already there and waiting, and had begun some preliminary talks. After seeing it, they came to a rather quick and shared conclusion—yes, this was the way out. Once they had agreed in principle, they began discussing what to do next. Yeltsin contacted Nursultan Nazarbaev, president of Kazakhstan, and asked him to fly in immediately. It was important to have the support of this highly regarded leader as well. Nazarbaev promised, but when his plane landed in Moscow, he called to say that there were technical difficulties, that he couldn't come. The tension grew. After all, what we had here was the de jure liquidation of a de facto crumbling nuclear superpower. After signing the document, Yeltsin, with Kravchuk and Shushkevich present, telephoned Yevgeny Shaposhnikov, told him of their decision, and informed him that the three presidents had agreed he should be appointed commander-in-chief of the joint armed forces of the Commonwealth. Shaposhnikov accepted the appointment. This was followed by a call to George Bush, who listened and took the information under advisement. Finally came the call to Mikhail Gorbachev, and the difficult conversation with him.

Returning to Moscow by plane on that December evening of 1991, I kept thinking: If Gorbachev had responded to the signing of these accords by applying military force, might he have saved the Soviet Union? Of course, the final answer to that will never be known. And yet it seems to me that such an attempt at the time would have been utterly hopeless. Gorbachev's authority, and the authority of all Soviet governing bodies, for that matter, was already a mere illusion; and the army, which had been used to prop up that authority so often, was hardly likely to be budged. We had passed, in August 1991, that fork in the road where it might have been possible to sign a Union agreement and so preserve the USSR in some form or another. Now, in December of that same year, a fait accompli was simply being given legal form.

While the heads of government were discussing what to do with the Soviet Union, we and our Belorussian and Ukrainian colleagues were busy with more prosaic matters — an attempt to coordinate action in the economic sphere. It was a difficult conversation. In the end, we worked out a compromise:

—Russia will push back the starting date of price liberalization from December 1991 to early January 1992, so that the other republics can better prepare.

—Russia promises to raise energy prices to match world standards in gradual fashion, spreading the increases out over the coming year, thereby giving Commonwealth states a chance to adapt to new conditions.

—Belarus and Ukraine promise to coordinate budget and monetary policy with Russia as long as they continue to use the Soviet ruble, and to limit the budget deficit to 6 percent of the gross domestic product.

—Belarus and Ukraine, in consideration of Russia's agreement to postpone price liberalization, will help supply Moscow and St. Petersburg with food products in December.

I had doubts from the very beginning whether our opponents would keep their part of the agreement. But neither did we have any wish to raise prices on energy within interrepublic trade just to receive massive amounts of their newly printed rubles in exchange.

My fears were borne out in a matter of days. There was an uproar in the Ukrainian parliament: why should we give Russia meat when we don't have enough for ourselves? Thus the laws of barter economy promote isolationism, not integration.

Chapter 7

The Terrible Winter
of Ninety-one

- Moscow in December
- Liberalization of prices
- Press hysteria
- The decree on free trade
- The strange market at Detskii Mir
- Changes in the village
- Aleksandr Rutskoi
- New denominations
- Western aid
- Ruslan Khasbulatov
- The government's fate is sealed

$\mathbf{A}$fter Belovezhskaya Pushcha, price liberalization was set to begin on January 2, 1992. This concession to Ukraine and Belarus would have had a less negative impact had the earlier deadline not already been announced. The extension, which raised inflationary expectations, slowed the turnover of goods even more. What manufacturer or trader would offer goods for sale when they knew prices were about to jump?

The government was working to determine which goods would remain, temporarily, under state price controls. Breaking down the perception held by both management structures and the public that a transition to a market economy mainly meant a long list of goods for which prices would be regulated was no easy task. Undoubtedly, the list had to include goods and services provided by natural monopolies: electricity, communications, rail transportation, natural gas. But making the list all-encompassing would be senseless. This would inevitably produce shortages, and then subsidies would again weigh down the budget, spur inflation, and create such price distortions that any reappearance of those subsidized goods on the market would be highly unlikely.

As interagency conferences and agreements torturously progressed, I was forced to keep cutting the list, while it, like a phoenix rising from the ashes, was reborn time and again, often with more luxuriant plumage than ever. There was a particularly fierce fight over two major groups of products—ferrous and nonferrous metals, and meat and dairy products. Regulating them would take much of the rest of trade, both in consumer goods and manufacturing resources, out of the sphere of free pricing.

We managed to beat off the attack. But overall, the list which was ultimately approved at a conference with the President was still clearly too long. The most serious consequences entailed maintaining government price controls not on consumer goods (by spring these were already being rather quickly and painlessly rolled back) but in the fuel and energy sector—primarily on oil and petroleum products. If I agreed to postpone the final decision for several months, it was mainly because winter was coming and the danger loomed that while energy producers and consumers were haggling over prices, several major cities could freeze.

Moscow in December 1991 is one of my most painful memories. Grim food lines, even without their usual squabbles and scenes. Pristinely empty stores. Women rushing about in search of some food, any food, for sale. Dollar prices in the deserted Tishinsky market. An average salary of seven dollars a month. Expectations of disaster were in the air.

When even today I am accused of having pursued an immoral and merciless policy that hit working people where it hurt them most, of adopting harsh measures that led to the loss of already "empty" savings accounts, that terrible picture of Moscow in winter always comes to mind. And I remain convinced that at that time, saving people from cold and hunger was the very highest form of morality.

Late in the evening of January 1, after making sure all the instructions, price listings, and organizational structures were in place, my wife and I went out for the first time in months—to a birthday party for Viktor

Yaroshenko, a journalist friend. As usual, it was a pleasant gathering. We argued about literature, chatted about the "thick journal" crisis.[1] We tried not to mention politics or the economy.

Beginning January 2, 1992, prices for the overwhelming majority of goods (with the exception of bread, milk, alcohol, and also public services, transportation, and energy) were freed, and regulated prices were raised. A 28 percent value-added tax was introduced.

The budget for the first quarter of 1992 was presented to the Supreme Soviet with no deficit. The Central Bank began a gradual shift toward a more restrained monetary policy, raised its interest rates, tightened its reserve requirements, and introduced restrictions on credit growth.

The severity of the economic situation in which Russia found herself demanded some rather unusual measures on the government's part. For example, given the weight of the money overhang pressing down on the market, and the paucity of product reserves, we temporarily lifted import limits and established a zero import tariff; this allowed stores to re-stock at least somewhat. Free imports in early 1992 were what actually catalyzed development of private commerce.

Quantitative limits on the export of finished products were also dropped; the only ones retained were the quotas on export of fuel and energy products and raw materials. Strict controls were established for the issuing of quotas.

The first reaction in the press was hysteria: "It's been two days since prices were freed, and there is still nothing for sale. . . ." "Now, five days after this hasty and ill-planned step, it's finally clear that liberalization will not do away with shortages. . . ."

Reason, of course, told us that it would be two or three weeks before the first results became visible, and yet we anxiously and impatiently waited for signs of improvement in the market. Would the stabilization measures be effective? Would they be enough to overcome the tradition, rooted in decades of Soviet commercial practice, of deficit distribution?

On the whole, the liberalization of prices on consumer goods proceeded without any of the excesses or disturbances many had predicted. The January jump in prices, as we had foreseen, led to a drop in the volume of goods in circulation and to gradual saturation of the market. Fiscal policy remained rather stringent through April. Simultaneously, a presidential order ratifying the basic points of the privatization program for 1992 allowed the process of an orderly transfer of government property to finally get off the ground.

In order to block a counterattack by state commercial structures and create the preconditions for real privatization in this crucial economic sphere, every store and distributing point had to become a legal entity and have its own bank account. The legal documentation that would permit broad-based auction privatization of retail stores would not be ready until March, and meanwhile state commerce had launched an all-out war to save the old shortage system. Under socialism, shortages were what made the position of salesclerk, retail specialist, or department manager a tremendous boon, the envy of practically every Soviet family. For those who worked in state commerce, a transition to a normal money economy, where the customer ruled, meant the collapse not only of existing stereotypes but of their prestige and social position as well. We discussed the situation and, at P. S. Filippov's suggestion, decided to draft a decree on freedom of trade—a normative act that would liberalize this sphere of activity to the maximum degree. The President signed it at the end of January, and it was immediately promulgated.

The next day, as I was driving through Lubyanka Square, I saw what looked like a long line stretched outside Detskii Mir department store.[2] Previously it had been rather empty around there. "It's a line," I thought, out of habit. "Probably something just appeared on the shelves." How amazed I was when I realized that these were not shoppers at all! Clutching a few packs of cigarettes, a couple of cans of food, or a bottle of vodka, wool stockings, mittens, or a child's sweater, people with the "Decree on free trade" newspaper clipping pinned to their coats were offering various little items for sale.

Tasteless? Ignoble? Vulgar? Maybe so. But to the best of my knowledge, babies aren't born into this world as perfect beauties either. Perhaps only the parents can see that a wonderful person will in time grow out of this tiny, caterwauling creature. If I still had any doubts about whether the Russian people's spirit of private enterprise had survived seventy years of communism, they disappeared that day.

We of course had to fight a long hard battle to preserve free trade, especially in the first few months, before private commercial structures had come together and before any good privatized retail stores began to appear or a network of chambers of commerce began to take shape. Notably unhappy with the decree were certain law-enforcement officials and district authorities whom we had deprived of the opportunity to practice their usual forms of extortion. At times they deliberately tried to make some places where local trade was concentrated look particularly seedy. However, be that as it may, it soon became clear that the basic task of eliminating shortages and changing people's attitudes toward private trade was being accomplished.

As expected, the most serious problems arose regarding products for which prices had remained under centralized control—bread, vodka, milk, sunflower oil, sugar. Working out a single subsidy plan for them, one that would sit well with every region of the country, was not merely difficult, but perhaps even impossible. In early January, I signed an order delegating decision making on most of these prices to local authorities. Depending on specific local conditions, we gave local authorities the right to refuse subsidies, thereby providing an impetus for market determination of prices, which would in turn do away with shortages and with lines. The leadership reacted differently in each region. Chelyabinsk and Nizhni Novgorod put the rights accorded them to quick use, and in those cities the supply outlook for the general populace began to improve. But there were other regions that stubbornly stuck to a policy of "regulated entry into the market," with all its attendant coupons, lines, generous subsidies, and further deterioration of the underfinanced social sphere.

Progress was very slow in restructuring agriculture. The basic directives for agrarian reform were laid out in a presidential order: reregistration of all collective and state farms, thus permitting property relations to be put in order; establishing the right of peasants to receive a land and property allotment upon leaving either one; and creation of a federal fund for redistribution of land to those who wanted to operate private farms, as well as providing financial aid to develop private farming.

The basic difficulties involved in reforming the Russian village are historical and social in nature. Throughout decades of collective-farm serfdom, young people in rural areas dreamed of sooner or later moving to the city. The institutionalization of second-class citizenship for peasants—no internal passports because peasants were assigned to their kolkhoz for life, a standard of living noticeably lower than in cities, limited opportunities to choose work they truly liked, and the paucity of cultural life or even everyday amenities—all this, year after year, gave young villagers, especially the energetic, smart, and confident ones, reason to move away.

So the one social stratum that might have jumped at the changes, supported them, made real use of the new rights and freedoms, was inevitably weakened. And of course the rural elite, the Communist gentry made up of kolkhoz chairmen and sovkhoz directors, were hardly burning with desire to give up their own privileged positions; and so they wrung every advantage they could out of the total dependence of their fellow villagers.[3]

And yet, despite the resistance, changes had begun. One indirect sign was that the number of livestock increased on private plots and fell on state and collective farms. Even more direct evidence was that by May 1992 there were over 100,000 individual small farms in Russia, and their number continued to grow rapidly. There was some hope that a level-headed, persistent, and consistent government policy could break the resistance of the agrarian *nomenklatura* and establish a market-oriented agricultural private sector grounded in clearly fixed property relations.

Unfortunately, these hopes were dashed by the unexpected appointment of Rutskoi as head of the agrarian reform process. I had first met Aleksandr Vladimirovich Rutskoi on November 6, 1991. Aleksandr Nikolaevich Shokhin, who had just been named deputy chairman of the Russian Federation government, and I decided to pay a protocol visit to the Vice President, introduce ourselves, and reach some understanding on mutual cooperation and coordination. Aleksandr Vladimirovich was

clearly pleased by the manifest respect shown him, and invited us to take
a look at some models of food-processing machinery whose development he was sponsoring. During our conversation someone brought in
a decree for him to stamp. Rutskoi looked at it, harrumphed in satisfaction, and signed it with a flourish. As far as I can guess, it was the order
"On the Declaration of a State of Emergency in Chechnya."

Rutskoi, who had only recently been promoted to general for his part
in the events of August, was hoping to make his mark as a military leader,
and personally charted troop movements on the map. Later, when the
situation began to deteriorate, he railed at whoever was within shouting
distance, and after the operation failed, he went looking for the guilty
parties. He came down on Barannikov hardest of all.

Late in October, at a session of the State Council, Yeltsin had forced
the question of price liberalization, and asked those present whether they
agreed it was necessary. Everyone, including Rutskoi, nodded yes. But by
November, Rutskoi was already engaged in some complex maneuvers to
avoid any responsibility for the unpopular decisions soon to be made. At
cabinet meetings conducted by Yeltsin, at whose left hand Rutskoi always
sat, the latter regularly brought up the issue of Ukraine, where President
Kravchuk was talking about declaring a state of economic emergency.
The idea of declaring a state of emergency obviously appealed to Rutskoi;
he really wanted to do something like that in Russia.

At the end of December, he set off on a tour of Siberia. The economic
situation was grave, and complaints were coming in from all sides. Rutskoi strove to separate himself as decisively as possible from the new
government and its plans. This was when he first mentioned the little
boys in pink knickers who'd decided to run Russia.[4] When he got back
he apologized, recanted, told us that he was totally misinterpreted, that
it wasn't us he'd had in mind, but the parliamentary faction called
"Change—a new policy."

This later would become a habit. He would come out with wrathful
denunciations of the government (those aimed at the President himself
were more restrained), then arrive at the airport from his travels with a
fistful of clippings from local papers, shake them in the air and tell us

how the central newspapers had gotten it all wrong, how that wasn't what he'd meant to say. Thus the conflict between the Vice President and the government rather quickly escalated from a cold war to a hot one. The problem was that around Rutskoi—a person, it seems to me, of quite limited abilities—there was a constant swarm of energetic hustlers who used him to lobby for a variety of commercial interests. They spun him all sorts of yarns about "serving Russia's interests," and dunned him for perquisites, privileges, and quotas. His hangers-on interpreted any refusal by the government to approve such extracurricular activities as a plot aimed at undermining Vice President Rutskoi's influence.

Granted, in February 1992, Rutskoi did attempt to patch up relations. He invited Gennady Burbulis and me to his office at the Kremlin for a chat. He began by stressing the need to reconcile, to be on a first-name basis, to be honest with one another. We took advantage of his invitation to say, in the sort of language he might understand, something like this: "Sasha, you don't know a thing about economics. Why keep butting in?" But on the whole the conversation was a friendly one. Nobody needed a war.

This was when Gennady Eduardovich was visited by what seemed to me a remarkably unpromising and dangerous idea—setting Rutskoi the task of reforming agriculture. An understandable enough idea, since agricultural policy had been the downfall of many, including the memorable and exemplary Yegor Kuzmich Ligachev.[5] I was categorically opposed to such an appointment. In the first place we were just beginning, with enormous difficulty, to make some headway in agrarian reform. Extremely significant presidential orders had been ratified. Kolkhozes and sovkhozes were being reorganized, land redistribution funds were being created, and we were supporting an emerging private-farm sector. And now all that complex, politically sensitive work would be handed over to someone who didn't know a hog from a hole in the ground, whose determination went hand in hand with rank ignorance. It was too great a price to pay for his political neutralization. And besides, there was no doubt that he would soon be complaining that people weren't letting him do his job, and he would try to dump the responsibility on someone else.

Nonetheless, the President approved the decision, and the consequences were quick to make themselves felt. A contradictory stream of
directives came forth from the Vice President and the Ministry of Agriculture, allowing the local-level agricultural *nomenklatura*, referring to
these very contradictions, to almost wholly block land reform and the
reform of agricultural enterprises. I soon become convinced that letting
the Vice President run agriculture was simply too dangerous for the
country; his determined *and* incompetent interference might cost us a
great deal. At critical moments during the agricultural year, especially at
harvest time, I made a point of asking Andrei Vladimirovich Kozyrev to
find Rutskoi some special and urgent mission abroad—preferably as far
away as possible. Fortunately, Andrei came through, and crops were har-
vested in a more or less organized fashion.

The fact that the Vice President was quite limited and ill-educated
was, of course, not news to me. Still, as work proceeded, and especially
when we ran into emergencies that required quick decisions, like the
events in North Ossetia and Ingushetia, South Ossetia, and Tadzhikistan,
I was stunned to learn that this heroic pilot was, to put it mildly, not all
that brave. Up to the very minute that a decision had to be made, he was
bursting with talk and energy. When the time came to act, and God forbid the President was away, and it was just the two of us—the Vice President and the acting prime minister—his passionate desire to foist the
decision making onto someone else came to the fore.

At first this was so much at odds with his established reputation that I
simply didn't believe it, and thought that I was probably mistaken. Later,
when this sort of thing happened again and again, I was persuaded that
yes, behind that dashing facade of the mustachioed man-at-arms lay a
vacillating and insecure personality. Later, in October 1993, Rutskoi's
anything but heroic behavior didn't surprise me a bit.

But that spring of 1992 the avalanche of telegrams and orders issuing
from the Vice President's office to rural areas was taken, everywhere and
in every way, as a signal to move from covert sabotage of agrarian reform
to active resistance. The chaos reigning in agricultural management, and
the impossibility of determining where the authority of the government

and the Ministry of Agriculture ended and that of the Vice President and his Center for Agrarian Reforms began, gave a tremendous advantage to those who wanted to preserve the foundations of the Soviet estate untouched.

We encountered opposition to these reforms in the financial sphere as well. I've already mentioned that in preparing for the reform we realized that an abrupt change in prices and income would require substantial emissions of cash, as well as a restructuring of the denomination structure of the money supply. My order to immediately print higher denominations, issued to the director of the mint, Leonid Vasilievich Alekseev, was accepted with full understanding, although his agency was still formally subordinate to the Soviet Ministry of Finance.

As it turned out, however, almost immediately after our talk, Alekseev was summoned by Khasbulatov and read the riot act: "You've been listening to these Gaidar types and spreading inflation." Given the legislative confusion of those times, determining whose order took precedence was no easy task. After this scolding, the head of Goznak simply lay low. All work on preparing new denominations was halted.

Meanwhile prices rose; and wages and salaries lagged behind prices, but also rose. With every passing day the volume of cash in circulation lagged more and more behind the demand, and Professor Khasbulatov's angry conversation with Mr. Alekseev resulted in real trouble. Because of the dearth of cash, delay in payment of salaries, pensions, and social benefits was becoming a mass phenomenon. And millions of people were in no position to care about who "up there" was right and who was wrong.

In order to make up for the two months foolishly wasted at the beginning of reforms, and to speed the printing of new denominations, the government made it first priority to give Goznak what it needed (for purchase of replacement parts, technical equipment) and tightened controls over cash circulation. But the crisis was becoming more serious, especially with the approach of the summer vacation season. In Perm, workers threatened to blockade the local mint if they were not paid what they were owed, and petitioners from outlying regions rushed to Moscow to declare that they simply could not return home without cash in hand.

At the height of the crisis we seriously discussed the possibility of minting and circulating gold coins in the most politically explosive regions. At the end of June 1992 the cash crisis began to abate. The political damage, however, was hard to repair.

Noncash circulation itself was, as they say, hardly a piece of cake. In my unfinished book, the one interrupted by news of the August coup, I had written that the response to price liberalization and the transition to a restrained fiscal policy in postsocialist economies across the board had been a crisis in payments. If a reasonable policy in the monetary sphere could be maintained for a sufficient time, the situation would stabilize itself on a level characteristic of stable market economies. Actually limiting the number of defaults would involve greater financial responsibility on the part of enterprises, as well as introduction of effective legislation on bankruptcy. Any attempt at combating defaults by increasing the volume of credit would merely reproduce and even increase the scale of debt, but on a new and higher curve of the inflationary spiral.

The fact was as incontrovertible as the setting of the sun. But drawing the proper conclusion from it was as hard for many directors of enterprises, and for their representatives in the Supreme Soviet, and for the practicing economists who supported them, as it was for our ancestors to acknowledge that the earth turns.

In Russia the factors giving rise to the payments crisis were complicated by the weakness of the microeconomic base for stabilization policy: privatization had not yet begun, enterprises had little financial liability, and legislation regulating bankruptcy was nonexistent. Moreover, changes in the accounting system linked to preparations for introducing a noncash Russian ruble slowed the movement of payment documents through the system, while many factory directors still firmly believed in the notion that products already shipped would automatically, sooner or later, be paid for.

If the cash crisis was the most obvious, most pressing issue of early 1992, monetary relations with the other states in the Commonwealth were a less visible but equally explosive one. The overwhelming majority of CIS states, having accepted initial liberalization measures as unavoidable, opted for a strategy of gentle, gradual entry into the free market, and retained price controls over a long list of consumer goods and industrial resources. They also retained a centralized planning system, and massive government commissions and funds distribution. What they got in return was a combination of rapidly rising prices and continuing shortages in all sectors of the market. Moreover, if at the beginning of 1992, administrative restrictions caused price-increase rates to lag behind those in Russia, they soon jumped considerably, leaving even the very high Russian rates of inflation in the dust. The Baltic states, it is true, chose a different route. They set a course for consistent market reform and definitive stabilization of a national currency. But in the first half of 1992 this whole group of nations with markedly diverse policies was still using the old Soviet ruble. Not only that, but all our ruble-zone neighbors had practically unlimited money-printing capacity. Over the first five months of 1992, money totaling 232 billion rubles was issued on the Russian market, while loans from the Central Bank to the Russian government amounted to 90 billion rubles. The danger we had foreseen—the monetary expansion of other CIS states at Russia's expense—was becoming a reality.

At this point, the strategy of many CIS states was to shift the bulk of their exports overseas to acquire convertible currency, meanwhile cutting exports to Russia across the board. This delivered yet another blow to Russian manufacturing, which used cotton from Uzbekistan, Tadzhikistan, and Turkmenia, nonferrous metals from Kazakhstan, and metal products from Ukraine.

Customs agreements were still conditional, the market transparent and permeable. As a result, an unpleasant and unstable situation developed. In Russia, as in the Baltic states, the tight monetary policy aimed at slowing price increases, especially at the wholesale level, was beginning to bear fruit. People were starting to think about their money, to refuse to buy products offered at artificially high prices that in no way reflected the consumer's real spending power. However, in those republics where the monetary policy had remained soft and flexible, people bought without bargaining, without calculating the cost: *We don't mind spending money. They can always print more.* This is a deficit economy, barter in its classic form. And as a result, the effectiveness of Russia's tight monetary policy was undercut. Under such conditions, tightening the policy even more would have been socially risky, and also fruitless. It gradually became clear that while the government was haggling over every kopeck, slashing expenditures across the board, and making enemies left and right, the former republics were calmly and prolifically churning out money.

A characteristic example was the issue of the Black Sea Fleet. In the spring of 1992 a debate over who owned the fleet was raging between Russian and Ukrainian authorities. Ukraine's chief argument was that "while Moscow is busy being cheap, we're spending money on both the fleet and the Crimea, never even counting the cost." And indeed, why bother to count if you can print all the money you need?

In early February, when it had already become obvious that a free market was beginning to take shape, at one of our regular evening meetings I proposed to my colleagues that we take advantage of the initial momentum of these changes, and of our opponents' disarray, to quickly and unexpectedly free prices on oil and petroleum products. But as discussion went on, the contrary opinion won out: Wouldn't it still be better to do as we originally planned, to wait until the heating season is over, to not rush things? The results, though, of this policy of caution were troublesome. Beginning in late February and early March, this very fight over liberalizing fuel prices would become the focal point for a gradual consolidation of the antireform forces. If you look through all the press coverage from this period, not just the Communist papers, it's apparent how widespread the hysteria over unfreezing oil prices had become.

In December of the previous year, many enterprises were still sanguine about the prospect of a price hike, and some were even hoping that henceforward their lives would be a bit easier. Many were certain that by continually raising prices on their own output they would be able to stay afloat without making any real changes. By the end of February, the directors of these concerns were beginning to realize that their suppliers and related enterprises would be resorting to the same tactic, and that everyone would eventually run up against that same ability-to-pay limit.

Hence the growing resistance to any measures aimed at liberalizing prices in the all-important fuel sector. Of course those oil producers who had ended up taking the fall—with fixed prices on their output but freed prices for their replacement and component parts and equipment—supported such measures. But almost everyone else was opposed. The argument was that if oil prices are five to six times higher, other prices will jump to the same level. From an economic standpoint this was nonsense, and within a few months, by June 1992, everyone in the country would be persuaded of that fact. But at the moment, when people had barely recovered from the shock of January 2, such an assertion seemed irrefutable. A whole conspiracy theory about the "global plot" to strangle Russian industry by freeing prices on oil and petroleum products grew out of this fear of a new crisis.

Pressure on the President increased. An avalanche of visitors informed him daily about the shady operation (or perhaps outright treason) these monetarists were plotting. The Supreme Soviet passed a resolution enjoining the government to make no changes in energy prices without its consent. What should have been a routine reform process in a crucial economic sector became a politically explosive issue. Recently initiated negotiations with the International Monetary Fund concerning a major loan gave the opposition a chance to cast the IMF in the role of chief instigator of the plot. Our government was assigned the part of its "obedient tool."

The initial response of Western political and financial elites toward Russian economic reform was extremely wary and cool. The Soviet Union—the West's historical opponent, but as such a guarantor of stability and predictability—had just crumbled. Gorbachev, so well liked in the West, was gone. It wasn't clear just what to expect from these new and unpredictable republics. Would they begin warring among themselves? Would they, God forbid, start trading nuclear strikes, as Russian and Ukrainian newspapers were warning in the fall of 1991? All this made

Western leaders anxious. And as far as the reforms already begun were concerned, Western thought was that over the past few years there had already been a great deal of talk, and a dozen or so official programs, so how did they know that this wasn't just more of the same? Better to wait and see.

Among the first to realize that this time Russia was serious about reform were British ambassador Rodric Braithwaite and American ambassador Robert Strauss—although it would be hard to imagine two prominent people less alike than this pair. Braithwaite was a career diplomat, an intellectual, a Russian expert. Strauss was a sharp-tongued American attorney known for never having lost a case, an archpolitician, and a former Democratic Party chairman who until his posting to Moscow knew next to nothing about Russia. They did, however, have one thing in common; both carried a great deal of weight in their respective governments. Proceeding from different assumptions, they had both by December 1991 come to the conclusion that Russian reform should be staunchly supported, and both did a great deal to persuade the leadership of Great Britain and the United States to do just that. By the time Yeltsin paid brief visits to London and Washington, D.C., in late January, when he spoke with Prime Minister John Major and President Bush, and I with the British finance minister Norman Lamont and Treasury Secretary Nicholas Brady of the United States, the ground was already well prepared. Our conversations were lengthy ones. I sensed that my interlocutors were genuinely interested in Russian affairs, and so went into great detail about what we were doing, what we were planning to do, what stages we had mapped out, and what difficulties we expected at each stage. There was already hard proof that these were more than just words: the overwhelming majority of prices had been freed, imports liberalized, budget expenditures reduced, and goods were finally beginning to appear in stores. Now was the very time to do everything possible to help a fledgling Russian democracy that could, if strengthened, help to open up new prospects of peace and stability worldwide.

After that January visit to London and Washington, the question of aid to Russia became part of the Western political agenda. Most important, the grain shipments from American ports which had so concerned me earlier were now proceeding virtually nonstop. In early April, President Bush sent Undersecretary of the Treasury Mulford to Russia for negotiations. Mulford informed me that Bush had made a policy decision to support economic reforms in Russia, and that within the next few days the Group of Seven (G7) would announce a major financial aid plan of roughly $24 billion. He asked me to lay out the optimal configuration of such a package. I was, of course, happy to oblige him. If the G7 nations were indeed willing to provide such aid, Russia's financial and foreign trade situation would improve substantially. The problem of maintaining sufficient grain stores until the next harvest would be solved. We could raise and resolve the issue of reviewing the unfavorable terms of our credit agreements with the Paris and London Clubs. We would be able to get additional low-interest, long-term loans from the IMF and the World Bank. However, I well understood that however crucial foreign aid might be, it alone would not solve Russia's domestic problems, and that when the vast expectations born of such massive financial support collided with Russia's grim realities, serious political difficulties were in store.

The winter of 1991–92 was a time of maximum strain and risk for the Russian government, but was also a period wherein we had a certain amount of room to maneuver. Traditional pressure groups were still disorganized. After August 1991, leaders of the agrarian and military-industrial lobbies who had been mixed up with the GKChP were no longer players. And even those others who had furiously criticized the ongoing reforms and who had hoped to ride to power on the crest of popular dissatisfaction had a vested interest in someone else doing the dirty work.

True, certain public figures who had come to power on the democratic wave thought it high time to put some distance between themselves and the reformists, to jettison them like so much unnecessary ballast. Here's Rutskoi in *Pravda*, saying that "the crisis in Russia which has emerged with particular clarity in these first few weeks following price liberalization is not something the people will tolerate for long. . . ."

Then there was Khasbulatov. At one time he had backed our plans for price liberalization, but by January 1992, at an official meeting with Italian senators, he was saying: "the situation is developing in such a way that it might be time to propose that the President dismiss his virtually ineffectual government."

Articles by Professor Ruslan Khasbulatov of the Moscow Economics Institute had caught my eye as early as 1988–89. Published in *Komsomolskaya Pravda*, they tended to reflect a rather simplified and rosy view, typical of market socialism, of the upcoming transformation. He had submitted some to *Kommunist*, and I had rejected them for publication on grounds of their banality. I met Khasbulatov in person in 1990, when my colleague Aleksandr Skrynnik, a special correspondent for *Pravda*, brought the newly elected deputy from Chechnya to see me at the economics section offices.

We had met again in the fall of 1991, after my appointment to a government post. I could see that he disliked me, but at first I didn't understand why. Later I learned from Yeltsin that Khasbulatov himself was vigorously campaigning for the prime ministership. Apparently he had decided that with the worst of the dirty work already done, it might be pleasant to run things for a while.

Khasbulatov had two undeniably strong points as a politician: an excellent understanding of bureaucratic intrigue and an ability to manipulate people. I watched with something akin to admiration as he doled out his favors, alternating between the carrot and the stick, as he played on deputies' weaknesses, their petty interests, as day by day he consolidated his control over the Supreme Soviet. Everyone well remembers how artfully he used the power of the bureaucracy to pass the resolutions he wanted. It was as if his very skin was sensitive to the mood in the hall, could literally feel the agitation, and he could sense when that agitation might be used to swiftly force a vote, or on the contrary, when he needed to let the hall have its say, tangle up an issue, drown it in debate. It may well be that for a long time my skepticism regarding Khasbulatov as an economist obscured the fact that here was a considerable political talent, one of the greatest to come out of the turbulent perestroika years. It seems to me that Khasbulatov had some inner feel for the Stalinist methodology of power, and that perhaps, consciously or not, he was trying to model and apply it. He eventually lost, but one must admit that he came very close to achieving his goal.

And so the winter of 1991–92 was our ally; we managed to accomplish a great deal. Looking back at our accomplishments over that period, I see that they did lay a foundation for a free-market economy in Russia. Yet by spring the overall political atmosphere had drastically worsened. The socially controversial policy dictated to us by force of circumstance had cut into the interests of every single major social group. The army and the military-industrial complex were feeling the pinch of drastic cutbacks in defense spending; the agribusiness complex felt it in the loss of subsidies for food products, the investment complex in reduction of budgeted capital investments. Tight fiscal policy had set caps on salaries for teachers, doctors, scholars and researchers, and managers. Forced savings accumulated under conditions of repressed inflation were now worthless, and this was a painful blow to older groups like veterans and pensioners. Industrialists and entrepreneurs were moaning about excessive taxation and blaming it for all their troubles. The failure of Vneshekonombank had stripped Russian enterprises of virtually all their hard currency holdings. And for this people blamed not the old Soviet government under Valentin Pavlov but the newly launched reforms.

We realized that no sort of maneuvering on our part could prevent the formation of a powerful pro-inflation political coalition. In the Supreme Soviet, a solid antireformist majority was already taking shape. By late spring, in our deliberations on political and economic issues, Russia's President was more and more often posing the anxious question: where was the popular base of support for our current policy? On the whole, from this time forward, the dismissal of the reform government was a foregone conclusion. The only question was when.

Chapter 8

An Accurate Forecast

- The Sixth Congress of People's Deputies
- The opposition regroups
- The President washes his hands
- Vitold Fokin and Leonid Kuchma
- Thoughts of resignation
- Privatization begins
- Vouchers
- The first billion dollars from the IMF
- Interethnic conflict
- The year's positive gains

The first frontal assault on the reforms came in April 1992. The place—
the Sixth Congress of People's Deputies of the RSFSR.

On the eve of the congress the President reorganized his government.
Burbulis remained state secretary but was released from his post as first
deputy prime minister. I was appointed in his place. This meant that, in
a setting where the President himself was head of the government, responsibility for day-to-day government business and for political defense of our chosen course would fall on me.

The shock of August had passed, there had been no harsh repressions
in the wake of the coup attempt, and the immediate threat of hunger and
wholesale economic collapse had receded. The opposition had recovered, and was thinking that in light of the hardships people had endured
throughout the initial stages of reform, now was the time to shout as
loudly as possible that it had all been done against the will of the congress
and the Supreme Soviet, or that it wasn't done right, it wasn't done the
way everyone agreed, or that it should have been done more gently or

more harshly, faster or slower but in any case differently, and that we had to stop right here, or even better—turn around and go back.

The flood of abuse and damnation directed at the government was rising: *The monetarists have bankrupted, sold out, ruined Russia.* One people's deputy, with much wringing of hands, informed the congress from the speaker's podium that in the first three months of Gaidar's reforms the birth rate had dropped precipitously. I pointed out to those assembled that in the light of insuperable physiological factors, we could hardly have undermined the birth rate in the space of three months, even if we'd tried.

Most of the deputies were not yet mentally prepared to take on the responsibility of a change in course. The economic realities of the recent past were too fresh in their minds, as was the obvious danger that any abrupt moves might not just send us back to square one but put us in an even more complicated spot than before. But the atmosphere of the congress, the nonstop nationwide broadcast of every session—when any deputy who walked up to the podium had the chance to outdo his rivals in publicly expressing his love for the people and at the same time point out to his constituency that he personally was not to blame for their individual woes—ratcheted up the excitement in the hall, and radicalized even the moderate opposition.

Almost on first vote, with no discussion, with no analysis of what was financially feasible, resolutions mandating the government to lower taxes, increase subsidies, raise salaries, and limit prices were adopted. They were a senseless assortment of incompatible measures.

At the same time, demands for a vote of no confidence in the government rang louder and louder. Presiding chairman Ruslan Khasbulatov skillfully orchestrated these into a thousand-voice symphony. He never formally put the no-confidence vote on the agenda, but did everything to ensure that all manner of criticism, even the most demagogic, was constantly in everyone's ears. Apparently not quite ready for a direct confrontation with the President, he didn't think that the moment for toppling the reform government had come; still, he wanted the government to come out of the legislative session weakened, demoralized, and obedient to the Supreme Soviet's will—or rather, Ruslan Khasbulatov's. In this desire to frighten but not kill (just yet, anyway) lay his weakness.

After the first day, the President did not attend any sessions, as if to distance himself both from the government he formally headed and from the parliamentary majority. Some of my colleagues were in a state close to panic. And they had good reason; these impossible resolutions bound us hand and foot. We couldn't move a muscle.

The threat was inarguably real. I called an urgent meeting at the Kremlin, in the Winter Garden. I proposed that instead of waiting passively for further developments, we should raise the stakes so high that the congress's hidden ambivalence would become clear to all concerned, thus forcing the deputies to make an unequivocal choice. After a brief discussion, the cabinet accepted the proposal.

The most cautious response to my de facto ultimatum-cum-collective-resignation came from Gennady Burbulis. Something about the idea bothered him, although he offered no counterarguments to my thesis that otherwise we wouldn't be able to do anything meaningful. It may have been that Burbulis, who had worked with Yeltsin much longer and knew him far better than I, understood one thing: our ultimatum was aimed, albeit less directly, at the President as well as the congress, that it was pushing him to make his own stance clear. And indeed, when I went to inform the President of the resolution, it was obvious that the idea didn't sit well with him. Before the Sixth Congress, his government had been merely a team of hired experts, technicians who enjoyed his political protection and authority. With this resolution the government became a player on the political scene. Boris Nikolaevich, with some doubt and dissatisfaction, shook his head, but nevertheless accepted his cabinet's resolution as a fait accompli.

When the recess ended, I immediately requested the floor and announced that since the government could not take responsibility for enforcing the policy mandated by the congress's resolutions, it was turning in its collective resignation to the President. I will never forget the silence that fell on that enormous hall. It seemed endless. Then the rumble of a thousand voices rolled through the archways of the Kremlin Palace. For most delegates, such a turn of events was unacceptable. Anything but responsibility! *After all, if the government resigns, we'll have to do it all ourselves.*

Legislative leaders began looking for ways to compromise. They convened a joint session of the presidium of the Supreme Soviet and the government, minus Khasbulatov. A Declaration of Congress expressing general approval of the reform was adopted, while earlier angry resolutions on economic policy were henceforth to be regarded as recommendations only.

It became clear after the majority's panic and retreat that an undeniable—albeit tactical and temporary—political victory had been won. Sergei Shakhrai then came to the President with a new idea: take immediate advantage of the demoralization in majority ranks and put my formal confirmation as prime minister to a vote. Yeltsin would in any case have to delegate these responsibilities to someone, and today would be the ideal moment for it. I was the last to be let in on the idea; Sergei Mikhailovich had broached it to the President first. Yeltsin heard him out, said that it was too soon, that the proposal wasn't ready yet and thus could fail.

Almost immediately after the session I sensed that those close to the President were insisting that he cut his high-handed reformers down to size, that he add some counterweights. It was at this point that industrial deputy chairmen began to sprout like mushrooms after a rain, and that exotic notions of eliminating the government's apparatus began to pop up. Any signs of a growing distance were covert, unexpressed, muted. Personal relations were as cordial as ever, and in cabinet meetings the President reiterated his support for our economic strategy. But anyone sensitive to the atmosphere in the higher echelons of power already knew that there was an unpleasant surprise in store for the reform government. A mere three or four months down the line, as relations between the President and the parliamentary majority openly and rapidly worsened, the April abscess started to fester.

In spite of consolidation among forces working against liberalization of fuel prices and for increased budget expenditures in all areas, the government did have opportunities to continue pursuing its previous policy, at least for a while. We dropped any retail price controls still existing on the federal level, including price controls on bread. We set fuel prices at six times their former rate, which in spite of panicky forecasts did not seem to particularly affect inflation dynamics. We abolished government price regulation on alcohol.

In May the Central Bank, at the government's urgent request, raised the interest rate on loans for the last time in 1992—to 80 percent. As of July 1 the currency was unified, and the ruble became convertible for current transactions.

The pace of privatization in trade, services, and the restaurant industry was picking up, and simultaneously the legal and organizational groundwork for privatization of major industries was being laid. The government, unsuccessful in pushing bankruptcy legislation through the Supreme Soviet in May, tried to set this mechanism so crucial to economic recovery in motion by presidential decree. Unfortunately that too was unsuccessful; the parliament rejected it.

In July and August the monthly inflation rate hovered at around 10 percent. After encountering serious financial problems, many enterprises were shifting their partners to a payment-in-advance system, and starting to closely monitor their ability to pay. The decline in output at many enterprises led to part-time employment and forced layoffs. Slowly but inexorably, unemployment was increasing.

The further we moved ahead, the greater the difficulties. It was a strange sort of movement. It wasn't like scrambling up some slope that might be steep and dangerous but at least was solid ground, where achieving your goal depended solely on you, on your own strength and endurance. It was more like struggling along some tortuous path through a bog—the ground shifts under your feet, the reeds cut, the mosquitoes blind you, and the first wrong step can send you stumbling off the trail into black ooze.

The greatest danger and the greatest anxieties were, as always, finances. Two problems fundamentally different in nature—interenterprise arrears and the cash crisis, which had peaked on the eve of the summer vacation season—prompted one single, ever more strident demand: *Give us money!*

The public was generally convinced that the government policy of strict monetary restraint was being conducted less for Russia's benefit than the IMF's. Some of the mass media, citing the opinion of certain "gentlemen and scholars," insisted to the public that rejection of such a policy would immediately set things right. In late spring sociological surveys showed that support for the government's policy was waning fast.

Now that, thanks to export credits, the grain crisis that threatened the country with famine had been weathered and the newly functioning market had reduced the need to import food, financial aid from the IMF became a political liability. Much has been spoken and written about the role played by the International Monetary Fund in the 1992 reforms, and the IMF catches it from both sides: from those who see the Fund as a tool in the imperialist plot against Russia, and from those who are convinced that in early 1992 a unique opportunity to use IMF aid to cement the reforms was wasted. In my view, the trouble with such judgments is their failure to understand what resources the IMF could realistically bring to bear.

The IMF is a large bureaucratic organization with a highly competent staff capable of solving the usual run of problems associated with repairing damage done by financial destabilization or reckless populist policy. By its very nature, it is absolutely unsuited to the resolution of large-scale political issues. At the same time, the collapse of the Soviet Union had presented the leading free-market democracies with a truly gigantic problem. Their enemy, confrontation with which had cost them trillions of dollars, had suddenly collapsed, and was undergoing an acute economic and sociopolitical crisis that could loose chaos on a large territory brimming with nuclear weapons. Strategically, the West's most important tasks were to help bring that chaos under control as quickly as possible, lay the groundwork for restoring government institutions capable of real action, and provide opportunities for economic stabilization—all of this being quite comparable to the set of problems born of the collapse of Germany and Japan after World War II. The question at issue was this: what would emerge from the rubble of the socialist empire? Something ugly, economically and politically unstable, a constant threat to the rest of the world, or a group of young but growing free-market democracies capable of speeding the growth of a global economy in the twenty-first century, a reliable strategic partner for the West?

I don't think that the leaders of the major Western powers were unaware of of the magnitude of the choices they faced. The trouble, in my view, was that there was no leader capable of filling the sort of organizing and coordinating role that Harry Truman and George C. Marshall played in the postwar restoration of Europe. The United States, on which, logically, the burden of coordinating Western efforts should have fallen, was paralyzed at the time by the standoff between the Republican administration of George Bush and the Democratic majority in Congress, and by the upcoming presidential elections. Germany, whose leadership, including Chancellor Helmut Kohl, understood the magnitude of Russia's problems perhaps better than anyone, was burdened with problems inherited from the GDR. Our relations with Japan were strained over the Kurile Islands issue, and moreover that economic powerhouse was clearly not prepared to take a leading political role in the West. England's John Major was sympathetic to our efforts, and was willing to help, but the country's economic resources obviously did not allow it to play an appreciable coordinating role. And so it turned out that collectively the leaders of major Western nations understood what was transpiring, were willing to act, but individually each one was trying for various reasons to shunt the burden of responsibility onto someone else. The natural outcome of these good intentions unsupported by any specific mechanisms for realizing them was that the West was forced to hand the coordinating role over to the International Monetary Fund (*It has solid financial resources, let it work on Russia*) even though it was clear that this large-scale political problem was something the IMF could not begin to handle.

When reforms began, we were not members of the IMF, and it took some time to join; any sort of financial cooperation was contingent on membership. In the critical months between January and April of 1992 as little as a few hundred million dollars of available currency reserves would have allowed us significantly more room to maneuver, but we had no access to them. And by the time the paperwork was finished, our stabilization program was coming apart at the seams. So the billion-dollar loan granted in July 1992 for replenishing currency reserves was now just belated support for efforts already expended in the first half of the year.

What the IMF can, perhaps, indeed be criticized for is its policy of trying to preserve a unified ruble zone. The leadership of the Fund, in the unique and quite peculiar situation that had taken shape, didn't know where to start. And as a result it very nearly brought all our efforts at introducing a Russian ruble to naught. We had to overcome not only political opposition from the former republics, who were holding on to their money-printing presses for dear life, but also opposition from the IMF. It was not until May and June 1992, when attempts to set up inter-republic mechanisms for controlling the monetary supply failed, and when the expansion of emissions credits from the Ukraine destroyed any hopes of stabilization in Russia, that the IMF leadership realized its mistake and agreed to the introduction of domestic currencies. But precious time had been wasted.

In time, the IMF gained a much better understanding of postsocialist problems and was able to adapt to conditions here. In 1995 its work with the government of Russia in conducting the stablization program was effective. However, all that came later.

In 1992, the stabilization of the food situation in the country had weakened any incentives linked to loans from international financial organizations. The elementary notion that these obligations were mutual, that without financial stabilization the reforms would not succeed, was not particularly popular with the public. And as a result, both sides, both the West and Russian public opinion, were becoming increasingly unhappy with one another. The International Monetary Fund was unhappy with Russia for not pursuing a consistent stabilization policy, without which foreign support for the budget made no sense. The Russian public was unhappy with the IMF because the promised loans were not coming through.

The ranks of the opposition were growing. And even young, energetic politicians who had once backed the reforms began distancing themselves from the government's unpopular course of action. Nizhni Novgorod's governor, Boris Nemtsov, urged us to give up our intentions of liberalizing oil and grain prices. All this, of course, could not help but affect the President, acutely sensitive to changes in public opinion. Time after time during our talks or during cabinet meetings he returned to the question—why not replenish working capital, even if it requires a new currency issue? Moreover, it was apparent that our arguments against doing so no longer seemed sufficiently convincing to him.

The CIS countries were another problem. At the moment, almost all of them were attempting to combine a "soft" entry into the free market with preservation of large-scale government price regulation and export of inflation to Russia. At meetings of CIS presidents, the most popular economic topics were the need for mutual cancellation of offsetting debts and addition of working capital by currency emission, the peril of liberalizing fuel prices, the perniciousness of any ideas hatched by the Russian government in relation to dividing up the ruble zone, and the necessity of keeping intact major barter agreements between successor states. At such meetings Yeltsin felt extremely uncomfortable, and it was not hard to understand why. He was clearly irritated when again and again I was forced to tell this community of presidents assembled for a friendly chat just how wrongheaded their proposals—which seemed so compelling to them—really were. Subsequently, after colliding with the harsh realities of market economics and seeing how easy it was to lead one's country to the brink of financial catastrophe, many of the presidents who took part in these debates began to radically revise their economic stance, and began supporting forceful reforms. But this didn't happen overnight, and at that time they were united in the view that the chief obstacle to economic cooperation within the CIS was the "doctrinaire" monetarist policy of the Russian government.

My relations with the CIS took a rather singular form. It was Askar Akaev, president of Kirghizia, who probably defined it best when, at one meeting of CIS heads of state in Bishkek, he said, "We've got one Gaidar for the lot. He's everyone's prime minister." Indeed, when Russia initiated reforms, and by so doing made them unavoidable for the rest of the CIS, politicians in the newly independent states now had an opportunity to point a finger at cruel and heartless Gaidar, who had come up with some unthinkable scheme, and say that however they might wish to do otherwise, they were compelled to take a similar route, although they would of course do their best to ameliorate the hardships their peoples would have to endure. What was particularly convenient was that Gaidar wasn't their prime minister—he was Yeltsin's. And so they were in no position to order him to do anything, or to force his resignation. The game of "bad Gaidar" went on at a high emotional pitch at first, and then abated a little, and by the middle of 1992 wasn't really taken seriously anymore. The presidents themselves, especially late in the evening after a snifter of cognac, would joke about the rules of the game. But nonetheless, rules are rules. They'd been laid down and must be reckoned with. It's a great pity that the Commonwealth nations couldn't bring themselves to ride the first wave of reforms, and that each of them tried to extract some unilateral advantage from the new situation. As subsequent events were to prove, this approach led to losses for all of them, collectively and individually.

Of those countries late in undertaking reforms, Ukraine was an especially sad case. At the end of 1991 and beginning of 1992 the Ukrainian political elite had steered a course toward the "soft option" for entry into the free market, with the assumption that it could make maximum use of the unlimited currency-issue opportunities of a unified ruble zone and fifteen independent central banks. In the words of Ukraine's then prime minister, Vitold Fokin, "Why hold down the budget deficit when you've got your own printing press?" As early as 1990, the Central Bank of Ukraine had already begun granting loans unapproved by the USSR Central Gosbank to the Ukrainian government and Ukrainian enterprises.

At the beginning of January 1992, without warning, Ukraine introduced its own domestic currency unit, while retaining the use of the Soviet ruble for noncash transactions. What emerged was a monstrous economic hybrid: a mixture of common noncash currency with a separately issued cash unit. It was then, after the introduction of the *kupon*, that I realized that yes, we had to talk with Fokin and try to reach some agreement, but one thing we could not do was count on any commitments being fulfilled. Of course, other republics were also guilty of exporting inflation to Russia, of taking advantage of new opportunities, but hardly on the scale of what Fokin was doing. If I were to name the one person who did the most to hinder CIS monetary stabilization efforts in 1992, Fokin could probably rightfully claim first place.

Beginning in July 1992, when republic accounts were given correspondent account status, and automatic export of the money supply to Russia became impossible, it was clear that Fokin's policy had no future, and that, politically, neither did he. But earlier in the spring of 1992, when Russia had not yet had time to create its own monetary system, the salary of, say, a professor in Kiev was several times greater than that of a professor in Moscow. At a time when the Russian government was pursuing the tightest of fiscal policies, the Ukrainian government was pursuing the loosest. At this very time, too, Ukraine's "soft reforms" were being touted as an example for us to follow by people who had no idea what that "softness" was costing.

The preservation of widespread price controls, which encompassed 60 to 70 percent of their product range, plus the loose fiscal policy, prevented the Ukrainians from doing away with shortages. In essence, their economy was functioning in an inflationary mode that was both repressed and open—rapid price increases as well as queues and coupons.

For privatization, the path they chose was perhaps the least promising of all. State trade monopolies were being privatized on a lease-with-option-to-buy basis, and were without exception duplicating all the worst features of state-run commerce, exacerbated, in turn, by their total irresponsibility.

There wasn't a single crazy idea that the Russian opposition didn't toy with, and that the Ukrainians didn't adopt. Working capital was regularly "topped off," offsetting debts were mutually canceled, inflationary credits were granted, attempts were made to preserve numerous subsidies, and privatization was linked to compensation for the public's lost savings. And all this of course went under the banner of safeguarding the welfare and interests of working people.

The suicidal consequences of such a policy were fully felt when Russia finally managed to gain its monetary independence. The currency issue of 1993, locked inside Ukrainian borders, resulted in a burst of inflation. Prices rose at ten times the rate of Russian indicators, which were high enough in themselves. By autumn of 1994, Ukrainian salaries lagged far behind Russian ones, at something around twenty dollars a month. The young nation, unable to cover its obligations, was on the brink of bankruptcy.

Of course one can't deny that there were people in the Ukrainian government who were trying to pursue a reasonable economic policy, but their opportunities to do so were extremely limited. I would like to mention one of them: Aleksandr Lanovoy, a young market economist and scholar, who in 1991 and 1992 headed the Ministry of Economics. He and I met in Moscow very early in 1992. We discussed the problems associated with the gradual rise of prices in mutual trade to world market levels. To the great consternation and disapproval of his delegation, Lanovoy sat down with me to sketch out charts and analyze options. It was obvious that he understood that the current policy was leading nowhere, but that he had no support at the higher levels of government. We had a pleasant and interesting dialogue, but I could assume from the start that he was unlikely to accomplish even a part of whatever agreement we might reach.

We later met at a meeting of CIS presidents in Tashkent. Relations between the Russian and Ukrainian governments were rather strained; there was strong anti-Russian sentiment among the Ukrainian political elite. Nonetheless Lanovoy approached me and we set up a meeting. We met late in the evening, and took a long stroll through the grounds of the presidential residence. He told me frankly that it was impossible to do anything meaningful toward market reform in the current political atmosphere. He asked my opinion on prospective Russian economic policy vis-à-vis Ukraine.

In November, Leonid Kuchma, the newly designated replacement for the outgoing Fokin, flew to Moscow for talks with Yeltsin and with me, his chief goal being to restore mutual understanding and friendly relations. He and I spoke in some detail. It seemed to me that he genuinely wanted to make some positive changes, to get the stalled reforms moving again. Perhaps he didn't yet have sufficient understanding of how to do that, but at least it was clear to him that Fokin's policy was headed for a dead end. It was obvious from the start that he was a completely different sort of person, straightforward, with no desire to scheme or dissemble. He himself brought up the issues of putting monetary relations in order, of a full-fledged introduction of a Ukrainian domestic currency into noncash circulation, and of the need to put an end to the chaos in the payments system. We spent some time in consultation. He asked me about key areas for transformation. Granted, he didn't have a clear or well-defined picture of what needed to be done—vestiges of the socialist-manager mentality still got in his way—but at the same time he obviously wanted to move forward, to pursue a meaningful and on the whole pro-reformist policy. Another thing was obvious: Kuchma genuinely did not want to play the usual anti-Russian card so prevalent in Ukrainian politics in 1991 and 1992, and was striving to normalize economic and political relations with us, to place them on a civilized, cultured, and honest footing. Subsequently I was persuaded that we could rely on the Ukrainian prime minister's word. Not everything was in his power to accomplish, and not everything turned out the way he wanted, but at least during the short time that we worked together, there was never any conscious deception. And that was precisely why I always tried to support him.

Back then, at our first meeting, Kuchma had said that he wanted to bring Lanovoy back into the government (he had left by this time), and asked me to phone him and convince him to take the offer to rejoin the Ukrainian cabinet. I contacted Lanovoy and told him that in my view, despite all the difficulties and the dearth of qualified staff, Kuchma had a genuine desire to do something, and I suggested that he help. Lanovoy replied that he considered the Kuchma government doomed from the start and didn't want to get involved with it. To some extent he was right; Kuchma was not head of the Ukrainian cabinet for long and had little time to accomplish anything. Nonetheless, I think that it would have behooved Lanovoy to help Kuchma. Later Lanovoy became involved in politics, and in 1994 ran for president and received a small percentage of the vote. It wasn't until spring of 1996 that he finally joined Kuchma's team as economic adviser. For all their differences, Lanovoy and Yavlinsky seem to have several things in common. Both worked in governments that were unwilling to pursue reforms, and both resigned. Both later entered the political arena. Even their appearance is strikingly similar, their manner of speaking, their attitude toward people. Perhaps like situations create like personalities.

My "twin," I think, was Viktor Penzennik, who joined Kuchma's government in the fall of 1992 and almost immediately earned the fierce enmity of Ukraine's populist parliamentary majority. He was persistent, tough, and clearly disinclined to fret over his own popularity and political future. He in fact pushed hard to get the deeply mired wagonload of Ukrainian reforms back on solid ground. He wasn't able to do much. After Kuchma's dismissal, his own departure was a foregone conclusion. But along with the hatred of the parliamentary majority, he had earned the trust and regard of those who were indeed striving to radically change the direction of their country's economic development. It's no accident that after Kuchma was elected president, and had begun carrying out a program of radical free-market transformation in the midst of a severe economic crisis, he summoned Penzennik to join the government and appointed him first deputy prime minister. Penzennik's task was to develop both the strategy and tactics of transformation.

We met again in the spring of 1995 in Kiev. Viktor was rightfully proud of the results they had managed to achieve in the preceding six months: the pace of inflation had been slowed and structural reforms had begun. He was full of plans for further changes. At the same time, the price of success was high; he had become the politicians' favorite target. It was clear that the president would have to either sacrifice him or, at the very least, shift him to a different post and curtail his authority. Several months later that's exactly what happened. Viktor had to say goodbye to the post of first deputy prime minister, and his authority was limited. He was considering whether to accept the new appointment or refuse it. My advice was to stay. Politically motivated staffing maneuvers were unavoidable in a situation as complicated as the one Ukraine was in. The main thing was not the post itself, but whether or not any possibility of influencing the course of events, of pursuing a meaningful line, would still be there. It was clear that Kuchma wanted to stay on the road to reform, and that meant there was work to be done.

I was glad that, despite all the hesitations and retreats, economic reforms in Ukraine continued through 1995 and 1996. Our neighbor began, with some difficulty, to catch up, and currently the idea of a soft entry into the free market no longer enjoys any popularity there.

But all that was to come later. In May 1992 the Kremlin held a conference on oil and gas issues; heads of major enterprises were invited. The plan was to discuss the progress of reforms in this critical area, as well as the financial situation of the enterprises and restructuring of oil pumping and refining concerns. Vladimir Lopukhin, the fuel and energy minister, had prepared several important framework documents for the conference and was to present a report. But the President opened the conference by announcing that he had made a decision to remove Lopukhin from office and to appoint Viktor Chernomyrdin, chairman of Gazprom, the government's new deputy chairman for fuel and energy.

Differences of opinion with the President over appointments had come up early on, as the government was being formed. There were later disagreements as well. We would talk them over and then together make the final decision. This time things were different; it was all decided behind my back. I won't deny that this was a serious blow. It wasn't just that I hadn't been consulted, and that a friend and cohort who had done much to reform a crucial branch of the economy was being forced to resign; it was the realization that my ability to argue my case to the President had been undercut, and that I could no longer take his support for granted. And in this particular political situation that inevitably threatened to change the shape of the reforms.

Immediately after the conference, Yeltsin called me and apologized, saying that he had tried to warn me, but unfortunately hadn't been able to get me on the phone. The usual political formalities. My first impulse was to tender my resignation on the spot, to divest myself of any responsibility for the unavoidable, negative, and painful consequences of retreating from reform, or simply slowing it down. And it wasn't hard to see that things were headed in that direction. It was a natural step, and probably a politically profitable one. In any case, Grigory Yavlinsky, who was well versed in such questions, told me later that this was my chance, and I'd missed it. But at the time I wasn't thinking about my own political career, I was thinking about our job. Everything we had achieved was still extremely fragile. The Russian ruble was not yet established. A massive privatization program was ready, but not yet launched. In short, the reforms were still largely reversible. Of course I could have made the beau geste, but that would have wiped out everything we had worked so hard to achieve.

And yet the thought of resigning remained. That evening I canceled several meetings and conferences, and freed up some time to think. I realized that remaining in the government would mean fighting a series of rearguard actions, watching the possibility of making meaningful decisions shrink while at the same time continuing to bear full responsibility for the inescapable consequences of a weakened fiscal policy and a retreat from reforms. But leaving would mean surrendering a position that was by no means lost, refusing to give battle at the critical time, when crucial structural reforms were ready to be put in place at any moment. After considerable thought, I decided to stay and continue my work. The deciding argument was that in spite of all the problems, I still had powerful enough levers in hand to influence current policy.

My chief headache was still the Supreme Soviet, where reform politics might as well be a red flag waved in front of a bull. The government barely managed to fend off proposals whose financial consequences would prove nothing short of murderous, and since the President had removed himself from direct leadership of the Soviet of Ministers, the job of holding off pressure from industry lobbyists fell to me. I tried to break up the pattern of direct cooperation, the links connecting industrial ministries and Supreme Soviet committees and commissions and the Central Bank—links that allowed them to bypass the Chairman of the Government and make economically dangerous decisions on their own.

On the whole, a retreat, a slackening of fiscal and monetary policy, became unavoidable politically. In May and June the budget deficit's contribution to the growth in inflation was small, but increasing rapidly.

The debate over the 1992 budget in the Supreme Soviet in early July was the apotheosis of financial irresponsibility. The parliamentary budget oversight committee, commissioned by the leadership of the Supreme Soviet, projected an unimaginable increase in tax revenues for the second half of the year. Over government protests and warnings, the Supreme Soviet took only two hours to pass amendments increasing government financial obligations and the budget deficit by 8 percent of the gross national product.

Relations between the government and the Central Bank were one of the main policy issues in the years between 1991 and 1994. At the end of 1991 the Central Bank of the Russian Federation was wholly subordinate to the Supreme Soviet, which in practice meant subordinate to its chairman, Ruslan Khasbulatov. The office of the chairman of the Central Bank had a direct phone line to the Supreme Soviet, and this telephone, to the best of my knowledge, got a good deal of use. I knew little of Grigory Matyukhin, then head of the bank, other than that he was close to Khasbulatov (they had once worked together at the Moscow Institute of Economics) and had played an active role in the bank-and-budget wars between Russia and the Soviet government. By increasing the volume of credit and granting cheap loans to Russian enterprises, Matyukhin had assured himself the political support of those in power. None of this instilled much optimism. To begin such a complex series of changes without being able to rely on shared understanding and cooperation between the government and the country's leading bank was dangerous.

In November we had tried to solve this problem by taking advantage of the additional powers accorded the President; we prepared an executive order transferring authority over the Central Bank to the president's office. This trial shot failed miserably; the order was immediately—and unanimously—blocked by the Supreme Soviet. Realizing that a cavalry charge wouldn't win us control of the Central Bank, we had to look for ways to compromise. The bank's leadership was, unexpectedly, willing to cooperate. Matyukhin himself rather quickly suggested appointing a key member of our team, Sergei Ignatiev, as deputy chairman of the bank, and gave him the opportunity to work on setting up a system of correspondent accounts with the republics and to supervise matters pertaining to the bank's overall economic policy. In our preparations for creating a separate Russian ruble zone, he turned out to be a useful ally.

In the first few months of 1992, the Central Bank limited the volume of loans provided to commercial banks. Each step toward raising the interest rate was a battle, and working with Matyukhin was no simple matter. At the height of crucial negotiations he was likely to disappear, simply drop from sight. And yet it was obvious that he supported monetary system stabilization, and was willing to carry it through.

At that time the main problem with the Central Bank, the one for which it took the most criticism, was the payments crisis, the sharp increase in the number of interenterprise defaults. A problem common to all postsocialist countries, it was complicated in Russia by the fact that the payments system was being restructured during those pivotal months of the reform. Matyukhin came under heavier and heavier criticism, and then the Chechen promissory-note scandal broke.[1] It was clear that his days as chairman of the Central Bank were numbered. We had to find another candidate and try to push him through the Supreme Soviet.

I talked with our supporters in the Supreme Soviet and tried to determine just which candidates might pass through its sieve. I consulted with Pavel Medvedev, who headed the subcommittee on banking. His answer was hardly comforting—in his view, neither Boris Fyodorov nor Sergei Ignatiev would be an acceptable candidate. Consultations with other parliamentarians confirmed that assessment. They named people who, as a rule, would be either impossible or extremely complicated for us to work with. But one candidate with a serious chance of receiving Supreme Soviet support was worth some thought. This was Viktor Gerashchenko, the last chairman of the USSR Gosbank. I had known of him for some time as a banker highly qualified to deal with foreign economic issues. He had worked in the foreign bank system and in the USSR Vneshe-konombank. Appointed to head the USSR Gosbank at the very height of the bank-and-budget war between the republics and the central government, he worked to keep the bank system afloat, to keep it from sinking into anarchy. I invited Gerashchenko in for a talk. My general impression was that he was ready and willing to work, and that he knew how to deal with the payments system. He assured me that he would work in close cooperation with the government. I decided to throw my support to him. This, apparently, was the most serious of my mistakes in 1992.

Once confirmed by the Supreme Soviet, Gerashchenko promptly showed himself to be a highly qualified manager and a forceful organizer. The bank began to function more precisely, more smoothly; less time was required for payment paperwork to pass through the system. But a single negative factor canceled all this out, and this was that Viktor Vladimirovich was unable to comprehend what should have been axiomatic for bank management during an inflationary crisis. He sincerely believed that accelerating the growth of the money supply by issuing more currency would straighten out the economy. I was to hear him make roughly the following argument many times in the future: Well, look—prices have gone up fourfold, but the money supply only twofold, which means there isn't enough money in the economy, which means that output is declining because of an insufficient money supply, so let's increase the money supply and grant more credit to the republics and to enterprises. I argued with him, presented my counterarguments, tried to prove how flawed such a policy was, tried to prove the obvious—that a drop in monetary demand is a natural reaction to an inflationary crisis and large-scale currency emissions. But changing the mind of someone with deeply rooted, firmly fixed notions about the interconnections within a free-market economy is not easy. In his heart he could not accept any other point of view. The case of Viktor Gerashchenko was clear testimony that the qualities required for commercial banking and those required for running the Central Bank were fundamentally differ-ent ones.

The results of the Central Bank's flawed policy were not long in ap-pearing. Rates of growth in the money supply jumped sharply, and the country stood on the brink of hyperinflation. Later, in September and October, when it became clear that the economy's response to monetary expansion was not increased output but a sharp drop in the value of the domestic ruble and a rapid growth in prices, Gerashchenko's enthusiasm for printing new money began to wane. We managed, with great dif-ficulty, to begin the tortuous process of fiscal and monetary stabiliza-tion all over again. But subsequently it was also clear that in his heart Gerashchenko simply did not believe in the efficacy of using monetary regulators to check inflation. Pursuing a stabilization policy when the head of the country's chief bank does not accept the very essence of that policy is a remarkably unproductive business.

Serious disagreements between the government and the Central Bank, as well as missteps in monetary policy, served to fuel rumors that Gerashchenko was deliberately out to damage the President and the gov-ernment, that he was playing the opposition's game. Quite honestly, I never believed any of those conspiracy theories and was convinced that he simply did not understand how prices, the interest rate, the exchange rate, and the money supply in a free-market and free-price environment were linked to one another.

In hindsight, knowing now the losses the Russian economy suffered thanks to this lack of coordination between the bank and the govern-ment, I try to imagine just what we might have done differently in May and June of 1992, when we were deciding who should head the Central Bank. We had very little room to maneuver. Then again, the most sensi-ble thing would probably have been to support Matyukhin, and try to prevent his ouster. All his organizational missteps were more than made up for by one single factor: he understood the primary task of the Cen-tral Bank in an inflationary crisis.

In July and August of 1992 the Central Bank began canceling mutu-ally offsetting debts and sharply increased its volume of lending. The rate of growth in the money supply, which between January and June held at about 9 to 14 percent per month, now leaped to over 25 percent. As is usual in such situations, the first symptom of a change in monetary policy was a shift in currency exchange dynamics. Up until the middle of May the dollar was dropping. We could sustain that trend through the middle of June, but only at the price of increasing hard currency intervention by the Central Bank. Continuing such intervention, given the bank's modest foreign currency reserves and the changed financial situation, made no sense. Beginning in mid-August, when after the standard one-month lag the ruble supply created in July poured into the foreign currency market, the dollar zoomed sharply upward against the ruble.

At the end of August, food price dynamics took a turn for the worse. The immediate trigger was the drastic upturn in wholesale prices for this year's grain, but the underlying reason was the shift in monetary policy. The threat of hyperinflation and monetary collapse was starker than ever, as was the possible forfeit of all reform policy gains.

While fighting these rearguard actions on the monetary policy front, I tried not to neglect privatization, without which the reforms could not possibly succeed. In the fall of 1991, as I put together proposals for government appointments and selected people for key ministerial posts, I had wanted to tap Anatoly Chubais, then an adviser to St. Petersburg mayor Anatoly Sobchak, for work on structural policy—the former Gosplan, the Ministry of Economics. But the experience of our colleagues in Eastern Europe suggested that the most labor-intensive and controversial area of reform would be privatization, and that meant that we needed a leader of very high caliber. Chubais filled the bill on all counts.

When late one night in Arkhangelskoe I told him that I could see him as head of the State Committee on Property—in other words, that he should take on the responsibility for developing and implementing a privatization program—the usually imperturbable Tolya heaved a deep sigh and asked me if I realized that he would then be the one man who, for the rest of his life, would be accused of putting Russia up for sale. I realized that, but nonetheless answered that if he, with his energy and organizational savvy, would take this on, there might be a real chance that a significant amount of property would be legally regulated and privatized. Otherwise the process would be spontaneous, uncontrolled, and therefore dangerous for society. And as far as any future reproaches were concerned—well, all of us would have to drink from that bitter cup.

There had been talk about the need to privatize ever since 1989. Beginning in 1990, the topic had, in one form or another, figured in every proposed but never implemented reform program. In the summer of 1991 the Supreme Soviet of the RSFSR passed a basic law on privatization. However, no broad-based systematic privatization work had begun. According to official statistics, as of January 1, 1992, in all of vast Russia only 107 retail stores, 58 cafeterias, and 56 service enterprises had been privatized. That was it. Yet these sparse figures didn't reflect the real picture. Between 1989 and 1991 semi-legal, uncontrolled, land-grab privatization had developed rapidly. Using Gorbachev's law on enterprises, which had granted unlimited rights to their directors, many heads of enterprises unabashedly took the sweetest pieces of state property and leased them either to themselves or to their family members—with option to buy—and then hurriedly transferred them to private ownership for a purely symbolic price.

In mid-November, when he took command of that little office titled RSFSR State Property Administration, Chubais immediately discovered that this office had neither any set standards, nor any structures, nor any people. He basically had to start from the ground up.

At the end of December the government convened to discuss and adopt basic principles for privatizing Russia. The document was signed by the President and then sent to the Supreme Soviet, and the process of creating a powerful federal structure capable of handling both organizational and legal tasks began. Russian and foreign experts were recruited to develop scores of normative documents.

In February there was a test run of mechanisms for the sale by auction of retail stores and the service sector. In March small-business privatization picked up speed, expanding to other regions of the country. Attempts by state commerce lobbies to organize popular protest against the auction of stores and commercial outlets got no support from the public.

The Supreme Soviet, again, was the center of resistance to privatization. Chubais reported on our program at one of its sessions. His program provided two options for privatization of state property, the choice of which would be left to the employees of the given enterprise. But in both options the following were taken into consideration:

—the interests of the work collective, including the right to acquire part of the shares at a discount from book value;

—the interests of managers, including shares for the management of the enterprise;

—the interests of local governing bodies, including profits from privatization to be passed on to the regional budget;

—the interests of citizens not employed in the private sector, including free privatization vouchers.

The program was not perfect, but was based on the idea of public consent. It was a working compromise that would allow for orderly division of property and would set in motion the market mechanism that would eventually lead to economically efficient redistribution.

In spite of government opposition, during debate in the Supreme Soviet a third option was added to the first two, giving employees the opportunity to buy 51 percent of the enterprise's shares at a discounted price, a faint echo of the Bolsheviks' "Factories to the workers!" which would later turn into a mighty bureaucracy and a tendency to avoid the harsh realities of the free market by hiding behind the employees. And it is no surprise that the ownership structure of enterprises privatized through this third option soon came to resemble that of industrial kolkhozes.

The government faced a choice: either insist on preserving the original idea in its pure form, thus slowing the process of redistributing ownership rights, or accede to changes that would distort the plan, understanding full well that the ownership structure that would emerge was hardly the optimal one. Loss of momentum was a luxury we could not afford, and so we made the concessions that would let the privatization mechanism, which would in many ways determine the further development of Russian economic reform, move ahead.

Initially the legislation on privatization did not provide for any sort of currency-like medium. We had proposed creating a system of registered privatization accounts and conducting transactions through these accounts. But at the very outset it became clear that in order to use this means we would have to create yet another system parallel to that of the savings banks, or else totally restructure the existing system, which would take considerable time and a colossal amount of money. In that case, real privatization would have to be postponed for at least a year. And this might, quite simply, deprive the country of its one window of opportunity.

The trouble with many of the privatization programs implemented in Eastern European states and the former USSR republics was that privatization documents were not tradeable. As soon as people realized that they had been handed something that couldn't be bought or sold, something that, as the saying goes, neither warms you up nor cools you off, interest in the whole idea of privatization dropped sharply. Therefore we decided that it was critical to introduce a tradeable privatization check that each holder would be free to keep or sell, thus turning it into an instrument of the emerging market economy. The question of what face value to put on the check was rather abstract, since the check's significance was social and psychological, certifying the bearer's right to a certain part of the property being privatized. Its actual worth would be determined by the size or amount of the privatized property, by the latter's financial stability, by the benefits belonging to employees. Finally, to keep things simple, we settled on a denomination of 10,000 rubles.

The President supported the privatization plan the government had designed, but he strongly objected to adopting the English word "voucher." At cabinet meetings he outright forbade members of his government to use what was in his opinion almost an indecent word, and we were supposed to talk about "privatization checks." Perhaps he was right, but language develops according to its own laws, not the government's, and tends toward maximum simplicity; the adopted term stuck, and Anatoly Chubais, apparently, is forever stuck being its godfather.

A significant part of the business elite soon recognized the opportunities unfolding as privatization progressed. If at the beginning of 1992 Russian industrial managers' image of happiness was still firmly fixed in the socialist past, when they were guaranteed resources, material supplies, technical backup, and if need be, state financing, now many of them were trying on a new social image, that of shareholders and heads of major private corporations.

Of course there was no small risk in all of this. The process we had started would eventually involve 148 million people. They were being handed some mysterious piece of paper with an outrageous name. We still had to make this voucher truly liquid, moving a huge volume of state property out to meet it; only then would the base of public support for reform begin to expand. So the critical problem was to keep up the flow of property offered for privatization. In order to work with it, we needed voucher investment funds. The State Committee on Property tried to regulate their operation, but there were a lot of them, and you can't track the activity of each and every one. Privatization, alas, always was something of a lottery, but its merit lay in the fact that for the first time in centuries the state was not taking property away from people, but trying to give them something back.

We realized that these 148 million people would not suddenly change their accustomed way of thinking, their hierarchy of values, their social priorities once they received their vouchers. A sense of absolute ownership of one's own property has to take shape gradually, over a number of years, perhaps even decades. You can't create it by fiat.

But we had accomplished the main thing. A demand for privatized property had appeared, and begun to grow, forcing local authorities to take privatization very seriously. They had to solve the problem of where their citizens could invest their privatization checks. Another nudge in that direction came from the inevitable tie-in between their local budget and revenues from small-scale privatization. And all of this was no longer just some fantasy dreamed up by romantic liberals, but a social reality that even its enemies had to reckon with.

Privatization began to create its own political base of support, and was becoming hard to stop. The majority stance in the Supreme Soviet in the fall of 1992 served as tangible evidence of that. For all the hysterics surrounding the August decree issuing vouchers, the majority apparently could not bring themselves to make the simplest and most unequivocal decision—to veto the privatization program as adopted, to stop privatization in its tracks. Once the first privatization checks were issued, this became politically impossible.

And so, in military parlance, you might say that between May and August of 1992 the government, under assault by superior forces, was in retreat, conducting rearguard actions, attempting to hold the line in crucial areas, but in several sectors continuing to attack.

Soon after the April congress, Yeltsin appointed deputy chairman of the Supreme Soviet Vladimir Filippovich Shumeiko first deputy prime minister of Russia. Now, for the first time since reforms began, there were two first deputy prime ministers. I had actual control over the key economic ministries, and my team made up the government. Still, the emergence of two centers of influence around a President who was clearly wavering, who was uncertain that the chosen course was the right one, seriously impaired our ability to pursue a meaningful policy. All the more because there were other centers as well; the government had little real influence on either the Central Bank or the Pension Fund. The industrial ministries could easily deal directly with industrial committees in the Supreme Soviet. And although personally Vladimir Filippovich was perfectly loyal to the current policy, the very diffusion of decision making gave lobbyists far too many opportunities to maneuver.

On June 13, the eve of Yeltsin's departure for Washington and his meeting with Bush, I received a call:

"Yegor Timurovich, what would you think about the idea of naming you acting prime minister?"

"I'd say frankly that in our current situation the idea seems reasonable. It would promote consolidation inside the government."

"Should I take that to mean that you are grateful for the trust I've expressed in you?" asked Yeltsin. I answered that yes, of course, I was grateful.

We met at the airport. Yeltsin informed his entourage of his decision and the already-signed order, and said that he was sending a written statement of confirmation to the Supreme Soviet.

From early April on, after Burbulis's resignation, I had been de facto head of the government, and had, as a rule, conducted the cabinet meetings. Both opponents and supporters of current policy were already calling us the "Yeltsin-Gaidar government." Still, until then my actual powers and responsibilities had been limited to exclusively economic issues. This was in keeping with Russian tradition.

Beginning with the turn of the century, Russia had had a number of so-called royal ministries—the Ministry of Defense, the Ministry of Internal Affairs, the Ministry of Foreign Affairs, the secret police. The heads of these ministries were empowered to report directly to the tsar, bypassing the chairman of the Council of Ministers. The Council of Ministers was authorized to deal with financial, economic and social issues. Such was the system under Witte, Stolypin, Kokovtsev.[2] In essence, this system was inherited by the Bolsheviks, who replaced the tsar with the general secretary, and then passed it along to the democrats, at which point the royal ministries became presidential ministries. Still, being appointed acting prime minister meant a genuine broadening of my actual rights, powers, and responsibilities. In Russia, especially the unstable, unsettled Russia of 1992, something was always happening, things that required intervention, involvement of government agencies—military and security agencies included. The President was not always there on the spot to ensure interagency coordination. So for me that meant getting involved in those problems, taking the responsibility for decision making.

In government work, you run into frequent demonstrations of the truth of the famous Peter Principle. Just a reminder—the idea is that, in a bureaucracy, people keep moving up the ladder as long as they can handle their jobs. And then, when they find themselves in a job that's too much for them, their career stalls. And that's where they stay. Of course in the tumult and chaos of 1992 this principle might have required some modification, but it was as valid as ever.

The story of deputy prime minister Georgy Stepanovich Khizha is an appropriate example. He had been a forceful general director of "Svetlana," then in 1991–92 an efficient deputy mayor in St. Petersburg to Anatoly Sobchak. He proved himself an excellent organizer capable of functioning in complex and difficult circumstances. So when it became clear that we would have to establish a new office of deputy prime minister for the industrial ministries, I (on the advice of Anatoly Chubais, who knew Khizha well) suggested that Yeltsin appoint Georgy Stepanovich to the post. Khizha got right down to work. However, it soon turned out that while he on the whole embraced the reforms, he was incapable of grasping the principles of managing the economy within a market framework; he looked at things the way a plant manager would. And therefore he proposed solutions that he thought would be helpful to enterprises, without the slightest understanding of how ruinous they would be for the national economy as a whole. From May on, Khizha was the chief proponent of increasing the budget deficit, monetizing the working capital, and mutual cancellation of offsetting debts. The unavoidable and abrupt drop in the ruble rate resulting from such a policy, and the increased rate of inflation in the fall of 1992, came as a complete surprise to him. The harsh and even sharp-edged dispute between Khizha and Chubais, the most consistent proponent of the reform policy, became a permanent feature of our government's work during the second half of 1992. On the other hand, I bear no grudge against Georgy Khizha; it's not his fault he had reached his level of incompetence.

Russian tradition has been that the military and security ministries come to the Council of Ministers on economic and financial matters only. But when a crisis is at hand, the prime minister has to deal with all sorts of issues. I soon became convinced that, at the moment, one critical problem with the machinery of Russian government was the passionate determination of all concerned to avoid decisions, the urge to hedge one's bets, to dodge responsibility. In the process of conferring on developments, let's say, on the border with Georgia, or in North Ossetia and Ingushetia, or in Tadzhikistan, if we didn't press our demands for action, the military, not surprisingly would hem and haw and point to the MVD, the MVD to the Ministry of Security, and so on and so on.

Without overestimating my own talent for deploying troops, I quickly realized that in such situations I had to take it upon myself to act, reporting to the President on my decisions, or else with all the hemming and hawing and pointing, nothing would get done. This is precisely what I had to do, for example, in Kabardino-Balkaria, where the summer of 1992 threatened us with a replay of the Chechen scenario of 1991. Reinforcements for internal security forces were urgently needed, but the MVD and the security ministry were arguing over who should provide them and whether the ministry could provide air transport or not. I had to step in to coordinate, by getting the leadership of the MVD and the General Staff to sit down together at one table and forcing them to act. On the whole, we did manage to stabilize the situation.

One thing that sticks in my mind particularly painfully is the November 1992 Ingushetia-Ossetia conflict. I remember well how it all began. For the first time in several months I had decided to sleep in on a Sunday, to stay home from work. Early in the morning, the phone rang. There were widespread disturbances on the border between Ingushetia and Ossetia. Weapons had been seized from a battalion of internal security forces. Fighting was in progress. The security ministry had somehow completely failed to notice the explosive situation. We found out only after the fact. There was a real threat that we would have another Karabakh, with its chronic fighting, in the making—but this time on Russian territory. The President was not in Moscow; he was on a nationwide tour.

I contacted the General Staff, and asked them to immediately transfer paratroop units to the area. I telephoned Viktor Yerin, and asked how long it would take to move in additional security forces, telling him that he had full military cooperation on air support. I ordered Georgy Khizha to fly to Vladikavkaz to head the government's operations group on site, and also sent Sergei Shoigu, chairman of the Committee on Emergency Situations, who had recommended himself well during peacekeeping operations in South Ossetia and Georgia, and in Moldova. I hopped into a car and headed to the airport to meet Boris Nikolaevich and report to him on the situation.

In Vladikavkaz there was massive unrest. Huge crowds filled the streets; people were demanding weapons. Khizha and Shoigu reported back, saying that if we didn't think of something fast, the situation would get out of control. People would simply seize the weapons depots. I took on a heavy responsibility by asking them to promise to issue weapons—but not until morning, and not randomly, but in some kind of orderly fashion, only with proof of official registration for military service, through the enlistment offices as official reinforcements for MVD units. The crowd began to calm down.

On the whole, the troops acted quickly and decisively. We managed to put out the fires, and clearly this wouldn't be another Nagorno-Karabakh. Yet we made two serious errors. In the first place, we located our office in Vladikavkaz, capital of one of the two hostile sides, which aroused suspicion among the Ingush that the federal government favored the Ossetians. Second, the command of the internal forces had been so slow to act that it was Ossetian militia rather than federal forces who entered Ingush villages. It's not hard to imagine how much trouble *that* caused. No high-ranking Russian government officials had yet dared show up in Nazran. And therefore I decide to fly out to the area and spend some time in both Nazran and Vladikavkaz to meet with military commanders and assess the situation.

Once there, I headed for Nazran first, in an MVD armored personnel carrier. It was no place for the faint of heart. There were signs of fighting and destruction everywhere. In the Prigorod district a large number of buildings were still burning. Not suprisingly, they were mostly Ingush houses. Ruslan Aushev met us at the border. I knew him well as chairman of the CIS Veterans of the War in Afghanistan Committee. He had just flown in. He was here to help stabilize the situation, but it seemed that he didn't really understand what had happened or what was happening right now. He said that using the personnel carrier was out of the question from now on—we'd be shot at. I got into his car; he drove. The cen-

tral square in Nazran was flooded with refugees, thousands of unfortunate people, victims of the politicians who were playing that simplest but
most dangerous of cards—radical nationalism. As we drove along, Aushev tried to find out what I thought about who was behind the whole,
terrible, bloody mess. Unfortunately, I couldn't help him much, because
the security ministry's reports were as worthless as ever.

Later there were negotiations with Ingush leaders and with a Chechen
government delegation, headed by Yaraga Mamadaev, which had arrived
in Nazran to try to prevent the spread of hostilities into Chechnya. There
was a difficult conversation with people on the square. At least I was able
to accomplish one thing, which was to dispel the Ingush belief that the
Russian government clearly considered one side right and one side
wrong in this conflict.

In Vladikavkaz, I met with military commanders, with the republic's
leaders, with the Supreme Soviet and the Provisional State of Emergency
Administration. We, as Russian government representatives, categorically refused to accept the notion of collective national responsibility. We
felt that returning the refugees to their homes in the Prigorod district
should be the Provisional Administration's top priority. This obviously
did not sit well with Ossetian leaders. It would clearly be a difficult process. Nonetheless the position of Russian authorities had to be clear-cut,
and any aid given to Ossetia for the resolution of its many problems had
to be linked to cooperation on the part of the Ossetian leadership in returning the refugees, and restoring normal living conditions, to what was
home and homeland for them too. Unfortunately, after my resignation,
the Russian government was unable to follow through on this.

Yet another place demanding constant attention from Russian authorities was Tadzhikistan. In 1992 the situation there grew increasingly
chaotic, and gradually slid into open civil war. Two forces stood opposed: one of them might very conditionally be termed Communist, the
other, Islamist. The Islamists were stronger in Garme and Nagorny
Badashkhan, the Communists in Kulyab. Both sides were attempting to
draw the 201st Division, garrisoned throughout Tadzhikistan, into the
conflict—or, at the very least, to get hold of its weapons. One very seri-

ous problem was that the division was made up largely of Russian officers and local troops. The latter were the ones both sides hoped to draw into the conflict.

The Russian-speaking population was fleeing the chaos-ridden republic. But rumor had it that local authorities were trying to stop them. We received information that the more radical wing of the Islamic forces was planning to use local Russians as hostages. The trouble was that we couldn't necessarily rely on the information our sources were giving us about the Tadzhikistan situation. The security ministry, as usual, had nothing concrete, the intelligence service's information was unreliable, and from our recently established embassy in Dushanbe we continued to receive, with several days' delay, utterly contradictory reports. I decided to go to Dushanbe to assess the situation firsthand and determine just what we should do. After meeting with CIS presidents in Bishkek, where the critical situation developing in Tadzhikistan was discussed in detail, I flew directly to Dushanbe.

In that city the atmosphere was grim, tense. From the look of the government security detail, it was hard to tell who they were planning to shoot—us, or each other. We negotiated with the Tadzhik government, then went to the 201st Division headquarters for talks with its commander, Major General Ashurov, and his officers. We flew over burning Kurgan-Tyube, where a battle was in progress, to visit a border-guard unit.

Our overall conclusion after all these talks was that the government of Adumalik Abduladzhanov had lost control of the situation, and of the country. If decisive action was not taken, the 201st would be drawn into the conflict. The very day of my visit a local serviceman had stolen a tank and driven it over to help "his side." This wasn't the first such incident. We urgently needed to reinforce both the division and the border units with Russian personnel. Clearly, anything developing in the next month would involve the use of military force. The threat to the Russian-speaking population was real.

On my arrival in Moscow I reported on the situation to the President. We agreed to take steps to reinforce the 201st, to make it an effective fighting unit instead of a hostage to warring sides, to keep its equipment out of the war. Colonel General Eduard Arkadievich Vorobyov, first deputy chief-of-staff for ground forces, was assigned to lead the operation. He had proved his worth while heading peacekeeping forces in Moldova. This emphatically well-spoken general with the soft, not particularly commanding voice was one of that small circle of military leaders who invariably ended up with the most difficult and dangerous assignments. In 1992–93 he and Colonel General Georgy Grigorievich Kondratiev often found themselves in that situation.

My experience in dealing with military leaders in a crisis has confirmed that the same law holds true in the army as in civilian life: a show of decisiveness and a loud, commanding voice are no proof of one's ability to take clear and decisive action when the risks are very high.

Just in case the worst should happen, we also formed a task force to prepare for the emergency defense and, if need be, evacuation of the Russian-speaking population of Tadzhikistan. The group was headed by Deputy Prime Minister Vakhtang Makharadze. Also brought in were the State Committee on Emergency Situations and the transport ministry; trains and transportation routes were mapped out, and a preliminary agreement was reached with President Islam Karimov of Uzbekistan on joint action in case of an emergency.

The situation in the republic continued to heat up, and a number of Russians, children included, were taken hostage. The threat had become a reality. Eduard Vorobyov and Sergei Shoigu, who had flown out to an area controlled by the 201st Division, were forced to take harsh and decisive action. An operation to reinforce the division and the border units with Russian enlisted personnel put an end to the theft of weapons in that area. Even though the civil war in Tadzhikistan has now gone on for more than four years, we have not had to mount a one-time, large-scale operation to evacuate the Russian population.

Just what a dangerous turn events can take if there are no systematic efforts to closely coordinate interaction between military and security forces became clear from the tragic events that did take place in Tadzhikistan the following year, when, thanks to the amazing sluggishness and inertia of the Ministry of Security, a Russian border post was almost totally destroyed.

I understood that only too well, and therefore was always willing to take the responsibility on myself if necessary. But when an emergency or a crisis subsided just a little, and I thought over what had transpired, I realized that I was no exception to the Peter Principle. I mean, what business did I have dealing with troop deployments—for which I'd never truly considered myself a specialist in the first place—instead of building a fiscal-and-monetary policy? Still, even with all these crises, the government's main worry was the threat of hyperinflation. We had suffered some setbacks, but the battle wasn't lost yet.

On July 1, 1992, correspondent accounts were introduced, and by fall of that year were activated throughout the entire ruble zone. Now we would not only receive information about monetary flows, but effectively control them on a day-to-day basis. The Central Bank of Russia had finally acquired a tool for regulating the dynamics of the money supply inside Russia. Monetary interrelationships with other republics now became a matter of conscious choice and policy rather than a race to see who could issue money fastest.

Beginning in July, after Russian currency circulation was made separate, we introduced convertibility in current operations, and the requirement that 40 percent of foreign currency revenue be sold to the Ministry of Finance at the reduced official rate of exchange was dropped. At the conclusion of negotiations with the International Monetary Fund, Russia finally received the first billion dollars of credit to add to currency reserves.

The food situation had changed considerably. A respectable harvest, greater than that of 1991, and increased state purchases combined with a now functioning market had relieved the government of a significant number of its concerns about keeping the public supplied with food. The noncash domestic ruble had once again made food exports to Russia an attractive proposition for other CIS states. On the whole, by the end of summer it was clear that the threat of catastrophic food shortages, so serious just a year before, no longer existed. The threat of a cash crisis, too, had disappeared, which did away with a major source of social tension.

Enterprises gradually began to adjust to the radically changed realities, including the drastically reduced volume of defense spending and new price proportions. The impact of the blow inflicted by the Vneshekonombank failure began to fade.

By the beginning of autumn, Russian military and security structures were regaining a certain ability to function. The creation of a Ministry of Defense, and new Russian jurisdiction over the army, while difficult, and fraught with reluctance and even resistance, was an improvement over the terribly dangerous situation of 1991–92, when the armed forces belonged to no one at all. I considered that one of the government's chief tasks in working with the military was to change the "fall guy" mentality that had recently, and not without reason, taken hold in military circles, when after Baku, Tbilisi, and Vilnius the political leadership had time and again ducked responsibility, hiding behind the army and trying to shift the blame onto it. That was why, when I demanded vigorous action to protect weapons stores, I signed a government resolution giving the army the right, when under attack, to use deadly force without hesitation.

The peacekeeping operation to separate the forces involved in the Georgian-Ossetian standoff in South Ossetia was, perhaps, our first success in easing dangerous interethnic tensions in years.

Among military and security structures, the Ministry of Security presented us with our most serious problems. Doubts about its reliability put the government in an awkward position. I made repeated but as a rule fruitless attempts to get information from this agency on corruption in the ministries and the government apparatus as a whole. Beyond eloquent pronouncements on the theme of fighting corruption, I got nothing. At first I thought that the more substantive information was going to the President. I talked with him about this several times. I explained how hard it was for the government to work in the dark, to walk through a mine field without any sort of detector. Then I realized that he had no reliable information either. However, all sorts of government and presidential papers, classified and nonclassified alike, were turning up on the pages of Communist and "Nazi" newspapers. In general, if the security ministry was working at all, it wasn't working for us. Unfortunately, the President still had complete trust in Viktor Barannikov at the time, and assumed that he simply hadn't got the machinery of managing the former KGB quite under control. The sensational incident exposing the security minister's own part in the corruption became known much later. That wouldn't come up until 1993.

By the summer of 1992 there were clear signs of a change in the country's global political position. To have your bread supply completely and totally dependent on creditors, creditors who know full well that you are insolvent, and to then try to puff yourself up at the negotiating table is hardly an enviable position. Now the normalization of the food situation and the growth of foreign currency reserves were letting us stand a little straighter and ask for fewer handouts.

At the Group of Seven meeting in Munich, in which Russia took part, we now tried to steer the conversation away from billion-dollar loans which would add to our already excessive debt and toward the opening of Western markets for Russian goods. In negotiations with our American counterparts I drew attention to the discriminatory practice of limiting market access for Russian uranium and space technology. In negotiations with the Europeans, the accent was on drafting an acceptable agreement between Russia and the European Union.

But the most striking changes occurred in relations with the other Commonwealth states. Since the introduction of the noncash Russian ruble, their policy on currency emissions and their experiments with a "soft entry into the free market" had been whipping up inflation rates not in Russia, but at home, and their domestic currencies were rapidly losing ground to the ruble. And now it was becoming clear: to pay for goods imported from Russia, you had to do one very simple thing—sell your own commodities to Russia and get Russian money for them. What had until recently been their best strategy—blanket limitations on exports to Russia, a shift in export orientation to anywhere else possible—

now began to break down. Interest in the Russian ruble, the Russian market, and economic cooperation with Russia was growing rapidly. Although still quite unstable, the convertible Russian ruble was creating a new focal point for CIS integration processes that could serve to replace the now-defunct forced cooperation of old.

In resolving the most urgent and painful problems vis-à-vis our CIS neighbors, problems like the Black Sea fleet, the growing strength of the convertible ruble and the rapid devaluation of the *kupon* had an impact both on the process and the outcome of negotiations. Draft projects to create a free-trade zone, a customs union, and to coordinate monetary policy began to have some real ground under their feet.

In summing up this complex year of both defeats and victories, we might say that the government, in retreat between May and August, thereafter considerably strengthened its position, and created the basic preconditions for a successful stabilization policy. A convertible national currency for current transactions was introduced; foreign currency reserves were in part restored; agreements, with acceptable and far more favorable terms than the previous year's, were reached with creditors about rescheduling payment of Soviet debts; a system of working markets had taken shape; the food problem was solved; privatization was progressing; and the private sector was growing quickly.

It now appeared that we could confidently move along this path and lower inflation rates. But it only appeared that way. The year had been too difficult, too contentious, and relationships with too many people had been ruined. Moreover, that barely flickering light at the end of the proverbial tunnel had sparked a desire in all sorts of people to move us out of the driver's seat, to do a little steering themselves. It wasn't nearly so risky as it had been when we started.

In one of my first interviews, in November 1991, I had said that I would probably be forced to resign sometime at the end of 1992, and that the probable excuse would be budget policy and differences with the Supreme Soviet. That forecast turned out to be fairly accurate.

Chapter 9
Dismissal

By the end of November it was quite clear to me that at the next Congress of People's Deputies there would be a change of prime minister. Of course, from time to time messengers from the opposition and the so-called centrists showed up, bearing promises of support were I to bring one of their people into the government and agree to the dismissal of some of mine.

They were particularly vociferous in demanding the heads of Aleksandr Shokhin, deputy prime minister for foreign trade relations with the CIS, Pyotr Aven, the minister of foreign trade, and Andrei Nechaev, the minister of economics. They proposed alternative candidates for these posts. Chubais they wouldn't touch, apparently realizing how senseless it was to even broach the subject of his possible dismissal. Especially active were Arkady Volsky and his colleagues in the Civic Union, who in exchange for the above, promised the support of the industrial managers' lobby widely represented in the congress.[1] Both privately and publicly, I responded frankly that such a deal was out of the question.

After some sober thought, I concluded that I could of course try to hang on as acting prime minister after the legislative session, in an even weaker position than before, with an unfriendly Central Bank and a hostile Supreme Soviet, but that it would be more helpful to our cause to get the congress to confirm a prime minister with whom we might regroup forces, and continue the work already begun. I suggested that the President choose the latter option. I recommended Academician Yury A. Ryzhkov, the Russian ambassador to France, as a candidate.

The president answered, "I'll think about it. And we'll see how the congress goes. . . ."

The congress opened with a mighty overture—a speech by Ruslan Khasbulatov, largely based on the text of a report prepared by the economics section of the Academy of Sciences and the Reform Foundation. Whole blocks of quotations were lifted from the report. He gave an undeniably powerful populist performance, and drew a simple and understandable picture for the people's deputies: A struggle was being waged in Russia, a struggle between two paths of development. One of these was monetarist, American, and vile, and it was down this path that the current government was trying to drag the country; the other was socially oriented, Swedish, dear to the hearts of the majority of people, Russia's salvation.

The congress was spellbound. How simple and remarkable it all was! Deputies in the hall traded proud and meaningful glances; it turned out that they were not really industry lobbyists trying to squeeze totally unsecured money out of the treasury, not demagogues handing out unfulfillable promises to the voters, not at all. They were staunch warriors in the fight for good socialism, Swedish-model socialism, in Russia!

I usually wake up early, but the following day a phone call from the President woke me earlier than usual. "Yegor Timurovich, I hope you have an answer for that demagogue?"

That morning I appeared before the congress with a summary of the work the government had accomplished so far. But it was more than a summing-up; it was an attempt to define the utterly new qualitative stage in the country's development begun in August 1991. Therefore, departing somewhat from the style of this book, I'll permit myself to quote, with substantial cuts, from the record:

Mr. President! Mr. Chairman! Esteemed members of the Congress of People's Deputies!

A little more than one year ago our government began its work. We knew at the very outset what an enormous responsibility rested on our shoulders. One can study the experience of others, build theoretical models, conduct sociological research, study trouble spots in the economy as much as one likes, but still, until the real transformation begins, no one can say how an enormous nation will react to a fundamentally new mechanism for regulating society and the economy. Will there be breakdowns in the basic social support systems, will uncontrollable social conflicts arise in this highly militarized nation, a nation bristling with nuclear weapons?

This very fear of responsibility was what shackled the energy of the last Soviet governments, what underlay their lethargy and eventually led to the collapse of the Soviet Union. The paralyzing effects of this fear also showed in the performance of Russia's first democratically created governing bodies in the eighteen months leading up to the autumn of 1991....

This very situation—when everyone was tired of the endless talk of reform, when it was clear to everyone that the old system was not working, that it was falling to pieces before our very eyes—was what made the Fifth Congress possible, what allowed the President to assume additional powers and also the responsibility for finally setting the actual reform process in motion.

In this situation, having taken the levers of control, we of course could not allow ourselves the luxury of leisurely chats on what to do first. All the more so because, as a specialist in the field, I can assure you that a theoretically tested and proven answer to the question of what, if done first, would guarantee a successful reform, simply does not exist.

We grounded our work in one simple principle: if the old system of management has stopped working anyway, we should do all we can to set the market mechanism in motion. And over the next year we proceeded from that assumption. It is now possible to look at some initial results, to analyze what worked, to examine and assess our own mistakes and try to learn some lessons from them.

The first and chief thing which we did manage to accomplish was to get the reforms moving, to set the market mechanism in motion. Granted, things are far from perfect. Granted, our market is far from being the competitive ideal. There can be no doubting the fact that it is still weighed down by the vestiges of a traditional command system. And yet the further we advance, the more obvious it becomes that production is beginning to respond to changing demand, that managers are beginning to think first and foremost about sales and marketing, that money is moving to center stage, that the economy is becoming monetarized, that for all the imperfections of our consumer market, the problem of standing in line for hours just to buy something, anything, is beginning to recede in the face of the other, more serious problems—of which there are many—resulting from a weak, not yet fully functioning market economy.

One of our most important tasks, once we had engaged this market mechanism, was to avoid any breakdowns in basic social support systems. You remember the tone of the last year's debates both here and in the domestic and foreign press. The topic under discussion was not the projected cuts in tank, mineral fertilizer, or cotton textile production for 1992. It was mass hunger, cold, paralysis in the transportation system, the collapse of a state and a society.

None of these occurred. The threat of hunger and cold is gone. We have passed through the most difficult period of adjustment to reforms without any major social cataclysms. For all the talk about mass dissatisfaction with reforms, we have been able to maintain social stability.

It might seem paradoxical, but it is a fact: through these ten months of very difficult reforms the number of instances of time lost to industrial strikes has dropped by a factor of six compared to 1991. It has become harder to pull people away from work to demonstrate or protest. If in April there were 152 strikes with 154,000 participants, in October there were only four, with a total of 3,000 participants. For all the enormous hardship these transformations entail, for all the difficulties we must overcome along this path, the Russian people have proved themselves much more intelligent and perspicacious than many of their rather patronizing politicians are willing to admit. People understand exactly how necessary these transformations are, they are ready to work, and work hard; they are not ready to rock the boat of their own well-being.

Our task was to ensure that privatization actually began, to move from words to deeds. We were not able to achieve everything we had hoped to. We have fallen behind in the 1992 privatization program, and apparently it will not reach all its goals. Judging by our progress thus far, it is clear that by the end of 1992 roughly 40,000 enterprises will have been privatized— which is to say we are taking slow, weak, but already quite real strides toward the formation of a multisector economy.

The issue which determined to what extent we would succeed in getting through the year without serious or even disastrous upheavals was the issue of foreign currency and our interaction with the international financial community. We were forced to begin reforms with no foreign currency reserves, with an absolutely unmanageable Soviet debt, with obligations to repay around $20 billion in debt in 1992 alone, but without any money to cover it, with a pressing need for critical imported resources. . . . After some complex negotiations, we were successful in rescheduling the debt and reducing the $20 billion to roughly $1.5 billion, without halting either imports or the flow of new credit. Last year we had the opportunity to bring in roughly $14 billion in the form of bilateral loans and loans from international financial organizations, and use these as the basis to finance critical imports, primarily grain, but also medicine and a number of crucial manufacturing components. If there had not been such an opportunity, I must tell you honestly, the threat of famine in the spring of 1992 would have been quite real, and the drop in livestock numbers would have been not 3 percent, as it is now, but 40 percent. Where, in our opinion, did we fail?

Our greatest setbacks were in the areas of financial stabilization and of monetary policy aimed at propping up the ruble. We had hoped that tight fiscal and monetary policy measures would allow us, month by month, to bring down the rate of inflation, bolster the real exchange value of the ruble vis-à-vis the dollar, fix it at a realistic level, and then move to a convertible ruble at a fixed rate.

In the first few months we seemed close to achieving this goal; rates of growth in the money supply were low, the budget was essentially balanced, inflation rates were dropping from one month to the next, the ruble was stronger against the dollar. Unfortunately, beginning in June, there was a considerable weakening of both credit-and-monetary and fiscal policy, and the rate of growth of the money supply shot sharply upward. It has increased by almost 2.5 times in the last four months. Naturally, this has had an impact on the rate of exchange, breaking the downward trend; it led, after the usual two-month lag, to a shift in price dynamics, a spurt in price growth for the second half of August. There is no doubt that this setback is a serious one, with dangers for both our current situation and prospects of reform. . . .

How does the situation look today? It is indeed very, very grave—critical, I would say. The real gravity is such that it is hard for me to understand why the esteemed chairman's aides felt compelled to demonstrate that fact by resorting to figures that do not quite accurately reflect the reality.[2] For example, looking at the statistical abstract which has been, I hope, handed out to all of you, it is not hard to see that housing construction has in the last ten months dropped not by two-thirds, but by 27 percent. Nor is it hard to see that capital investments in the domestic economy totaled not 17 billion, but rather one trillion five hundred million. Education was allocated not 21 billion, but 600 billion. And so on. I won't bother going into the many other similar misunderstandings.

If it is necessary to demonstrate the real gravity of our current economic situation, it can be done using figures that do in fact correspond to reality. And here we find what is perhaps the most serious of all—dangerously high rates of inflation. By October, as a result of a weakened credit-and-monetary policy, we saw inflation rise to a rate of 25 percent per month. That is already close to 50 percent—technically, the borderline level for hyperinflation, when money circulation speeds up abruptly, when there is unregulated currency flight and a general breakdown in monetary circulation with fatal consequences for the integrity of the economy and the state. This is precisely why implementation of a consistent anti-inflationary policy remains a crucial priority for any responsible government.

One could, of course, cite other frightening statistics as well. But one can also find statistics that testify to the beginning of weak, but positive shifts, that point to the fact that since August the crisis has become more and more structural in nature, that over the last three months output rates for a number of important consumer goods have moved steadily upward.

However, in general, the point is neither to frighten oneself with the terrible statistics of disaster, nor to comfort oneself with marked positive changes. Much more important is the question of what to do to stabilize the situation, to bring it under control and thus lay the groundwork for an economic recovery.

In yesterday's speech, Ruslan Imranovich Khasbulatov presented his reading of the alternatives facing Russia today, of the economic and political choice that we must make. The gist of it is this. There are two models: the monetarist, American model, and the socially oriented European (Scandinavian) model. We must choose which society we wish to live in (Scandinavian or American) and, proceeding from that, build an economic policy for Russia's immediate future.

No matter how hard I try, I find it very difficult to find any correlation between this set of alternatives and the very difficult practical problems that the Russian economy is forced to confront on a daily basis. . . .

Of course, if we do our work very well and very effectively and do succeed in creating a multisector economy and putting an end to the absolute rule of bureaucracy, in clearing the way for private enterprise and integrating our country into the world market, then perhaps in three or five years we will indeed want to discuss what type of society we want—American or Scandinavian. Unfortunately, I am not sure our performance so far merits such discussion.

Let us try, however, to focus on the practical issues that lead to differences of opinion between us and the Supreme Soviet. Naturally, these differences arise in relation to the passage of the 1992 budget. The Supreme

Soviet adopts a budget, then writes in additional expenditures amounting to 1,300 billion rubles. What is this—socially oriented policy and market economics? Its result has been to exacerbate budget problems in practically all regions of the country, cause a crisis in regional budgets as well as a drastic increase in expenditures in the federal budget and in its obligations, a drastic increase in the money supply in July and August, and an acceleration in the rate of inflation beginning in the second half of August. If this is a socially oriented market economy, then pardon me, but Ludwig Erhard must be turning over in his grave.[3] Resolutions like this, unfortunately, are the object of an entirely different realm of theory—the study of economic populism, problems of chronic poverty and stagnant underdevelopment. . . .

The real dilemma facing our society today, unfortunately, is much more difficult and dramatic than some simple choice between American and Scandinavian models. The criminal delay in undertaking a long overdue structural overhaul of the economy, in carrying out long overdue economic reforms, both pulls and pushes our economy downward, into the abyss of underdevelopment. A mighty but terribly militarized economy, weighed down by its own archaic structure, is trying to pull itself out of crisis. Which way will we go? Will we find a way to pull our country out of underdevelopment, will we find a way to steer a steady course toward joining the community of civilized free-market states? So that later we can choose whether we want high taxes or "cheap" government. Or will the momentum of decline, the momentum of collapse, pull us even further down, toward a chronically unstable financial system, and thus toward exceedingly low savings and low investments, toward an ailing industrial complex protected by trade barriers, toward chronic poverty, and hence toward political instability, to the constantly shifting pleiad—so familiar to the "third world"—of populist politicians and authoritarian dictators? This, I am profoundly convinced, is the real, and far bleaker, alternative to our current socioeconomic policy in Russia.

Of course it is very easy to slip onto the first path, the path of underdevelopment. All one has to do is be drawn into a dangerous confrontation between the different branches of government and slow down the free market transformation. And then we are sure to go the way of Africa, or Latin America.

But getting off that dangerous path requires a good deal more. It requires precise and clear-cut answers to the most painful questions facing our economy today; it requires sustained and coordinated action by all branches of government. . . .

Further on in my report I underscored our most pressing policy issues: what we were doing to curb inflation and to prop up the ruble; investment issues and the question of how to stimulate commercial bank activity; and the tasks facing the agribusiness complex, including development of a private-farming sector. And of course, privatization issues: the relationship between central and regional authorities; foreign trade. And most detailed of all— our view of problems in the area of social welfare and the measures that should be implemented there.

I ended my report with the following words:

Esteemed members of the Congress of People's Deputies! In the very short time allowed me by parliamentary procedure, I of course do not have the opportunity to go into great detail on all the areas in which the government is working, on all the things we consider essential to the stabilization of the Russian economy. But I would like to emphasize once again that the real situation, the real opportunity to maneuver here, is to an enormous extent determined by the country's currency situation, by its lack of reserves, by the exceedingly dangerous inflation situation, by the deformation of the economic structure, by a massive number of factors that any governing body must face, whether it wants to or not.

We are not standing on some enormous square where we can calmly discuss which road leads to a bright future. We are on a narrow, tiny track. Only by moving carefully along it can we find our way out of this very grave crisis, can we enter the commonwealth of civilized peoples. Without concrete, constructive, creative, and responsible work by all Russia's governing bodies, stumbling off that track will be all too easy. This is the assumption from which we proceed, in all our work. Thank you.

In reporting to the congress, I above all wanted the deputies to understand that we had no intention of altering our course.

In the debate that unfolded afterward, Ruslan Khasbulatov sent his strongest orators out on stage last: their job was to finish the government off. At the time, this meant Aman Tuleev and Nikolai Travkin. Tuleev, chairman of the Kemerovo Regional Soviet, gave an offhand but colorful address in which he related how he had begged Gaidar for bread money for the Kuzbas on bended knee, and how Gaidar had turned him down flat, the villain. The speech made an impression. But then Travkin, chairman of the Democratic Party of Russia, administrative head of Shakovskoy district, a seasoned political fighter and the opposition's key orator, slipped up. The day before, newspapers had printed the revelations of a certain lady who claimed that she'd slept with Khasbulatov but had turned Travkin down. Cut to the quick, he started making excuses, explaining that he hadn't particularly wanted to sleep with her, but that if he had wanted to, she would have. His criticism of the government came off a little blurred.

A new battle now raged around opposition attempts to force through constitutional amendments circumscribing the President's powers. Its initiators thought that victory was at hand, but came up several votes short. It was a serious defeat for Khasbulatov; much ado—and again nothing. At a meeting between the President and the delegations' council, one of the opposition leaders suddenly brought up the idea of a package deal, the essence of which was that the President would appoint military and security ministers with the approval of the Supreme Soviet, and the opposition would give the nod to Gaidar as prime minister. The idea was utterly unexpected, improvised, but the President liked it, and immediately agreed.

Before the confirmation vote on prime minister the President asked how many votes I thought we might win. We needed, it seems, 524; I replied that I thought we would get no more than 450 or 460, that they wouldn't keep their word. Boris Nikolaevich shrugged in disbelief—that simply couldn't be, at least 540 or 550 deputies would support us. After the vote, which confirmed that I was right, I went to my office on Old

Square. I called Yeltsin; it was clear that he was in a bad mood, for he took any sort of deception very hard. He asked, "Well, Yegor Timurovich, you're still smiling? What are we going to do now?" I answered that I saw no reason to cry about it, that since they had broken the agreement I would go ahead and "act" as prime minister for the time being, and then we would see.

The next day, shortly after seven in the morning, Viktor Ilyushin, the President's chief aide, telephoned me, passing along the order to convene the cabinet at 9:30 at Old Square. I had a bad feeling about it all. As she saw me off, Masha remembered *A Roadside Picnic*: "So, you've stepped in the witch's jelly, have you?"[4] I understood perfectly well that I was less the reason than the excuse for a new spiral of confrontation.

I called an urgent meeting of members of the government. There was some hope of persuading the President not to make any ill-calculated moves. But no, I was told that he wouldn't attend the meeting; he was going directly to the congress. Gennady Burbulis called and informed me that Sergei Mikhailovich Shakhrai was on his way, he was bringing some papers: don't be surprised—it's all for the best, it's the right decision. The conviction grew that I had got the other foot in it too. In his statement, the President proposed holding a referendum on confidence—confidence in the congress or himself, either one, and should the results so warrant, early elections. His proposal was entirely constitutional and within the limits of the law, but, in my view, poorly prepared and, chiefly, very ill-timed. To appeal to public opinion because the congress has just failed to confirm the man who freed prices, the man generally identified with a very painful time in the country's life, was a remarkably bad idea.

For all that, having come to know Boris Yeltsin quite well, I realized that trying to hold him back right now was utterly useless. It would just make things worse. I assembled the ministers, informing them that the President had resolved to let the people decide. I called on them to keep things in order. The point of the meeting was that the political situation was extremely serious, that they should allow no acts of provocation in any of the systems within their official purview. The response of many of the industrial ministers was, as I expected, negative. Their industries were already in crisis, and a referendum would require all sorts of un-planned-for expenditures, and major ones to boot. It was clear that in the coming months, as we prepared for and conducted this referendum, there would be no sense in even talking about a meaningful economic policy. And the upshot of it all? Economically—we lose. What we might win politically was anyone's guess. We watched the President's address on TV; everyone was quiet and grim.

Yeltsin accused Khasbulatov of becoming a tool of the forces of reac-tion. He proposed to hold a referendum. Khasbulatov walked out. The President, in turn, urged his own supporters to leave when he did. They hadn't been warned, they hesitated, and only a small number left with him. Nothing was going right.

The opposition's first tactical victory at this juncture was in maintain-ing a quorum; the congress was lawful, it could function, it could adopt resolutions. We'd stung the opposition, scared them a little, but it hadn't hurt them much, and after a moment or two of disarray, they regrouped. One right after another, the minister of security came before the con-gress, and the minister of defense, and the minister of internal affairs. Barannikov's speech was particularly distasteful; it was as if he was tak-ing an oath to serve the congress. The defense minister and the internal affairs minister said nothing cogent, but the very fact of their appearance instilled confidence in the majority. The impression was that the Presi-dent had no real backing, no real force behind him. The congress went on with its work, adopting one distasteful constitutional amendment af-ter another.

Meanwhile the President went to AZLK and gave a speech to the workers there.[5] We talked back and forth throughout the day. At first he seemed primed for battle, ready to attack. But he's also an astute politi-cian, and within several hours he realized that his bombshell was a dud. "Well-wishers" streamed in, asking him to review his referendum plans.

Valery Zorkin came to see me to argue that for the sake of civil accord I should refuse the nomination for prime minister.[6] I replied that for the sake of civil accord I might well refuse much more than that, but that it was important to be sure that this was compromise rather than capitulation. My principle is never to get into a fight unless it's absolutely necessary, but if I've gotten into one, then I fight to the finish. Even if you have taken a wrong step, you try to fix it. The main thing is not to worry too much, be consistent, and build up initiative. Clearly, neither the parliamentary majority nor Khasbulatov himself was popular with the people. And that meant we might be able to shift the focus of the conflict away from the unfortunate issue of naming a prime minister, and toward areas significantly more important and understandable to the public. We had to secure the support of groups that had traditionally backed the President and the reform policy. Therefore, I tried to convince Yeltsin not to make any unilateral concessions.

Zorkin's address, in which he called for negotiations between the executive and the legislative branches, to be mediated by the Constitutional Court, seemed to offer an opening for an acceptable compromise. Out of these negotiations, in which Nikolai Ryabov headed the parliamentary team and I headed the President's, came a formula for agreement. Its basic points were as follows:

— The congress would repeal the most unpalatable of the constitutional amendments it had adopted.

— An official referendum would be conducted on the issue of confidence in the President and the congress, thus cutting the Gordian knot of *dvoevlastie* and clearing the way for early elections.[7]

— The President, after reviewing proposals by parliamentary factions, would nominate several candidates for the post of prime minister. Congress would hold a preliminary vote and the top three vote-winners would advance. The President would then present one of these three to the congress for confirmation. If that candidate was not confirmed by the congress, the President would appoint an acting prime minister.

Given the situation, this was the best we could do. The President saved face, did not have to back away from the referendum, and gained some room to maneuver in his choice of prime minister. Yeltsin and Khasbulatov did not attend most of the negotiating sessions. When they eventually did appear, the formula was essentially already worked out and agreed upon. I suggested that the President support it; he agreed. Khasbulatov obviously did not like the draft agreement, but could not afford to isolate himself, to look as if he opposed a national consensus.

Deputies who supported us were genuinely enthusiastic about the agreement. The opposition was glum. Khasbulatov was able to push it through solely by virtue of his talent for manipulation. Almost immediately after the vote, representatives of the opposition put him through the wringer, accusing him of appeasement. He apologized, explaining that "the devil made him do it." We felt that we had managed to turn a defeat into at least an honorable draw. The only thing remaining was to resolve the question of prime minister.

On the eve of the vote, Boris Nikolaevich invited members of the government to a supper. The mood was cheerful, and everyone had the sense that the terrible storm of an unmanageable confrontation had somehow missed us, passed us by. Taking advantage of the lively conversations my colleagues were having, I asked to speak to the President privately and told him that as things now stood, especially after all that had transpired, I thought that any attempt to keep me on as prime minister was too dangerous; it would only give the opposition more chances to destabilize the situation. Since at this point, in spite of all my attempts at persuasion, Yury Ryzhkov was firmly refusing to become a candidate, I suggested nominating and backing Vladimir Kadannikov, who I believed was both willing and able to pursue a consistent policy of reform. I added that if he were to be appointed, my colleagues and I could also remain in the government and continue our work. The President promised to nominate him and said that he would see how the voting progressed.

On the following day the initial roster brought to a vote included the secretary of the Security Council, Yury Skokov; the first deputy prime minister, Vladimir Shumeiko; the deputy prime minister, Viktor Chernomyrdin; Vladimir Kadannikov; and me. The President had turned down a number of unacceptable candidates proposed by various factions.

In the preliminary round, Skokov received the most votes, with Chernomyrdin close behind; I was a distant third. Kadannikov, whom Yeltsin had formally backed, had spoken out for reform a little too fervently in his speech and so dropped out of the running right away.

After this vote I had a talk with the President. I knew Yury Skokov rather well from having worked with him previously, and was firmly convinced that under no circumstances should the job of running a Russian market economy still in its infancy be handed over to him. He could very easily smother it in his overly enthusiastic embrace. And, quite honestly, I was not at all certain that in critical situations he would stand by the President and not get nervous and maneuver for position. I told Boris Yeltsin this. Subsequently, in April 1993, my apprehensions were confirmed.

My attitude toward Chernomyrdin was far more complicated. After the President had gone over my head and appointed him deputy prime minister, our working contacts had been quite normal. He dealt with his oil and gas complex, was both efficient and dependable, didn't get mixed up in general economic issues, and, in my view, was handling his responsibilities rather well. He wasn't interested in elbowing anyone else aside for the position of prime minister and had said from the very beginning that he would withdraw his candidacy if necessary.

If chance had tapped him to head the Russian government in late 1991, before the beginning of reforms, he would in all likelihood have gone down the same sad road as the USSR's Ryzhkov, Russia's Silaev, Ukraine's Fokin, and Belarus's Vyacheslav Kebich, whose work experience and mentality closely resembled his. None of them ever managed to cut the umbilical cord between the government and the socialist economy. Of course now, at the end of 1992, we had a fundamentally different situation; it was a matter of continuing something already begun rather than building something new—and yet. I remembered how cruelly Chernomyrdin had, in his Gazprom days, brought to heel some gas-complex directors who had taken it into their heads to act independently. For a monopoly industry it was the right choice, but would he decide to make it again for all of Russia?

I told the President that as things stood I could not withdraw, since I was not sure that my successor would continue a reform policy. But if he felt he had to back another candidate, then I asked that it be Chernomyrdin.

After our conversation the President invited Chernomyrdin in, then Skokov, then me again. He said that the gap between me and Chernomyrdin, in terms of votes received, was just too great. He had decided to recommend Viktor Chernomyrdin for the post, and asked me to withdraw my candidacy. I answered that unfortunately I couldn't do that, that I wasn't convinced that Chernomyrdin would consistently follow through with economic reform, although I did consider him the better choice of the two. It was painful to look at Boris Nikolaevich; the decision had obviously not been an easy one. He really didn't want to abandon a position he had announced just a few days earlier, to show weakness. I said again that I was ready to support his appointment of Chernomyrdin, but that, regrettably, I couldn't relieve him of the burden of having to choose.

I returned to the hall and told my colleagues in the government seats around me that in a few minutes Boris Nikolaevich was going to propose Chernomyrdin as his candidate. The deputies from the democratic blocs could not believe what had just happened, and rushed over to Yeltsin to persuade him to propose me instead. He brushed them off wearily—the decision had been made.

After an energetic speech by Chernomyrdin, in which he promised to build a market, not a bazaar, and to carry through with reform without impoverishing the people, I left the hall and went to prepare for the transition.

On the eve of the congress, members of the cabinet had announced that they would remain in the government only if I remained at its head. In a less formal setting, members of my team who were not on the cabinet but had come along with me to begin the reform said the same. However, when my dismissal became a reality, I decided that dragging them out of the government with me would be extremely unwise. The real battle to preserve and strengthen the reforms still lay ahead, which meant that the stronger the positions of pro-market members in government, the better.

I gathered my colleagues to say that I freed them entirely from any promises to collectively resign, and that I thought that they could work with Chernomyrdin. Moreover, I asked several of them, including Anatoly Chubais, to stay and continue the fight.

I met with Chernomyrdin and briefed him on the areas he hadn't dealt with before: finance, money, foreign currency. He wanted to know whose opinion he could rely on in such matters. We consulted on staffing issues. I talked quite openly about what I saw as my colleagues' weaknesses and strengths. Of course it was now up to him to decide whom he would work with, but he still didn't know our team very well, he could make mistakes, and after all I wasn't handing over the keys to some beer stand, but to the government of Russia itself. On the whole, I advised him not to be in a hurry to make any sweeping changes in personnel, but to think about inviting Boris Fyodorov, who was currently Russian director for the World Bank, to rejoin the government.

There was, perhaps, only one sore point in terms of personal relationships after my ouster, and that was Aleksandr Shokhin. Aleksandr and I had worked next door to one another in Shatalin's department in the big glass building on Profsoyuznaya Street; we were among Shatalin's favorite students, and our families had been friends for years. He was without a doubt a highly competent expert on socioeconomic issues: income disparities, poverty, household savings. Between 1987 and 1991 he had served as Eduard Shevardnadze's economic adviser, and then as head of the Ministry of Foreign Affairs economics section. I was very happy to see him appointed Russia's minister of labor in the summer of 1991. Shortly thereafter, that fall, he became one of the chief framers of our joint program.

In the government's first few months of work he had the complicated and thankless task of overseeing social policy, which, under the circumstances, I thought he managed quite well. For me, it was extremely important that in these first critical months the social agenda be defended by a qualified and competent person who understood the general idea behind the reforms as well as the limits of what was possible. But by spring of 1992 Shokhin's relations with the Supreme Soviet were at the boiling point, and the deputies were vigorously and stubbornly pressing for his ouster. At the beginning of April, Aleksandr came to my office, laid out the situation, and said that in this post it was unlikely he would be able to pursue any kind of meaningful policy and that he would prob-ably be one our first casualties. I agreed and, in the process of reorga-nizing the cabinet, got him out of the line of fire by assigning him to foreign trade and CIS relations. There was a mountain of work to be done there too, and it was politically less controversial. He accepted gratefully, and then proved his worth in negotiating with the CIS, preparing for liberalization of foreign trade relations and developing an agreement with our creditors. Yet even here he was still under fire, and I had to per-suade Yeltsin more than once that dismissing Shokhin could do serious damage.

While working together in the government we met on a regular basis, candidly discussed both political and economic issues, and stole a few hours, usually late at night, to visit each other's homes. I never imagined that our friendship could fall hostage to political squabbles. But that is precisely what happened. On the evening of my dismissal he stopped by and said that for a long time now he'd been wanting to tell me what he thought I was doing wrong, and that he'd finally made up his mind to do it. In other, simpler, words: friendship with an ousted prime minister was an encumbrance, it tied his hands.

Several months later, when rumor had it that I would rejoin the gov-ernment, Aleksandr was the first to call and congratulate me. Then again, it's not for me to judge. For my part I still respect his professionalism, but I've lost a friend. Politics and power hardly promote kinder, gentler hu-man relations.

That same evening a very distraught Naina Iosifovna Yeltsina called. She said something like this: you're young, you're smart, think of some way to help Boris Nikolaevich; he's not so young anymore and he's taking all this very hard. I tried to reassure her, and told her what I truly thought—that nothing was lost yet, that everything was still ahead of us.

The next morning Boris Nikolaevich called. He proposed that I become his chief economic adviser. I answered that I had to turn him down because my appointment would cramp the new prime minister, and I knew all too well how dangerous it was to double up on economic leadership. I didn't want to get in his way. But I said that I was always ready to help the President, whether I held official office or not.

Chapter 10

Dvoevlastie

- Far from newspapers and telephones
- Some theoretical conclusions
- Leszek Balcerowicz
- A call from Chubais
- You can't hitch . . .
- Chernomyrdin and Fyodorov
- The Supreme Soviet goes on the attack
- On Vasiliev Slope
- The duel with Rutskoi
- The sword of Damocles
- I accept the President's offer

*P*odmoskovye. The first three days I slept, slept, and slept some more. What a joy to wake up, look out the window at the snow-covered branches of the fir trees—and then fall asleep again. When I finally went out, I heard the wind whistling and the snow crunching underfoot; I saw a friendly mutt. Over by some open water on the lake someone was sitting at his fishing hole, keeping an eye on his float.

"Are they biting?"

"Nah, not much, just a bit."

The normal, live, big world was coming back to me, with all its smells and sounds. And suddenly that long, long, narrow, absurd room in the Kremlin, once a whole enfilade that Stalin had ordered redone so that it could house Party congresses, seemed so far away. Now there was a truly monstrous "corridor of power."

The emotions I first felt after my dismissal were very complex and very contradictory. A mixture of relief and bitterness. The relief was that an enormous weight had been lifted from my shoulders. No longer did I have to answer for everything that was happening in the country. No more anxious telephone calls—an explosion in a mine shaft somewhere, a train wreck somewhere else. I no longer had to make decisions affecting people's entire lives, or deny whole regions or enterprises or scientific institutions the financial support they needed to survive. I didn't have to be responsible for the many imperfections of a young democracy. All of that would now be someone else's headache. And still—there's the sinking feeling that no longer can you do what you think the country needs done, events will take their course regardless of what you do, you'll watch from the sidelines and see mistakes that you're in no position to correct. It was worrisome. Just how many mistakes would there be? Would they undo everything that had been done, with such difficulty and at such cost, to establish a market economy in Russia?

Suddenly I realized how much I'd changed, how I'd aged. Only one year had passed since I'd joined the government as a young, energetic thirty-five-year-old, and now I felt at least fifteen years older. And it wasn't even a matter of insults and injuries, but that after this crazy year my whole perception of life, of people, had changed radically. The most unpleasant part was that I'd grown harsher, colder. At the same time, I had an infinitely better idea of how real power works, how decisions are made, how the switches that direct that heavy train called Russian history are pulled. And in general I noticed that overall I had begun to see events I knew well enough from history books in a different way, almost from the inside out; I had begun to see life more concretely, more vividly than I had before. I realized that, like it or not, politics are less a choice between good and evil than between greater and lesser evils. And I had a better understanding of people who in their time had gritted their teeth and chosen the lesser evil, and closed their eyes to its flaws.

Practically anyone who leaves a position of power experiences the inevitable syndrome that I call "the elevator's broken." The phrase comes from a true story. Once upon a time an ousted Politburo member walked into Party headquarters on Old Square, stepped into the executive elevator, and for the life of him could not understand why it wasn't moving. He had forgotten that you have to push a button. It was habit. Politburo members never pushed buttons; their security detail did it for them.

Of course, for those who govern only for a short time, the syndrome doesn't acquire quite such anecdotal proportions, but you do get a sudden and unavoidable sense that everything has stopped revolving around you. Hundreds of everyday problems crop up, problems that yesterday you didn't have to deal with. Time expands, and you can again measure your life in hours and days rather than seconds. Adaptation to this new reality depends entirely on the person. Those who have sense enough to understand that all the fanfare had nothing to do with them as people, but is intrinsic to the office they held, adjust to private life rather quickly. But I have seen people who, after working in government, could never readjust to ordinary life without the trappings of power. I feel sorry for them.

A dismissal, as opposed to a high-level appointment, provides a wonderful opportunity to take stock of your relationships with those around you. I invented a special unit of measurement, a measure of constancy in human relations, that I called "one chub"—short for "one Chubais." However our relative social status might change, Chubais and I have never let that affect our relationship. Unfortunately, more often than not I now measure constancy in terms of "centichubs," "millichubs," and even "microchubs."

My family greeted my dismissal with relief. The strain under which my father, mother, wife, and even children had lived over the past year finally eased. I heard rumors to the effect that I was leaving the country, going off to Chicago or Harvard to join my beloved monetarists. It had never occurred to me to do anything of the sort. I'd never had any desire to leave Russia, much less now.

My plan was quite clear—I would return to the Institute of Economic Policy. They were expecting me. One year earlier, before leaving, I had assembled the staff and said that I hoped to continue working with them. I would stop in, and we could brainstorm the latest economic predicament. How naive I was.

But in a way I never really said goodbye to the institute. Many of its leading experts followed me into government work. Andrei Nechaev became minister of economics, Vladimir Mashitz became chairman of the Committee on Cooperation with the CIS, and Sergei Vasiliev took over the government's Center for Economic Reforms. Other institute staff found work in the apparatus. And even those who had stayed in academe regularly did reviews and analysis for the government, and developed normative legislation.

On returning to my duties as director, I also renamed the institute, giving it a devilishly cacophonous name—the Institute for the Economy in Transition.[1] The explanation for its very awkward acronym may be that my brain was still suffering the effects of long-term stress and wasn't working too well at the time. Vladimir Mau, Sergei Sinelnikov, and Aleksei Ulyukaev returned to the institute with me.

Gradually the fatigue passed, my head cleared, information came pouring in about the country's economic life, and with it came the new and not entirely pleasant sensation of having been suddenly moved from the driver's seat to the passenger's side. You still feel responsible for everything, and when you see a pothole or a rut or a log across the road—or, dispensing with the metaphors, any sort of economic mess—you keep wanting to fix it, to give orders on the spot. And then suddenly you remember that you can't do anything, you're just a passenger.

I recalled my meeting with Leszek Balcerowicz, minister of finance and acting prime minister of Poland, just a year earlier, in December 1991. We had never met face-to-face before. Once or twice we almost ran into each other at economics conferences. But we had a number of friends in common: his deputy at the Polish finance ministry Marek Dombrowski, his adviser Jacek Rostowski, and Russians Pyotr Aven, Konstantin Kagalovsky, and Sergei Vasiliev. I think it was Aven that Balcerowicz stayed with when visiting in the late 1980s. He had no money for a hotel.

It was Leszek's lot to be the first to launch serious reforms after the collapse of the socialist economy, and therefore he had a particularly difficult time of it. By the end of 1991 he had major transformations, economic liberalization, the opening of foreign trade, and a developing private sector to his credit. At the same time there had been a precipitous drop in industrial output, continuing high rates of inflation, and increased wage and salary disparities. A good overall assessment of what transpired is given in Grzegorz Kolodko's book *Missed Opportunity*. No one knew at the time that these reforms would lay the foundation for the dynamic industrial growth of 1993, or that in 1996 Poland, with its impressive growth in industrial output, would become the fastest growing country in Europe, one of the most dynamic in the world. Or that very soon the whole world would start talking about the Polish economic miracle. All that came later. At the time, Balcerowicz—one of the most unpopular, the most hated people in Poland, the man who had "robbed" the people—was on the verge of being sacked. Several weeks after our meeting, he in fact was. Leszek obviously already knew. We talked, and I tried to extract as much as I could, in terms of practical experience, from our conversation—especially the sort of detail that you won't find in any analyses or articles or books.

The crisis of collapsing socialism had begun earlier in Poland, and reforms had begun there earlier as well. Despite the differences in our economies, I had grown used to regarding Poland as the reference point by which we could gauge and analyze the problems that Russia would soon face during free-market transformation.

In December 1991, I was also thinking about what had transpired in Poland from a personal standpoint. I would end up in roughly the same position. I, too, would be hated in a year or so, even if despite Russia's immeasurably more complicated conditions we managed to engage the market mechanism, warded off hyperinflation, introduced a convertible ruble, saturated the market, and created a base for economic growth. What can I say—it was hardly an inspiring prospect.

In the summer of 1992, I visited Poland. By that time Leszek had already left office, and was thinking, writing. Late one evening, after official protocol was taken care of, he and I sat for a while in one of Warsaw's taverns. We talked about economics, about problems of postsocialist transformation. It seemed that Poland was already starting to pull itself out of the crisis, pointing the way for other countries. Leszek never complained about the vicissitudes of life or politics, but his eyes had a sad look, like those of a pilot who'd been grounded. My thought was that if I lived long enough to be sacked, I'd eventually be in that same mood.

Later we met fairly often, exchanged economic literature, came to be friends. Balcerowicz was head of the liberal Polish party called Freedom Union. Gradually the public came to better understand what he had done for Poland. But I'll never forget the expression on the face of one of the leading economic reformers of the twentieth century, just a few months after his ouster.

In December 1992, I decided to take a leave of absence and go somewhere far away from newspapers and telephones, to work in peace. After all, since August 1991 I had been able to read current economic literature only by fits and starts. I wanted to fill in the gaps as quickly as possible.

A rather clear-cut overall picture emerged. The economic transformation of the early 1990s in Eastern Europe and the former USSR was a reaction to a natural crisis in the socialist model and to the collapse of the political, economic, and military-security structures that had ensured the functioning of those states. This historically inevitable challenge confronted a variety of nations substantially different in their size, economic structure, and in the degree to which their domestic market mechanisms had remained intact. An analysis of how these countries attempted, each in its own way, to meet the challenge and articulate a suitable economic policy suggests a number of general conclusions. The following are the most important:

—A drastic decline in output is an inevitable result of the crisis in socialist microeconomic regulation, and of forced, accelerated restructuring. Industrial production declines by at least 30 percent of the achieved maximum, a condition that lasts for at least three years. Given the increasing inefficiency of traditional mechanisms, any delay in engaging the market mechanism merely leads to a decline in output before reforms even begin (USSR, 1990–91). Countries that begin radical transformation first are also the first to see a resurgence of economic growth (Poland, 1993).

—The most crucial factors determining both the difficulty of engaging the market mechanism and the losses associated with doing so are a function of the scale of financial distortions bequeathed by socialism, and of the overall plight of the national private sector. Given these parameters, the countries with the most favorable conditions for introducing reforms were Hungary, which had a sizable private sector, an existing market, no monetary overhang, and limited distortions in monetary flows; Czechoslovakia, the only socialist country to have maintained its traditional financial stability up to the eve of the revolution; and Poland, which had maintained a private sector within a socialist framework. It was in these countries that progress in establishing a market economy was swiftest, and the drop in output smallest.

The former Soviet republics were left not only with massive financial distortions and an undeveloped private sector, but also with a record-breaking military burden. At the start-up of reforms, they also lacked any regulatory levers whatsoever, including full-fledged central banks. This, too, made it difficult for the economy to adapt to fundamentally new conditions. Here we should also add an important psychological factor: over years of Communist rule, people had unlearned the skill of working independently—the foundation of a market system. Further, in postsocialist economies inflation is first and foremost a monetary phenomenon. Liberalization of prices transforms repressed inflation into open inflation. Practically everywhere (except Hungary), the initial jump in prices has been roughly twice that of preliminary estimates. Under a restrained monetary policy it is possible, in the space of a year, to bring the price growth down to no more than 2 to 3 percent per month, and thus open the door for investment in domestic production.

As a consequence of the above—and much more might be added to this—those countries that have been consistent in their pursuit of radical reforms have effective mechanisms for microregulation of the market in place within two or three years after reforms are initiated; they also have a rapidly developing private sector, an open economy, and an acceptable level of monetary stabilization. At first glance it might seem that once they have paid for their exit from socialism with a decline in output, they can then confidently move forward on a path of sustained growth. However, the reality is much harsher. Even after the most immediate problems are solved, the socialist model still leaves a complex legacy of long-term problems, primarily social and political in nature, for those attempting to return to a capitalist path of development.

The launch of a yet-imperfect market mechanism and the expansion of a legal private sector invariably cause a rapid increase in social differentiation that is especially painful for former socialist countries where a "leveling" mentality once reigned. This, too, can lead to serious political conflict. The pauperization of significant population groups set against a backdrop of conspicuous consumption by the nouveau riche can, over the long term, serve as a breeding ground for political radicalism.

Just as with traditional capitalism, one possible antidote to the intensification of social inequities is dynamic economic growth; however, a combination of several negative factors can substantially complicate a breakthrough in this direction for postsocialist nations. The socialist model of development was based on reallocation of resources through the state budget, which provided financing for investment projects. The role of nongovernmental sources of accumulation, primarily individual savings, was insignificant, while the strict political control which permitted a high level of centralization of financial resources in the hands of the state hindered attempts by various social, professional, or institutional groups to reallocate resources to their own advantage.

And therefore the first consequence of any weakening of political control in these countries in the late socialist era was to undermine the effectiveness of the state financing mechanism, to collapse the state budget, to effect an inflationary crisis. The state, deprived of its traditional levers of coercion but still burdened by the weight of paternalistic duty, was no longer able to finance accumulation at even minimal levels. Attempts to solve the problem by deficit financing only exacerbated the inflationary crisis.

The drastic reduction in state capital formation then led to a grave crisis throughout a wide range of industries. There was deterioration in capital assets at a time when the society was unable to mobilize those vital investment resources capable of financing a structural overhaul of either industries or enterprises now dealing with the fundamentally new conditions of the free market. Herein lie both the roots of the profound crisis in postsocialist economies and the essence of the problems that must be solved in the coming years. Lacking this, dynamic economic development will be impossible.

In the meantime we have a stalemate: our old sources of financing have stopped functioning but new ones have not yet begun. Recently legalized private ownership initially cannot provide any guarantees of stability, and that reduces incentive for private investment, especially long-term investment. At the same time, the level of voluntary household savings—an important source for financing market development—has historically been low, which is natural for countries with poor populations and relatively highly developed social programs.

All of the above allows us to answer the question of what needs to be done in order to guarantee dynamic economic growth, and consequently civil accord, in postsocialist nations. The requirements are macroeconomic stability and low, predictable rates of inflation, an open economy plus access to promising markets, clear-cut guarantees of property rights and a respectable level of financial liability, high levels of individual savings and investments, and effective programs to aid the poor and to maintain political stability.

There is only one little problem. *How* are the countries caught in the postsocialist trap going to make this happen? Plenty to puzzle over. But even so, after analyzing, for the umpteenth time, our government's actions, I come back to the same conclusion—that the road we took was the right one.

This was something understood, if not always publicly acknowledged, by many who took part in economic policy-making during the fall of socialism in Russia. I'll cite only one opinion here, that of former first deputy prime minister of the USSR, Vladimir Shcherbakov. Here is what he said in an interview with *Izvestia*:

I've never criticized Gaidar. I know full well that he had no other choice. Economic processes have their own internal and inescapable logic. This logic, with which any Russian government would have had to contend at the time, was determined by our very industrial structure, which took decades to evolve and which could change only with the passage of considerable time. . . . When administrative control crumbled—as was inevitable—price liberalization became equally inevitable, as did the devaluation of savings built on the old economic base. Given such conditions, one can only be amazed at how few mistakes Gaidar's team actually made. Another team might have made more.

Out there, away from Moscow, with piles of statistics, heaps of economic journals, and stacks of dissertation abstracts in front of me, I didn't listen to the radio, watch television, open a newspaper, or, of course, pester my colleagues still in the government. It seemed easier to get rid of the "driver's syndrome" that way. But on January 8, 1993, Anatoly Chubais tracked me down by telephone to say that the government had decided to freeze prices and there was panic in the consumer market. He was trying to get the measure rescinded, but was having difficulty and needed help.

What had happened? Chubais laid out the situation for me in a few words; later the whole picture took on clarity and form.

The opposition took Chernomyrdin's appointment as a major victory. The pages of *Pravda* and *Sovetskaya Rossiya* were filled with letters addressed to the new prime minister, calling on him to put an end to Gaidar's anti-people policy. Here's a typical excerpt from the December 31 edition of *Pravda*:

A terrible evil is being done with this whole market debacle—what's being created is the most ineffective, small-scale but simultaneously most wasteful type of economy. It puts all the republics of the former Soviet Union at risk. As Russia goes, so go the republics. As we speak, the "reformers" are keeping the promise that Yeltsin himself made on television: "We'll bring the rest of the republics along." Blinded by hatred of everything the Soviet people have achieved, they are actively dragging us down into the abyss. Who will stop them?

We appeal to our fellow Russians—you are our only hope! We appeal to Chernomyrdin—do not betray Russia, her future lies not in free markets, not in private property that separates people from one another, but in an economy rationally organized on the basis of progressive socialist principles, on a collective spirit. We appeal to the scholars and scientists, the deputies who have kept faith with the people: unite, so that you may save Russia from reforms that will bring ruin upon her, and all of us together.

On his very first day in office, a storm of financial requests and demands swept down upon the new prime minister. His words about markets "but no bazaars," about reforms but no drop in standard of living, had given heart to the habitués at the government trough. His words had given birth to the hope that Chernomyrdin was not all that staunch a monetarist, and that with a little pressure they might squeeze some money out of him. Some had already managed to do just that, which set off a panic. After all, you can accept the fact that the government isn't handing out any money, but when the clever guy next door gets some, and the industry or the major enterprise you run ends up with nothing— it's intolerable.

Chernomyrdin's government, while still in the process of organizing itself, was already caving in, retreating. In the latter half of December the volume of credits from the Central Bank already exceeded the amount of deficit financing in the previous year's entire budget! Meanwhile, loans from the Central Bank to commercial banks totaled 160 billion rubles per month from September through November, and in December approached 900 billion. On the whole, the volume of Central Bank lending had increased by more than 150 percent. All this meant that any effects of the previous autumn's policy of restraint were now canceled out, and that the country was again on the brink of hyperinflation.

Meanwhile, in ministries and agencies the paper chase was on— useful papers, harmless papers, dangerous papers. One of the agencies whose leadership had functioned professionally enough within the old management system, but had enormous difficulties in adapting to the new situation and its new demands, was the Committee on Prices. Once a powerful organ with offices at the House on the Embankment,[2] by the early eighties it had become a locus of opposition to economic liberalism. Its colorful former director, N. Glushkov, had often warned the Party leadership about those nasty little ideas being professed at the Central Economics and Mathematics Institute. This was the committee that during the tenure of its chairman Valentin Pavlov had drafted the price reform that ultimately brought down Ryzhkov's government. In 1992 the Committee was stripped of its independent status and subordinated to the Ministry of the Economy. Lira Ivanovna Rozenova, a conscientious and highly qualified specialist, was assigned to head it. Yet for all her competence, her heart was still with administrative price controls. She had little faith in newfangled ideas about managing prices through overall demand or the money supply. From the depths of the Committee, now and again, proposals to freeze prices—at least on *something*—would surface. Reluctant to offend sweet Lira Ivanovna, I would nonetheless send them back, gently suggesting the Committee focus more on controlling prices within natural monopolies—something they had coped with in less than optimal fashion—and on reducing the scope of administrative regulation of prices in areas where it had obviously outlived its usefulness.

The Committee's next proposal to expand administrative price management came in November 1992; I shunted it off in the usual fashion, again recommending that the Committee redirect its attention. It's quite possible that this was the very proposal that had landed on the new prime minister's desk. As far as I can tell, it must have happened on the eve of 1993. The document was presented to him as "Gaidar's will and testament"; supposedly Gaidar had already been leaning in this direction, but ran out of time. Chernomyrdin quickly and decisively signed off on it. A New Year's gift to the Russian people.

The combination of an economy pumped up by loans, increasing inflationary expectations linked to changes in the government, and attempts to freeze prices was quick to produce results. Russian consumers, who understood where all this was leading, rushed to buy up products while they were still available. There was a wave of panic buying. With high weekly rates of inflation, the saturation index on the consumer market took a downturn. That was why Chubais had searched me out and asked for some urgent help in repealing this ruinous measure.

When I resigned, I had vowed not to interfere in the management of the economy. But this was too much. To let everything that had taken such effort to achieve go down the drain, to see the whole country lined up, dependent on ration coupons—it was just too much.

I immediately tried to contact Chernomyrdin, but couldn't get through. I then called the President and said that I was very alarmed, and asked him to read the memo I was about to send him and to rescind the decision on prices. And in general to curb the inflationary appetites of his new government. Several days later I learned that the ill-starred resolution had been rescinded.

The vacillation and ambivalence that from the very outset had manifested themselves in the policy pursued by the government were a characteristic of Russian economic life throughout the second half of 1993. The Far East episode is telling in this respect. Although its economic significance was relatively slight, it still cast a bright light on this government's working style, through which our time-honored national tradition was beginning to peek out: *Issue yet another high-level decree to make people at least a little happier.*

In January the government had enacted new regulations on motor vehicle operation. Along with some solid, technical provisions that were both reasonable and useful, the regulations included a ban on cars with steering wheels on the right. It seemed logical enough; the roads would be safer. But no one gave any thought to the fact that increased imports from Japan to the Russian Far East had made cars with right-hand steering a widespread means of transportation in that part of Russia. An enormous region literally rose up in defense of its rights. The government was forced to repeal that decision.

It was obvious from all the zigging and zagging that the government wanted everyone to both have their cake and eat it, to provide financial support for industry and agriculture but at the same time keep the fragile, new, but functioning market regulators from breaking down. This ambivalence also took individual form: the first deputy chairman of the government and minister of economics, Oleg Lobov, was a resolute proponent of active government regulation, while Minister of Finance Boris Fyodorov was an equally staunch liberal and anti-inflationist. As a result, government policy was literally moving along two different, at times contradictory, lines.

Pressure from proponents of "support for industry" and "reforms without impoverishment" led to the adoption of new subsidies for bread, mineral fertilizer, livestock feed, et cetera. Week after week the government reviewed and approved new federal programs requiring generous budget allocations to increase centralized capital investments, to support the various regions of the country. The overall number of budget commitments grew incessantly.

If all the resolutions adopted by the government in the first half of 1993 had been financed in their entirety, a collapse of the monetary system, and hyperinflation, would have become unavoidable. But the Ministry of Finance was in no particular rush to do anything of the sort. Despite government promises and obligations, it held federal budget financing to approximately 20 percent of the gross domestic product, covering these expenditures with tax revenues and Central Bank loans beginning with borrowing both in the domestic market and from international financial institutions.

It worked just like the standard two-detective scenario in classic crime stories. The good cop understands everything, tries to help people. That's Prime Minister Chernomyrdin. But he's got trouble—he just can't handle the bad cop, aka Minister of Finance Boris Fyodorov.

The problem with such a tactic, and indeed with any disingenuousness in economic policy—or any other—is that while it temporarily takes the edge off the conflict, it leads to unpleasant consequences. Obligations undertaken by a government are not just idle chatter; they are immediately incorporated into enterprises' manufacturing plans, into their finance plans, and they materialize as orders for component parts and materials. And when it suddenly turns out that the whole thing was a bluff, that no one's paying for anything, then the government itself exacerbates the payments crisis. Moreover, by setting an irresponsible example, it gives enterprises leave to follow suit: *If even the state doesn't make its payments, then why should we?* It would be hard to come up with a better way to help the extremists and the radical opposition.

In any case, during the first half of the year the rates of growth in the money supply were held to roughly 20 percent. Between March and the end of June monthly rates of increase in consumer prices hovered at around the same level. But we were sitting on a budgetary time bomb. You can't postpone the choice of direction, playing the good cop–bad cop game forever. Eventually you have to choose.

There was one more key area of economic policy at the eye of the storm—privatization. Our strategic advantage here was that the process had already begun, that 148 million vouchers had been distributed. Stopping it or trying to roll it back was by now a very risky proposition, and probably impossible. The parliamentary majority wavered between a passionate desire to ban privatization and fear of the political consequences of such a step. Its tactic, then, was to let someone else strangle privatization. More concretely—to let the regional soviets strangle it. The Communist regional soviet for Chelyabinsk, obviously acting on orders from Moscow, passed a resolution suspending privatization within the borders of the region. A number of other regions followed suit.

Chubais realized that if this was not nipped in the bud, the battle was lost. He dropped everything, flew to Chelyabinsk, and appeared on regional television, telling the public just who it was who wanted to take away their right to own property and how they planned to do it. He explained, argued. Pyotr Sumin, former first secretary of the Chelyabinsk Communist Party regional committee, now chairman of the Chelyabinsk regional council and up for election as head of the regional administration just a few days hence, capitulated, assembled the regional council, and repealed the resolution. Privatization in the region continued, and in Chelyabinsk's wake, other regions retreated as well.

Infuriated by the failure of this campaign, parliamentary majority leaders got involved directly. Without formally halting privatization, they proposed introducing a number of amendments into existing regulations, which would have utterly paralyzed any work in progress. Chubais raised the stakes, played the giveaway game, drafting a directive on total cessation of all privatization measures, accompanied by an explanation of the consequences of such a decision. What the Supreme Soviet had thought would be a quiet squeeze play suddenly turned into an all-out battle on the very eve of the referendum.[3] At the very last moment, frightened by the possible consequences, the opposition retreated.

Beating off attacks from all sides, including those by industrial ministries that had sensed a weakening in State Committee on Property positions, privatization managed to forge ahead; this was perhaps the most positive thing to take place in the Russian economy in 1993.

Agricultural reform, however, went down in total defeat. The weak and unsteady sprouts of 1992 didn't survive the change of government. The number of peasant, or family, farms had by December 1992 reached 180,000 and had, out of inertia, increased in early 1993 as well. By late spring of 1993 the growth stopped. Local authorities were returning most of the lands in the federal redistribution fund to reorganized kolkhozes and sovkhozes. In the vast majority of regions, local administrations were making it much harder for people to quit the kolkhoz and receive land.

Though there was no need for them, government procurement quotas remained in force. It was a wonderful opportunity for the agrarian lobby to put the brakes on any development of a market for agricultural products, to dump all the processing costs on the government, and then, with the government by the throat, force it to pay prices far higher than the going market rate. The financial obligations taken on by a faltering government were unrealizable, and far exceeded what had been budgeted. Cutting social programs would not plug this hole. The already complicated financing situation was becoming harder and harder to control. The budget bomb now had a lighted fuse.

After my dismissal, I had turned down various offers to join this or

that political organization; I was sure that I would positively and absolutely return to research. I considered my forced involvement in government business in January 1993—over rescinding the decision to
freeze prices and curbing the excessive generosity of financial policy—
an isolated episode, unfinished business in the transfer of power. But
gradually I came to understand that backing out of politics was impossible. We were the ones who had launched the massive and difficult
reforms that had so drastically changed the country's way of life; we
had solved some old problems but at the same time created new ones.
Therein lay our moral responsibility—my moral responsibility—for
the consequences. And no matter what course events might take, no dismissal from government could free me from that responsibility. Someone else had been sitting in the prime minister's seat quite some time
now, but there were people who still furiously condemned "Gaidar's
anti-people policy," and others who still defended it. You can't run away
from that, and you can't hide. And now, perhaps even more than when I
was at the wheel, I felt the pain of all those missteps and the mistakes.

To shut myself up at home, at my desk, to bury myself in institute
business, to declare that I had been misunderstood and unappreciated,
and that I was washing my hands of it all, that seemed dishonorable. All
the more so because the political situation was becoming more complicated; there was a growing sense of danger, premonitions of a conflict
whose outcome could very well decide Russia's fate.

A major internal source of political instability in 1992 and 1993 was
the Constitution of the RSFSR as part of the USSR; in other words, the
constitution of a state that had no real independent status. It was a decorative facade created to conceal and prettify the simple fact that Russia
had no laws of its own, that instead it had only the absolute power of the
USSR Central Committee. Once that pivot—the statute on the guiding
and directing role of the Party—was removed, everything in this solemn
text became rather shaky, ill-defined, and ambiguous. However carefully you might now read this hurriedly patched and repatched text, you
could find no clear-cut, unambiguous answers. What were the limits of

presidential or governmental or congressional or Supreme Soviet prerogative? What were regional or municipal authorities allowed, or not allowed, to do? And what if these bodies passed conflicting resolutions? The result was constant wrangling, legal chaos.

For example, Ruslan Khasbulatov, who was after all a mere deputy chairman of the Supreme Soviet, signed a resolution establishing the independent status of an enormous Russian manufacturing concern, Russian Nickel. Well, fine, I supported this gigantic and unique enterprise in Russia's Far North becoming independent; moreover, I tried to help move things along any way I could. But, does some paper with Khasbulatov's signature really oblige anyone to do anything? No answer.

Or let's take another example. After reviewing competing projects for developing a portion of the Sakhalin shelf ("Sakhalin-2"), a government expert commission decided to award an American-Japanese consortium the right to conduct a feasibility study. Even before it was finished, in fact immediately after the award, disgruntled competitors forced through a Supreme Soviet resolution nullifying the outcome of the bidding. And this sort of thing was happening everywhere.

Another characteristic example of the anarchy born of *dvoevlastie* was the situation in Chelyabinsk region in the fall of 1993. The regional Soviet had set dates for electing the regional administration head. The court had canceled those elections because of procedural violations in organizing them. The elections proceeded anyway. The Supreme Soviet recognized the victor, Pyotr Sumin, as lawful head of the Chelyabinsk regional administration. The government and the President continued to recognize acting head of administration Vadim Solovyov. Some district and municipal chiefs went over to Sumin's side; others stayed loyal to Solovyov.

There was more to come. The Central Bank and its Chelyabinsk branch recognized Sumin's authority. The Ministry of Finance continued to consider Solovyov head of the administration. The commander of the regional militia was on Sumin's side; the city militia commander was loyal to Solovyov. There followed a stream of contradictory directives, total chaos in funding, and no one in control. Chernomyrdin demanded that Gerashchenko reaffirm Solovyov's authority; Khasbulatov called Gerashchenko and demanded that he support Sumin.

Obviously, in a situation like that the machinery of state simply cannot work, and the result is a power vacuum, anarchy. The state's own weakness in the face of crucial tasks—providing legal safeguards, maintaining legal order—becomes a catalyst for crime.

In such a situation, stable economic activity, long-term contracts, or major investment projects were simply impossible. Moreover, the very structure of Russian governmental authority was constantly being shaken loose, and could not stabilize itself.

The First Congress of Russian People's Deputies had long ago resolved that a new constitution should be drafted, and then put to a referendum. But the leadership of the Supreme Soviet was deliberately dragging out the process. The leadership could, after all, redo the old constitution as often and as much as it liked—reworking it here, trimming it there, decorating it with studs and geegaws, and then using it to club its political opponents.

The parliament functioning throughout that period in Russia was perhaps one of the most irresponsible in the history of democracy. A resolution passed by the Supreme Soviet privatizing deputies' Moscow apartments (temporary, government-provided quarters) showed just how morality, as restraint, had been switched off, how the majority of deputies were ready to start privatizing the whole country for themselves and their relatives. Draft legislation titled "On Inherited Deputyship," a parody of current lawmaking practices that one of the very few democratically inclined deputies circulated on the Supreme Soviet floor, hardly sounded like a joke anymore.

The President was in a difficult spot. He, the Russian state's highest publicly elected administrative official, the guarantor of its security, could see that the absolute power of an irresponsible congress was becoming a serious threat to the country. At the same time the President had no established constitutional authority to protect the country's citizens from that threat. He could not set new elections, nor had he the right to call for a referendum on the issue, to seek support in the express will of the people.

Given these circumstances, Boris Yeltsin chose to compromise, make concessions. The Supreme Soviet majority read this as a sign of weakness and seemed to be merely awaiting the signal to pounce on its already weakened prey.

The opposition saw the change of prime minister as a defeat for the President. Khasbulatov was again riding high, and the December agreement was forgiven, or rather was now regarded as proof of his political sagacity; the clever guide had merely led his followers to their goal by a roundabout, safe path. Why should the opposition now, after this victory, keep any agreement reached at the Seventh Congress? They annulled it; there would be no referendum. When asked his opinion, the chief justice of the Constitutional Court, Valery Zorkin, initiator of the agreement and its guarantor, replied that it would be better for Russia this way.

Yet the leaders of the opposition again made a serious misstep in overestimating their success, and chiefly in showing an inexcusable disregard for public opinion. Soon, as the Eighth Congress progressed, the demonstrative and unconcealed arrogance shown by the majority in so lightly dismissing its sworn obligations, the frank unwillingness to listen to the voice of the people, to ask the people's opinion, set off a great wave of protest in Russia.

By the time the President went over the head of the Supreme Soviet and directly addressed the people, calling for a referendum, the situation was far different from that of the previous December. The meaning of what was happening was now clear to everyone. This time the President's call met with a wide response.

True, not everyone recognized the shift in the public mood, or recognized it right away. Vice President Rutskoi, misreading the situation yet again, went over to the Supreme Soviet camp. Khasbulatov was obviously pleased as he opened his emergency session; he could hardly conceal his triumph. He, too, was certain that the President had taken the fateful step toward his downfall. The Constitutional Court hastily ruled that the President had acted unconstitutionally, and its chief justice, peacemaker Valery Zorkin, shed a couple of crocodile tears: "I pity you, Boris Nikolaevich."

Now, thinks the opposition, we have them! Chernomyrdin, who was so unanimously applauded at the congress and with whom Khasbulatov was so friendly and courteous, will falter, the ministers of defense and internal affairs will distance themselves from Yeltsin, and impeachment is sure to follow.

But time was passing. Chernomyrdin seemed in no hurry to disassociate himself from the President. It was ruining Khasbulatov's mood. He could no longer hide his annoyance, and traded barbs in public with the minister of defense. On the day when the congress Khasbulatov had called into emergency session was to vote on the question of removing the President from office, democratic forces held a rally at the Kremlin's Saviour (Spasskaya) Tower, on Vasilievsky Slope.

The morning was sunny, windy, and cool. The columns of marchers gathered on Tverskaya Street, descended to Manezh Square, across Lubyanka, and then along the embankment to Red Square and St. Basil's Cathedral.

This was the first time I'd been out in public since my dismissal. My father and I marched together, side by side. It was a joy to see not only my comrades-in-arms, but also those democratic leaders with whom I'd argued and fought a year earlier, as well as some Yeltsin supporters who had seemed ready to back away from him after the December change of government but today were joining ranks with us. On Manezh Square I looked over my shoulder, and saw that all of Tverskaya Street, as far as the eye could see, was overflowing with people; a sea of people filled the center of the city. We moved out onto the embankment, as new columns of marchers hurried toward the bridge from the Zamoskvarechye side.

The marchers were cheerful. People might be anxious enough inside, but it wasn't visible now. There were songs, laughter, jokes, demonstrations of goodwill: "Let the veteran through!" "Look out, there's a pothole here!" "Calm down, everybody." Even the slogans and the banners were upbeat, witty. It's too bad I can't remember them all.

The rally was held beneath the ancient walls of St. Basil's. From time to time the speaker, who was saying true and needful things, whom people were following attentively, would be interrupted by a dissatisfied rumble; he would turn around in dismay and then, realizing what the matter was, smile and continue speaking. Behind him, some opposition deputies were up on the parapet, observing the rally.

Now it was my turn to speak. But I barely had time to get my first words out when I sensed that the attention of this enormous audience had shifted. Out through the Saviour Gate came the President; he climbed to the speaker's platform. Beside him was a glum and preoccupied Chernomyrdin. The President told the rally that the vote count had begun, but that whatever the result, he would not recognize any decision by the congress until the people had their say in a referendum. Ovation. Yes, apparently there's no other choice. But I mentally ran through the worst-case scenario: say the congress of deputies votes to impeach. Rutskoi is sworn in. The country would have two presidents, possibly two prime ministers, and at least two ministers each for defense and internal affairs. Who could say how the military and security ministers would react. Would it all come down to fighting in the streets of Moscow?

Yeltsin and his entourage returned to the Kremlin. I had to finish my speech. So I said what I thought. However dangerous it might be, however difficult, Russia would not relinquish its hopes and its freedom so simply, on the whim of some deputies who had lost all touch with the people.

Speakers, speakers, speakers. It was dark now. The rally went on. Spotlights played over the heads of the crowd. Late in the evening the President again ascended the platform, this time with a large and cheerful group around him. There were not enough votes to impeach. Sensing that they had gone too far and that the public mood had turned against them, the congress had agreed to a referendum. Now Khasbulatov's chief hope lay in formulating the questions to be put to Russian citizens as artfully as possible. The first question was to be a vote of confidence or no-confidence in the President. The second, logically, should have been a vote of confidence or no confidence in the congress; instead, it asked whether people supported continuing the economic policies launched on January 2, 1992.

It was an excellent move. It would be difficult, even for me, to answer that second question on the ballot with a short and unequivocal "yes." After all, economic policy at the time was not uniform. It was a battle, there were gains, retreats. And certainly not everything that Chernomyrdin's government was doing was to my liking, let alone to the liking of others. And no matter how much you remind someone of yesterday's queues and mass shortages, what's important to him are not all the sad yesterdays, but today, this day. And this day was not an easy one. Drastically higher prices, lost savings. And no one was obliged when answering yes or no to consider the fact that we were paying the price for seventy years on a dead-end road, plus five years of Gorbachev's on-again, off-again perestroika.

So even if the President won his victory, and won a personal vote of confidence, a loss on the second ballot issue would render that victory worthless. (*The people may support the President, but they don't support his policies.*) A few days before the referendum the opposition brought out another trump card. Vice President Rutskoi hauled his "eleven suitcases" full of compromising materials into the Supreme Soviet, and demanded to be broadcast live by both radio and TV.[4]

The long, emotional speech contained a varied and unpleasant assortment of real facts on abuse of power (materials he should have handed over to the prosecutor's office long before, instead of hiding them away in his suitcases for a rainy day), rumors and absurdities concocted in absolute ignorance of actual events, and deliberate distortions. My name figured in the speech several times. It turned out that I was the one who shipped off the gold reserves and squandered all the emeralds. And in general, the entire executive branch, except for the scrupulously honest Vice President, was up to its ears in thievery.

What can I say—it was a serious blow, and it had done its job for the moment. By the time everything was sorted out and made sense of, the referendum would be over. And how can you give a President a vote of confidence when his own Vice President is saying that the entire government is a gang of crooks?

When I was still in the government, the ritual accusations of corruption had somehow never stuck. But that evening, after Rutskoi's speech, Masha and I went to a new performance at the Moscow Art Theater, something we'd long been planning, and for the first time ever I could feel curious glances directed my way. (*Just think, he wolfs down the whole gold supply and then sits there like nothing happened.*) It was very unpleasant. The only way out was to confront Rutskoi directly, in front of millions of television viewers, where I could demonstrate in detail the absurdity of his accusations, cite numbers and facts. But would he agree to such a dialogue, to a duel?

I gave a very angry interview for the popular television program *Itogi*, in hopes of getting him stirred up a little. The next morning Oleg Poptsov, president of Russian Radio and Television, telephoned to say that Rutskoi had agreed to meet for a radio broadcast. I asked that television crews be invited as well. When Rutskoi's entourage saw the TV cameras, there was consternation and much waving of arms, but Rutskoi himself, grimacing, agreed to let the cameramen stay. After our conversation, I left the studio in a rotten mood. Although I had caught Rutskoi in one exaggeration after another, and explained how decisions on the sale of gold and on gold reserves are actually made and implemented, how in 1992 the gold supply had for the first time in years actually grown rather than shrunk; although I tried to show how groundless his crude notions of economics really were, I had the feeling that he had literally drowned it all in a flood of words. According to the timers, Rutskoi had talked roughly two and a half times longer than I had.

I couldn't watch the broadcast because I was leaving for St. Petersburg that evening. Not until I arrived there did I learn, to my surprise, that public opinion had awarded me a clear victory, and that the effect of the "suitcase speech" in the Supreme Soviet had been by and large neutralized.

On April 26, the referendum votes were tallied. They were unbelievable; practically no one had expected this. The President had not only received overwhelming support, but 52 percent of those who voted expressed their support for continuing the economic policy begun in January 1992. And so to the implied question "Do you want to go back to the bright Communist future?" the majority of Russians answered "no."

After the opposition's crushing defeat in the referendum, it seems to me, Yeltsin was convinced that the political issue was resolved, that the terrible Damocles sword of *dvoevlastie* no longer hung over Russia. Now all that remained was to move confidently toward passage of a new constitution and, on that basis, conduct new elections. The people's opinion—democracy's court of last resort—was clear.

A number of the more perspicacious parliamentary leaders realized that as well, and accepted the Supreme Soviet's defeat. Nikolai Travkin resigned his office as deputy and began to prepare for new elections. N. Ryabov, a deputy chairman of the Supreme Soviet who had recently been one of Khasbulatov's chief sources of support, went over to the side of the probable victor.

The impact of the referendum on the conduct of the Central Bank also became obvious. Ever since the fall of 1992, the two weakest links in monetary policy had been technical credits to other Commonwealth states and low rates of refinancing, which were spurring an artificial demand for centralized credits and additional growth in the money supply. The problem of technical credits, a ruble-zone legacy, had become particularly acute after Chernomyrdin's first meeting with the leadership of Kazakhstan, when, not yet current on what was happening, he had agreed to abolish the system of interrepublic correspondent accounts. Thus this bastion, which had taken such effort to build in defense of the still weak Russian ruble, suffered a major breach. A stream of worthless money soon came gushing through it.

By spring, Kazakhstan had elbowed out Ukraine as the leading exporter of inflation to Russia. Ministry of Finance attempts to control technical credits issued by the Central Bank from Russia to other CIS republics had borne little fruit. But at the end of April, with the referendum, the situation changed radically. The hole in the ruble zone was plugged, and the faucets pouring out technical credits were turned off. Financial cooperation with other CIS governments moved onto the generally accepted track for intergovernmental export credits. Separation of the ruble zone for noncash circulation was complete. The future looked promising. Simultaneously, the Central Bank began to move toward raising interest rates to a realistic level.

But while the parliamentary majority's political defeat and the need for early elections was obvious to many, Khasbulatov and those around him were hardly ready to admit the fact. Perhaps had the President taken more vigorous action in those first days after the results of the referendum were announced, they might have resigned themselves to the inevitable. But while the President delayed, waiting for a civilized gesture of capitulation from his vanquished political opponents, the shock passed, and the same old logic prevailed. (*If we're not being disbanded, that means they're afraid of us. And if they're afraid of us, why should we pass a new constitution and agree to elections? We can do as we please!*) After the First of May celebrations, when the opposition provoked a number of bloody confrontations on the streets of Moscow, it became clear that there would be no capitulation, that the deputies would not go forward with new elections.

And while the President was working on a new constitution, organizing wide-ranging discussion and review, leading a constitutional conference, the momentum of the referendum victory began to dissipate amidst the calm of summer vacations and seasonal chores like gardens and dachas.

At the end of July, I received an urgent call from Andrei Vavilov, first deputy minister of finance. He was alarmed. He told me that he was in charge of the ministry in the absence of Boris Fyodorov, who was in the United States, and that a monetary reform had just been announced. The Ministry of Finance had not been informed and was not ready. The population was outraged. Vavilov gave some details: the total amount people were allowed to exchange was extremely small, and the time allowed for exchange was limited; the formal justification for the reform was to defend against ruble intervention by the former republics. He

asked me whether it was possible, in my opinion, to do anything to salvage the situation.

All this sounded like total idiocy, to put it mildly. Of course the problem of a shared currency and separate noncash circulation was real, and
it was serious. It had been much discussed, and the only reasonable solution was to halt the free boxcars of cash Russia continued to deliver at
CIS request. If CIS states wanted to buy rubles—fine; Russia would export them as soon as it received U.S. dollars instead of just a thank-you-
very-much in exchange.

Of course, an ultimate solution to the problem would require negotiations with the republics, in fact rather complex ones, but that was different from simply whacking someone over the head with a currency
surrender. The Ministry of Finance had long ago proposed such negotiations, back when Russian cash was indeed being shipped to the republics in boxcars. Now, in one stroke, agreements were being violated
and economic circulation disrupted. And, naturally, this threw the door
wide open for a variety of financial machinations. After all, you could
make a killing on the difference in exchange rates between the old cash
currency, the new currency, and noncash rubles in Russia and the former
republics. If you wanted to help the speculators, you couldn't have
dreamed up a better way!

The inevitable result would be massive dumping of rubles into Russia
and panic buying of all sorts of commodities, plus accelerated inflation,
ruined vacations, queues at savings banks. It was all painfully reminiscent of the Pavlov money reform of January 1991.

I racked my brains: was there any way to salvage the situation? Unfortunately, there wasn't much we could do. It couldn't be halted now, as
much for financial reasons as for political ones; faith in the currency to
be surrendered was already undermined, and you couldn't restore that
by decree. The inflationary impulse had been sent, and was working. The
only thing that could and should be done now was to try to limit the social damage. I got through to the President and told him that in my view
a serious mistake was being made. To make up for it, we had to raise the
limit on the amount people could surrender, extend the deadline, and

keep smaller-denomination banknotes in circulation for the present. The President promptly agreed; apparently he was looking for just such a solution. But all of this couldn't make up for the political and economic damage done.

For the opposition it was a dream come true. By the end of summer it became clear that the government's economic policy was crumbling. Commitments to specific levels of government grain purchases and grain prices, which far exceeded the state's capacity to fulfill them, exacerbated the budget crisis and rendered it unmanageable. Ministry of Finance proposals for immediate reduction of government obligations and for expenditure plans got lost in the bureaucratic maze. The acrimonious polemics within the government, especially between the heads of the Ministry of Finance and the Ministry of Economics, underscored the absence of any uniform policy.

In August, thanks to the currency reform, rates of price increase on consumer goods jumped to 26 percent. The Supreme Soviet was now crafting a financial bomb capable of blowing up the entire economy—a resolution requiring the government, in the fourth quarter of the year, to pay out everything that it had promised, and that the Ministry of Finance had underfinanced, in the three previous quarters. The government tactic of making generous commitments but stingy allocations had thus led us to the brink of an abyss. It was time to choose: either the swift collapse of monetary circulation or painful measures aimed at cutting government obligations, along with an honest statement from the government (*what we can pay, we will, but what we can't, we won't commit to*).

The political situation had grown drastically more complicated. The unpopular currency reform, as might have been expected, provoked a good deal of dissatisfaction in society. The opposition had gained a counterargument: would Russians really support policy like this in a referendum? It became clear that the congress would not adopt the new constitution, nor would it set early elections. Not only that—it would raise the stakes once again, and ignoring the constitution, try to remove the President from power. If need be, it would lower the number required for a quorum, expel some of the deputies who supported the President, and simplify the impeachment process. In *Rossiskaya Gazeta*, the mouthpiece of the Supreme Soviet, Yeltsin's impeachment was being predicted regularly from one edition to the next.

Everything spoke to the fact that constitutional resources had been exhausted. The people were asked their opinion in a referendum, and an unequivocal answer came back. Now, in spite of it, a coalition of Communists, nationalists, and just plain hustlers were demanding the removal of a President for whom Russia had shown convincing support. And that meant that the President had little choice: to capitulate, and thereby betray the trust shown him by Russians who had twice voted for him, or to suspend the work of the congress and by his own authority set new elections. It was also clear that in this situation the battle would be decided on strength alone, and it was very hard to predict which of the two sides would be stronger at the decisive moment. Much like our position at the beginning of the reform, we now faced a choice between two options: the first was passivity, inaction, and certain defeat; the second was exceedingly risky, but had some hope of succeeding. Opting for force ran up against the question of how the "force structures" (i.e., the military and security structures) would react. Whose side would they take? At the time, no one knew the answer. But even now, after the fact, when the tragic events in Moscow have become history, I ask myself: was there another way out, a peaceful one? And I can't think of any. *Dvoevlastie* was consuming the state system, dooming any and all efforts aimed at economic, social, or administrative stabilization. This enormous country, simply, could no longer live under a government in a constant state of chaos and paralysis, when decisions made by one branch of government were automatically canceled out by the decisions made by another, and no one could say which side was right. Democratic traditions in Russia were not so sturdy as to withstand such overload. We all know how the *dvoevlastie* problem was resolved in 1917.

On one of these September days, after a presidential council meeting, Boris Nikolaevich approached me and asked whether I would agree to rejoin the government as first deputy prime minister. I answered that

I would have to think about it. Soon thereafter Chernomyrdin invited me to his office, reiterated the President's offer, and said that the situation, as I no doubt knew, was extremely complex, and that my help was needed. Political issues were not discussed, but as far as the economy was concerned, the prime minister averred that he was ready to proceed with reforms.

I got the sense that over these last few difficult months as prime minister, Viktor Stepanovich had come to understand a good deal. We also discussed several personnel changes that would be required, were I to accept the offer. Accepting it was no simple thing. Whatever happened, I would still have to mop up somebody else's spilt milk, and answer for the spring and summer promises so generously handed out but so impossible to keep. All the positive things we had managed to accomplish in 1991 and 1992 — eliminating the threat of famine, filling the stores with goods, converting the ruble, and creating a free market that had one way or another started to function — all this had become part of ordinary life, and it neither surprised nor particularly gladdened anyone by now.

If I were to return, I would again face the hard and dirty job of hauling away someone else's garbage. Responsibility for a clearly difficult policy in the fall was not likely to bring in democratic votes in the upcoming elections, and moreover would take away any advantage of being in the opposition. And besides, it was far from clear how the head-on collision between the President and the congress would turn out. But whoever was in the government at the time would have to deal with it.

All this was obvious — and yet it wasn't important. The country had a dangerous battle ahead. Its outcome was impossible to predict. It was also of fundamental importance for Russia's future. Sitting it out on the sidelines, watching from the bench, was impossible.

I called the President and the prime minister, and said that I would take the job.

Chapter 11
The Battle

- The President makes a decision
- The opposition raises the stakes
- Sergei Glaziev's unpleasant surprise
- Attack on city hall and Ostankino
- Appeal to Muscovites
- The rebels are driven back

On September 16, 1993, immediately after I called and agreed to rejoin the government, the President announced my upcoming appointment. Actually, he was supposed to make the announcement at a previously planned meeting of financial experts, but this meeting was canceled for some reason; instead Boris Nikolaevich went to visit the Dzerzhinsky Division, and it was there that he informed everyone. It came off as quite militant.

Nonethless, no decree had yet been issued, and that evening I had to leave for several days on regional Russia's Choice business.[1] As long as the official appointment hadn't yet been made, I decided not to cancel the trip. People in Rostov and Voronezh were expecting me.

Rather late in the evening on September 18, when I was already in Voronezh, Sergei Aleksandrovich Filatov, the President's chief of administration, called; he told me that the decree had been signed and asked me to come back to Moscow immediately, and see him as soon as possible; we needed to talk, to consult. At around noon on Sunday I arrived at his dacha and discovered that the President had decided to suspend the Supreme Soviet session, declare new elections, and hold a referendum on the constitution. Filatov had been assigned to come up with a political scenario for what might follow. He told me that he had some serious concerns about the whole thing. He asked my views on the situation.

After the Supreme Soviet had openly ignored the popular will to continue reforms, so clearly expressed in the April referendum, and had rejected one reasonable attempt at compromise after another, this decision was no surprise to me. And yet, it was one thing to think through options and alternatives, and quite another to watch the flywheel of a violent conflict with unforeseeable consequences unwind. Moreover, this seemed like the least opportune moment for it. That important element of suddenness, of surprise, was lacking; the leaders of the intransigent opposition were expecting Yeltsin to make just such a move, and were ready for him. More than that—they had clearly provoked him to it. How else could you interpret Khasbulatov's stunt, when he had insulted the President personally in front of millions of television viewers? It was obvious that he was deliberately trying to throw Yeltsin off balance.

I answered Filatov by saying that in my view it would be more useful to bide our time, keep Khasbulatov's team guessing, make them nervous. Why do exactly what the other side expected, at the very moment they were best prepared? Besides, it was clear that occupying the White House right now—that is, actually stopping the Supreme Soviet session, itself a crucial prerequisite for success—was not possible. Filatov asked me to phone Boris Nikolaevich, to meet with him and talk it over. All this made it obvious that Filatov shared my doubts. I headed home with some uncomfortable thoughts going through my mind. A direct collision was about to become harsh reality.

I had for a very long time, throughout all of 1992, decisively rejected any ideas about resolving conflicts with the parliamentary opposition by confrontation or force. But by 1993, I was firmly persuaded that the current Supreme Soviet majority was at the beck and call of people who refused to recognize any sort of ethical framework or democratic standards. In other words, this democratically elected government was itself becoming the chief threat to democracy. History had seen this happen more than once.

The President's plan for escaping the constitutional cul-de-sac did not presuppose any repeal of democracy. His key idea, his main goal, was to set new and free elections, the speedy conduct of which made perfect sense, given that the parliament's political line had so clearly diverged from the will of the people as expressed in the referendum. Of course, should Yeltsin be defeated, the prospects for his comrades-in-arms were grim; the Communists and nationalists would hardly play nice. Yet if the plan succeeded, the pendulum might well swing back sharply in the other direction. In place of a power crisis and a gelatinous government we might have a drastic and disproportionate increase in Presidential power and the breakdown of the whole system of checks and balances. That was precisely why it was such a pity that the majority had so categorically rejected the way of compromise. Still, from long-standing acquaintance, I knew that Yeltsin was not the sort of person who would use his victory to attack free speech or refuse to hold elections, or to establish an authoritarian regime.

But if you take the path of direct and open confrontation, you then must be ready to use force if necessary. And it was hard to predict how the "force structures," the military and security structures, would behave. Certainly not everything hinged on the high command. In a situation like this, much depended on chance. The fate of our enormous country might well turn on how some obscure major behaved, how some senior lieutenant interpreted an order, or what their sergeants did. It was impossible to second-guess.

On Monday, September 20, after a consultation, Chernomyrdin asked me to stay behind; he, too, asked for my assessment of the situation. I replied that I understood the motives behind the decision, that I saw how highly mobilized the opposition forces were, but that I thought the timing was bad. I realized then that we were of the same opinion. Viktor Stepanovich inquired whether I had spoken with Yeltsin on the issue, and if not, was I planning to? We agreed that I should call right away and request an urgent meeting.

I managed to reach the President almost immediately. He said that he could see me at 16:00. As I was preparing for our meeting, I decided to catch up on current business. Whatever the anxieties, whatever the situation, the government still had to run. I asked for financial data, a report on implementation of the government's action plan, and information on normative documents already in the works as well as on those still stranded somewhere in the bureaucracy. I spoke with several ministers. Shortly before our meeting time, the President's office called and said that the meeting was being postponed until tomorrow.

On the morning of the 21st, I learned from Viktor Stepanovich that he had had a long and difficult conversation with the President the day before, had tried to persuade him to postpone implementation of the plan, and had mentioned my view on the matter. But the President's decision was final, and the order would be made public that evening. The President called almost immediately after, and apologized for not receiving me today either. It was clear that he knew what I wanted to talk about, and simply didn't want to waste time discussing an issue that was already decided. Still, I felt obligated to speak out, and to present my arguments. At one point it seemed to me that he was wavering; he was silent for a moment, as if weighing all the pros and cons, and then said, "No, that's it. The decision is made. There's no going back."

And so, as we counted down the hours until the decree was made public, events entered the critical stage. Now, much would depend on organization and coordinated action. Unfortunately, I had little hope that the necessary and proper action would be taken. It wasn't merely a matter of this or that person's organizational ability. This was an extraordinary situation, an emergency, that would inevitably leave its mark on everything—and everyone. All too many people would try to dodge responsibility, avoid making decisions. They would disappear, get sick, not do things, not understand things, et cetera. All at the very worst time, and at every level.

It would soon be time for the President's television appearance. Clearly, he would deal personally with the military and security structures. But there were a myriad of other issues that might turn out to be very important. I called in Shumeiko, Shakhrai, Chubais, Kozyrev, and Yury Yarov. We sketched out a contingency plan. The mood was anxious, but businesslike. Sergei Shakhrai was rather disheartened, troubled by forebodings that the Supreme Soviet might refuse to leave the White House, which meant it would continue to function, which meant inevitable defeat.

The overall shape the situation would take during the next few hours was easy enough to predict. The Supreme Soviet would refuse to disband, and the Constitutional Court would rule the President's decree unlawful. The congress would meet in emergency session; apparently there would not be a quorum, but it would declare itself empowered to act nonetheless, swear in Aleksandr Rutskoi, confirm a new prime minister and military and security ministers, and try to take over the administrative apparatus and bring the rest of Russia over to its side.

In these next few hours it would be crucial for us to shut down the White House television channel, which had been broadcasting live ever since August 1991, and to generally cut the White House off from the rest of the world—to shut down communications, water, electricity. We would have to quash any signs of insubordination in regional administrations and make sure that federal systems remained manageable. Our strategy was clear: avoid violent confrontations and provocations, maintain calm and order, and get the electoral campaign moving as quickly as possible by forming district and ward commissions, by nominating candidates. There was some hope that many of the deputies, isolated in the White House, would simply be unable to hold out, and would rush back to their districts to enter the preelection fray. Predictably, opposition leaders would try to forestall such a turn of events. They were scared to death of elections, they didn't want to run. If the President needed order and stability to win, they needed just the opposite—tension, fighting, blood. This meant that their chief hope lay in making the standoff as hostile as possible, and its resolution purely a matter of force. Under these circumstances, which were dictated by the actual alignment of forces, it was clear that the extremist wing in the Supreme Soviet would daily, or rather hourly, take on greater weight, eventually crushing the remnants of the moderate and centrist forces.

I stopped in at Chernomyrdin's office and showed him the draft of our emergency action plan. He approved it, but rejected the idea of cutting White House communications and other vital services. This would mean, after all, cutting those same services to many of the apartment buildings located nearby.

We began receiving information about Supreme Soviet actions. It was just as we had predicted. Rutskoi was now "President." He had given a fiery speech in which he accepted responsibility for the fate of the nation. He named new ministers to head the military and security agencies— Vladislav Achalov, Andrei Dunaev, Viktor Barannikov. It was a calculated move: the three of them all had their own people in these agencies; scores, hundreds of threads connected them with people personally loyal to them within the military, the KGB, the MVD. Surprisingly, the office of prime minister remained vacant. Some unverified information came in; supposedly Rutskoi had wanted to offer it to Yury Skokov, who in April had been removed from his post as secretary of the Security Council. But Skokov, it seemed, was lying low and had dropped out of sight.

After hearing about the Supreme Soviet's resolution approving the death penalty for "particularly dangerous accomplices" of the President, Viktor Stepanovich, grimacing, rethought his decision to delay cutting off the White House telephones and issued the appropriate order.

Someone brought in a letter from Minister of Foreign Economic Relations Sergei Glaziev; he was resigning. For me, this was an unexpected blow. That Barannikov would take the opportunity to switch sides was, honestly, something I had long expected, even back when he was considered one of the most reliable and devoted people around Yeltsin. In his dealings with the President there was always that touch of obsequiousness that automatically instilled mistrust. But Sergei Glaziev, someone from my own generation, an astute economist, an old member of the team. . . . True, on the issue of the government's role in managing the economy he tended to favor a "directorial" stance, while Sergei

Vasiliev and Andrei Illarionov tended more toward a liberal one. He liked, for example, the idea of an active industrial policy, of government selection of bid winners—the famous Japanese Ministry of Industry and Trade practice, which he hoped to apply here in Russia at the Ministry of Foreign Economic Relations, to which he had been appointed as first deputy minister in November 1991. After Pyotr Aven's dismissal in December 1992, I was happy that Glaziev was the one to fill the office. Of course, it had been obvious for some time that Rutskoi was singling out Glaziev for special attention, inviting him along on practically all his foreign trips, after which Rutskoi would make a point of singing his praises and telling me that there were some great people on my team. Just recently, in August 1993—after the latest exchange of fire and mutual accusations of corruption, which in this case also involved Glaziev—Chubais, Fyodorov, and I, having not the slightest doubt about Glaziev's personal honesty, did everything we could to defend him. Just the day before, the 21st, I had brought him and a number of other ministers in for a discussion of the economic situation. We had talked over the draft of a new import tariff, about a long overdue lowering of export duties, and about cutting the export-quota list. And now he had gone over to the other camp.

Truly, you can never know someone else's mind. Yet even if it wasn't justifiable, it was understandable. Here, on our side, there were dozens of smart, young, well-educated experts. Who knew what fate would have in store for Glaziev; he would end up around seventh, maybe fourth, from the top. But Rutskoi and Khasbulatov—well, they were pretty hard up. Moreover, they were the likely winners here. So who better than Glaziev to step into the role of prime minister? I wished I were wrong, but I couldn't discount the possibility that it was this simple train of thought that carried him to the other side of the barricades, and, after the December 1993 elections, took him all the way to the leadership of the Communist-nationalist bloc in the Duma.

With the exception of Glaziev, all the ministers continued to function as usual. Control over federal systems was maintained. The government operations staff met twice daily, morning and evening. The overall picture in the first few days looked favorable enough. Rutskoi's decrees seemed more comical than anything else. Attempts by the new ministers to "lead" were ineffectual. After a day or so of hesitation, the majority of local administrations expressed their loyalty to the President. Overall, the public was taking the whole thing in without any particular enthusiasm, with a certain amount of anxiety, but also with understanding. Now we had to take our success a step further; mainly, draw the opposition into the new election process. Unfortunately, within several days it became clear that this sense of relative calm was illusory. The situation quickly turned more and more complex. We had not occupied the White House, which remained a powerful locus of opposition; and its occupants began to play out their own scenario aggressively, trying to destabilize the situation with constant and ever greater acts of provocation. They were clearly looking to shed some blood.

Large numbers of weapons had been stockpiled in the White House. They were being handed out generously, no questions asked, but mostly to paramilitary types arriving from all over the country. And then finally one opposition objective was accomplished: the first blood was shed, in an attempt to seize the headquarters of the Unified Armed Forces Command, on Leningradsky Prospekt. Two people were killed, and several were wounded.

The government took countermeasures, strengthening the cordon around the White House and pulling in reinforcements from OMON and the militia.[2] But a militia forced to stand watch day and night under a soaking rain is a perfect target for opposition agitators and provocateurs. Now the government was on the defensive; it had to relieve its troops, ensure law and order. Its chance to take action and shift the balance in its favor had not yet come.

At meetings of the government's operations group, the deputy minister of internal affairs reported that his people were tired, that the opposition was actively agitating among them. It was crucial to bring in fresh units. Security Ministry representatives, from whom I was first and foremost expecting intelligence about what was happening inside the White House, and about possible attempts at provocation, told us instead that yesterday at x hours y minutes, two foreign intelligence operatives had approached the cordon, and that one of them, a Swedish diplomat, had told the French diplomat that . . .

The opposition was organizing rallies and demonstrations. They weren't large, but they were very aggressive.

On Tuesday, September 28, we had an idea: presidential and government representatives would set up interregional conferences with administration heads and chairmen of local soviets. They would get a sense of local situations and attitudes, and would encourage and reassure people. Help them get their bearings. I was assigned the Far East. On August 30, I flew to Khabarovsk.

There I got the feeling that everyone was waiting to see what was going to happen in Moscow. For the time being they thought that the President was stronger, and remained loyal to him. The regional soviets were hardly willing to be drawn into any outright confrontation; they were more or less neutral. The recently elected head of the Amur regional administration, who had already sworn his allegiance to Rutskoi, buzzed around me, peered into my face, and claimed that he had been slandered. He vowed that he was loyal.

On the whole, there was no real regional support for the parliamentary majority to lean on. Despite constantly repeated assertions in all sorts of commentaries that the outcome of the standoff would be decided outside Moscow, my conviction grew that in Russia elections and wars may be decided in the regions, but revolutions and overthrows are decided in the capital. I flew into Komsomolsk-on-Amur and visited some defense plants now reaping what was sown by the last year's shortsighted policies. On October 2, I returned to Moscow. Here, the situation continued to deteriorate.

An agreement to restore White House water, energy, and communication lines in exchange for a surrender of weapons held by the parliament fell through. But once again, the very prospect of such an agreement heartened the opposition. This too they interpreted as a sign of weakness on the President's part; they presented more demands. Attempts to negotiate through the Patriarch led nowhere. Barricades went up on Smolensk Boulevard.

All the same, I could see no reasonable tactics other than the ones we chose at the very start: avoid provocations and insist on new elections. But the parliament building filled with armed fighters was like an enormous mine capable of destroying the Russian state, and it lay at the very heart of the city. Sporadic reports began to paint a picture suggesting that the paramilitary fighters, not the official parliamentary leaders, were now the key force inside the White House.

On Sunday morning, October 3, the President called a meeting. Present were Viktor Chernomyrdin, Sergei Filatov, Vladimir Shumeiko, Oleg Lobov, Sergei Shakhrai, Pavel Grachev, Viktor Yerin, and several others. We discussed our visits to other regions of the country; many of us had just barely returned. The conversation was fairly calm. A rough summary might be as follows: for the time being, control over basic federal structures has been maintained, neither unrest nor major acts of insubordination are anticipated, and regional authorities are loyal and will hold elections. The situation in Moscow was not specifically discussed. The information that today was the day the opposition planned to make its move was something that the Ministry of Security either did not possess or had decided not to share with the rest of the government.

After the meeting I went to my office on Old Square. In the three days I had been gone, a massive amount of work had piled up, and I wanted to use this Sunday to sort out the pile. I had arranged for a three o'clock meeting with Professor V. Starodubrovsky, whom I had recently asked to set up an expert review of federal programs adopted in the past year, the idea being to isolate what was of principal importance. During our chat, at around four o'clock, a call came in from Aleksei Golovkov, who in 1992 had been my right-hand man, head of the government apparatus, and was now one of the chief organizers of Russia's Choice. He excitedly told me that there were major disturbances going on in the city, that the cordon had been breached and a number of militiamen disarmed, and that city hall was under attack.

It had happened, the very thing we feared most. The opposition had managed to turn the standoff into open war, to channel it into violence. The time for political maneuvering was over. Now readiness, organization, the will to act, to press—these would decide the outcome. The first small flames of another civil war were licking at the sky over Moscow.

Vyacheslav Bragin, chairman of Ostankino Radio and Television, called to say he had information that a column of trucks and buses carrying opposition fighters was making its way from the White House to the television station. He asked me to organize a defense.

This time around, my job in government was economics, and only economics. The only armed forces officially under my command were the three security men who had worked with me ever since I was prime minister. My fourth bodyguard, their newly appointed chief, dropped out of sight about midday. It was no surprise that today even direct orders would end up being carried out in slow motion.

Meanwhile, the telephone was ringing off the hook. People demanded action, help, protection. I called Yerin and relayed Bragin's request for support. He assured me that the team had already been assigned, units were on the way, and everything would be fine. I contacted the President and asked him if the Emergency Decree was ready. The President answered that it was being drafted, that Sergei Shakhrai was working on the text.

Again the anxious voice of Bragin on the phone: "Where are the reinforcements you promised? Those we have now clearly won't be enough." Oleg Poptsov, chairman of Russian Radio and Television, got on the line: "They'll be coming after us next, and over here by the Belorussky and Shabolovsky stations there are no defenses at all."

I needed an independent intelligence source, and I tracked down Aleksandr Dolgalev, one of the leaders of "August '91," an organization of people who had come to the White House's defense during the coup. His men generally had good information about everything going on in Moscow. I asked him to organize his people and to regularly—once every half hour—report on the developing situation.

The news now filtering in through a variety of channels painted a grim picture. Efforts by the internal affairs minister, who was clearly trying to do everything he could, had yielded no tangible results. City hall had surrendered, the OMON commandos were demoralized, and the militia was nowhere to be seen. Opposition fighters were acting boldly and decisively, ever more surely taking command of the situation.

We received information that an attack on the Ministry of Defense building had been launched. Not able to reach Grachev on the phone, I contacted his first deputy, Andrei Kokoshin. The general sense of chaos and indecision merely increased. I realized perfectly well how difficult it would be under these circumstances to get the army to move. Over the last few years we had said time and time again that the army should remain outside politics, that it should not be pulled into internal political conflicts. This became in some sense an article of faith, compellingly affirmed in August 1991. None of us had ever discussed the possibility of using the army in a political struggle. Even in the most extreme cases, the only question was whether to call in internal security forces, the militia, the security service. But events on October 3 had shown that the demoralized militia and internal troops were incapable of keeping order in Moscow, and meanwhile the armed detachments mounted by the opposition were about to clear the road to power for some irresponsible and dangerous extremists. It became obvious that we had to call in army units immediately.

But would orders reach them, would orders be obeyed? Might it not just happen that, as in August 1991, the military machine would refuse to budge, and we'd be left with nothing but communiqués and the appearance of action? No one—including the defense ministry and the President—could answer that question with any certainty.

The opposition had made an apt choice for its first strike. Its leaders had rightly assessed the potential of television, in this case the most powerful medium for influencing the situation. The capture of Ostankino, a television appeal by Rutskoi—these would have created the sort of atmosphere that would lead anyone still hesitating, in Moscow or in the regions, to declare their allegiance to the "victor." And all that separated Russia from the terrible things that might follow was a handful of Vityaz troops.[3]

The Ostankino channel went off the air. Things looked very bad.

Chernomyrdin had set a cabinet meeting for 19:30. But it was late getting started. The ministers milled around the doorway of the small auditorium on the fifth floor, quietly exchanging news. Or maybe rumors? People were saying that the Radio House next to Smolensk Square had been occupied. Also that something belonging to the Ministry of Communications was captured. And something else at the Ministry of Fuel and Energy.

Memoirs describing the atmosphere at the last meeting of the Provisional Government came to mind. I recalled Vladimir Dmitrievich Nabokov's words: "All the ministers were in the hall, except for N. M. Kishkin. . . . The ministers were clustered in little groups, some pacing back and forth, others standing by the window; S. N. Tretyakov sat down beside me and began to talk indignantly about how Kerensky had abandoned them, betrayed them, how the situation was hopeless. Others said that all they had to do was 'hold out for another 48 hours, and by that time troops loyal to the government will have reached Petersburg.'"[4] The evening of October 3 at Old Square seemed very like this.

Most surprising of all was the news about the capture of the State Customs Committee building. My first thought was—why? It was only later that I learned of "Rutskoi's list." He had assigned Customs the task of detaining members of the government who, he supposed, were about to make a dash for the border. They were to be arrested and promptly remanded to the White House for trial and sentencing. And although the list, which started with the chairman of the Soviet of Ministers, was quite extensive and included quite a few notable figures, neither the President's name, nor the defense minister's, nor mine was on it. Apparently this particular trio was not to be transported very far.

As I recall, we were still waiting for the meeting to begin when Yury Luzhkov appeared on the television screen. He appealed to the people of Moscow to maintain order and calm. To my mind, what he said had absolutely nothing to do with the real situation. Who exactly was supposed to maintain order and calm? The mercenaries storming the television station? The Russian citizens being robbed of their freedom this very night? You might call for order and calm if you were sure that there actually were troops loyal to the President, and that they would in fact obey orders. But now, when here in Moscow the fate of the nation was being decided, sending grown men off to bed like little children was absurd. Instead, we should be relying on the people who had twice, in August 1991 and April 1993, clearly chosen freedom.

Eight o'clock. The siege of Ostankino continued, and opposition fighters captured new positions. MVD forces were demoralized, and no army units arrived to back them up. The opposition had almost succeeded in convincing the populace that this was a mass movement and that the President stood alone. All this served to discourage anyone willing to help.

I decided that we needed to turn to the people of Moscow for support. First, I called Sergei Shoigu, chairman of the emergency committee. We had worked together before. Bold and decisive, he had proved his worth in other hot spots—Ossetia, Tadzhikistan, Moldova. I asked that he report back on what weapons his civil defense system had on hand in and around Moscow and, if the situation warranted, that he prepare to issue 1,000 automatic weapons and ammunition immediately. I could tell from his voice that he was nervous, that he understood quite well what an enormous responsibility this was. It was also clear that he would follow government orders.

I contacted Viktor Yerin. If we didn't make a public appeal, I said, things would get worse. He concurred and promised to help in any way he could.

I called the President and told him that I thought it expedient to appeal to people directly. He also concurred.

I directed Dolgalev to concentrate his people around the Mossoviet building. And I asked businessmen who had their own security forces to provide as much trained backup as they could.

I headed for the prime minister's office. Through the corridors of the

normally proper and decorous executive fifth floor, agitated civil ser-
vants scurried back and forth. One ran up to me and shouted, "Don't you
understand it's all over! In another hour they'll slaughter us all!"

Viktor Stepanovich was calm; he was holding up well. He requested
cash from the Central Bank in case of a blockade of the government's
offices. I passed along the order to the first deputy minister of finance,
Andrei Vavilov, and I myself informed the prime minister that I was on
my way to Russian Television to make an appeal to the people of Moscow; from there I would go to Mossoviet. Before leaving I just managed
to sit down in my office and sketch out a brief introduction for the *Echo
of Moscow* program. I took Arkady Murashov, a Russia's Choice colleague and former head of the Moscow militia, with me.

Moscow was deserted—no militia, no troops, no one on the street. In
the car we listened to triumphant opposition communiqués: *We are winning, or rather, we've already won. There will be no compromises, Russia
can do without this President. The Yeltsinoids' final hour is at hand. . . .*

We pulled up to Russian Television. The entryway was barricaded. After long and wary negotiations between my security men and the television station's, they finally let us in. Poptsov was very nervous. After the
attack on Ostankino, he was expecting an assault. He couldn't understand why no one was sending soldiers to protect the station. The way
things were, they would not be able to hold out for more than a few minutes. As we were talking, word came through that the Itar-Tass building
had been occupied.

I contacted Yerin again and asked for at least some kind of protection
for Russian Television. Now I could see for myself that they had no defenses at all. He promised to help.

The TV camera lens was already trained on me when I stopped and
asked to be left alone in the studio for a minute. Somehow the flush of
excitement had suddenly drained away, and in its place came a wave of
alarm for those I was about to call out of their quiet apartments and into
the streets of Moscow. What a terrible responsibility for their lives I was
taking upon myself. But there was no way around it. In reading and
rereading documents and memoirs about 1917, I had often caught my-

self wondering how it was that tens of thousands of cultured, honorable, and honest citizens of Petersburg, any number of military officers among them, could have let a relatively small group of extremists seize power so easily. Why did everyone keep waiting for someone else—the Provisional Government, Kerensky, Kornilov, Krasnov—to save them?[5] We all know how the story ended. That thought, probably, is what in the end outweighed my doubts. And so, without hesitation, with a sense that I was in the right, I made my speech.

After the TV appearance we went to the Mossoviet building. A little earlier, driving by, we had seen a small cluster of *druzhinniki*, volunteer patrols, at the entrance. Now the square was filling up with streams—soon to be torrents—of people coming up from the Hotel Moskva side or down from Pushkin Square. They were here! And they were already building barricades, lighting bonfires. They knew what was going on in the city, and had just seen television reports on the fighting around Ostankino. They were railing at the government, at the democrats, and probably at me as well, cursing us for not being able to handle that scum ourselves without putting people in danger, without dragging them away from their warm homes, their families. They were right to curse us. But they kept coming to Mossoviet. Oh yes, they were planning on sorting out later who was at fault, who didn't do what, or did it wrong. But right now they were coming, unarmed, to defend their country's future, and their children's. To keep another set of extremists from bullying their way to power.

Groups of officers, ready to arm themselves if necessary, were already forming around the statue of Yury Dolgoruky. But that was just in case of emergency. I very much hoped the weapons wouldn't be needed. The crowd reminded me of the one that stood in front of the White House in August 1991. The same eyes. The same kind, intelligent faces. But, perhaps, the mood now was even grimmer, tenser. Somewhere in this crowd were my father, my brother, my nephew. And I knew for certain that many of my friends, allies, and classmates were there too.

I made a short speech to the assembled crowd, telling them that the opposition fighters had been repulsed at Ostankino. I asked them to stay here, to stay concentrated in one place, to organize themselves into squads and if necessary be ready to provide backup for troops loyal to the President.

The main entrance to the Mossoviet building was closed. With some difficulty, crawling over barricades, we got in through a side entrance. Not too long before this, the opposition had controlled part of the building. A group of Mossoviet deputies had tried to organize a command point, but now Luzhkov's people had cleared the area. Luzhkov himself was animated, excited, even cheerful. I asked Murashov to set up communications between the *druzhinniki* and the militia. I contacted Viktor Chernomyrdin by phone to tell him about the situation here at the capital's center, and ask what was known about any troops moving up. On the whole, the picture was unclear, slow to change, but the opposition's first burst of activity seemed to be petering out.

I spoke to the crowd once more, and then it was into the car and over to the Saviour Tower, another gathering point. From the car windows I could see that Moscow was transformed, awake. Crowds of people, bonfires flickering, songs, ranks of *druzhinniki*. Now that they had come together, people sensed their own strength. They were confident.

At Saviour Tower on Red Square, where people had come on their own initiative, the mood was more anxious; they were having trouble getting organized. An officer approached me, introduced himself as a retired colonel, asked for orders, some help. Over at Mossoviet the ranks were holding firm. Here, perhaps, was our most vulnerable spot.

Back at my office I met with Chubais, Saltykov, Pamfilova, Vasiliev, and Ulyukaev. I eagerly asked them for news of everything that had happened in my absence. There was frustratingly little information. I asked the ministers to go out to the various rallies, to speak, to brace up the martial mood. In general, one night like this tells you more about a person's character than many long years of acquaintance. One of our people suddenly panicked and left. But the rest were calm, even courageous. For example, Vasily Vasilievich Barchuk, chairman of the Pension Fund Administration, was no longer young and had a bad heart. The evening that Ostankino had fallen silent, he rushed in from his dacha without changing clothes, ready to do whatever he could.

At around midnight there was finally a break in the situation. The illusion that this was an uprising against a hostile regime with no popular support began to dissipate. The President's supporters were coming out of their initial state of paralysis and disarray. By this time I was absolutely sure that we wouldn't let power in Russia fall into the hands of the Anpilovs, Barkashovs, and their ilk.[6] Even if the MVD wasn't able to restore order in its ranks by morning, and even if the army remained passive. If that happened we would simply arm the *druzhinniki* and take action ourselves. I had no doubt that we could do it.

Something came to mind from Fyodor Raskolnikov's memoir, *Kronstadt and Petrograd in 1917*: "If the Provisional Government had managed to muster the resolve, then by simply placing a pair of gun batteries on the banks of the sea canal it could easily have blocked the Kronstadt ships from getting to the mouth of the Neva. . . . But, fortunately, thanks to the general panic and dismay in the Kerensky government, that thought never occurred to anyone. . . ."[7]

At around two o'clock in the morning I spoke with Boris Yeltsin by phone. His voice was tired, even hoarse, but much more confident than earlier: The troops were coming! They've moved out! They were on their way to Moscow!

I could guess that it must have cost him dearly to make that happen. I told him that in my opinion, he, as President, should meet with the military even before their units entered Moscow. They should see him in person, and receive their orders from him personally. Otherwise the risk remained that the army still wouldn't begin to act. The victory would be ours in any case, but there could be more bloodshed.

At five-thirty in the morning the President called back to say that he'd done what I asked.

Anyone who didn't actually experience that evening of October 3, 1993, who didn't see the terrible danger looming over the country, who didn't have to call people out into the streets of Moscow, may have difficulty understanding my feelings when the first round of tank fire resounded over the White House. The first thought that came to mind was that now we wouldn't have to hand out weapons to all those people who had trusted in me; we wouldn't have to send them to fight.

October 5. Order is restored to Moscow, other regions profess emphatic loyalty, the threat of civil war has passed. But the political problems, of course, are far from resolved, and in some ways have become even more profound.

Chapter 12

Lost Opportunities

- The chief casualty is democracy
- Mercedes for the government
- Face-to-face with populism
- Inexplicable euphoria
- The leading role
- Elections
- Letter of resignation
- RDC in the Duma
- The creation of a political party

To sum it all up politically—on October 3 and 4, 1993, a brief civil war was fought in Moscow. Communist and nationalist armed units, acting with determination and forcefulness, were close to taking control of key points in Moscow—which meant Russia's key points as well. The armed forces hesitated for a long time, and went into action only after the public came out in clear support of the President. Over 150 people were killed at the Ostankino broadcasting station and the White House.

No radical opposition leaders or deputies were hurt. The one who perhaps disgraced himself the most was "President" Rutskoi, as he alternately called for the air force to bomb the Kremlin and for foreign ambassadors to ensure his precious safety, then later displayed his automatic weapon still in its packing grease as his chief alibi. Twelve tank rounds were fired at the White House—ten dummies, two incendiary.

After a time the tension of real battle, the tormenting anxiety that had enveloped millions of people throughout Russia and the world on the evening of October 3, when the outcome of the conflict was still undetermined, would disappear. Many of those who on that evening exhorted the President to take the most forceful action possible would soon utterly disavow their own words and hasten to assign him sole responsibility for everything that took place. And the image of tanks firing on the White House would long remain in public memory, sowing doubts about the stability of Russian democratic institutions.

Unfortunately, there was a price to be paid for the political elites' inability to compromise, to avoid the use of force, and it immediately became clear that the first casualty was democracy itself. On the morning of October 3, President Yeltsin was still only one of many players on the Russian scene, the first among equals, conducting complex negotiations mediated by the Patriarch, trying to find his way out of the political cul-de-sac. On the morning of October 5, all the power in the country was in his hands. We had leaped from gelatinous *dvoevlastie* into a de facto authoritarian regime that a good part of the nation, tired of *dvoevlastie* and wishful of a restoration of normal order, would support or at least not actively oppose.

Outwardly, this manifested itself in a change in Yeltsin's own position, and could be felt in the behavior of those around him, as well as in how the leaders of the Moscow and regional elites and the CIS heads of state now dealt with him. Essentially, this was when the first jarringly lordly notes began appearing in the President's voice. In October 1993, more than at any other time before or since, the choice was Yeltsin's—which path would Russia take? And he made his choice. In this radically new situation, the constitution now submitted to the voters was not the balanced compromise worked out the previous summer at the constitutional conference, but a much more rigid and typically "presidential" version. Still, Boris Yeltsin had enough sense to avoid a sharp shift in the direction of authoritarianism. The state of emergency was soon lifted. Outspoken opposition newspapers, *Pravda* and *Sovetskaya Rossiya*, continued to appear on newsstands. No censorship, either "harsh" or "mild," was introduced. Instead, a date for a referendum on the new constitution and election of a new parliament was set.

The democratic forces' prospects for the upcoming elections hardly looked bright. Until October 4, *dvoevlastie* was something the public knew and acknowledged, which meant that the President and his government had to answer for the country's plight only to a limited degree. Now that *dvoevlastie* had been eliminated, the government could no longer plead mitigating circumstances. Meanwhile, by fall the economic policy time bomb that had been lit back in spring and summer of 1993, the policy of generous commitments but actual underfinancing, had exploded. Unfulfilled promises of payment for military procurement orders, payments for grain already delivered, subsidies guaranteed but never introduced, and delays in paying doctors' and teachers' salaries and military pay had all turned into a terribly acute political problem.

Moreover, the government could not justify itself in any way. It is in fact dishonest to promise something and then not do it. But to keep every one of those empty promises handed out so generously in the months previous would have undermined the Russian economy, its monetary system; it would have meant stepping onto the path of financial ruin, the consequences of which were so vividly coming to light in our neighboring states—Ukraine, Belarus, Kazakhstan.

In spite of staunch resistance by Minister of Finance Boris Fyodorov, surplus monies far exceeding the Russian economy's means were still flowing into the agricultural sector in an attempt to keep obviously unprofitable and unviable enterprises afloat.

Every country's economy has its so-called lag—the time between the moment or the period when the government drastically increases the amount of money in circulation and the moment when the corresponding rise in inflation rates begins. When we initiated reforms, we could only guess what that time lag, given the specific conditions then prevailing in Russia, might be. Now, in the fall of 1993, that figure had defined itself rather clearly—it was five months. The reverse phenomenon occurs at the very same interval; only in four to five months would any tightening of monetary policy make itself felt in a drop in the rate of inflation. Hence the austerity policy to which the government, seeing a genuine threat of hyperinflation, had returned in September and October 1993 would have no real effect on restraining price growth until February 1994. And the elections were slated for December 12.

If you set yourself no moral boundaries, if your chief end is power and the end justifies the means, then creating an economic base to ensure an election victory isn't particularly complicated. It would be enough, now that the opposition had been crushed, to pump up the volume of lending by the Central Bank, pay off all debts at one blow, and give compelling proof on a level that any family can understand of how kind, generous, and loving a stronger government could be if only the opposition weren't always throwing a monkey wrench into the works. And you could worry about paying for it all with an inflationary spurt later, after the elections were won.

But for me that was out of the question. It would be dishonorable to do that to the country. And besides, life wouldn't end in December 1993. How would we get ourselves out of our financial mess afterward? Yet the problem created by unfulfilled obligations was real, and there were no easy solutions. The only reasonable thing to do in the situation was to promptly stop any further advances or promises, and cut the flow of state obligations. All resources from current tax revenues should be used to repay first-priority debts.

The government decided to eliminate grain subsidies, to stop issuing the low-interest loans that were overburdening the budget, to give up indexation of state capital investments for the fourth quarter of the year, to begin a graduated increase in housing rents, and to review all federal programs passed in 1993 — concentrating our meager resources on what was essential, what the budget would bear.

This was the only way to go. But I soon became convinced that, given the changes within the government, my own prospects for effectively carrying out such a policy were quite limited. The feed subsidy story was graphic proof. That summer the agrarian lobby, after squeezing the government to pay wholesale prices far exceeding current market value of grain, proceeded quite unabashedly to seek budget subsidies for agricultural enterprises that would use this expensive grain to manufacture livestock feed. The logic was admirable: first use budget money to pay me sky-high prices for grain, then give me some more because this grain is so pricey. The government had wavered and promised to pay, but then for lack of money in the budget had not even begun to do so.

Firmly convinced that if there was clearly no money for it, we ought to say so right off, I raised the issue and pushed through a resolution officially eliminating any yet-unpaid subsidies for feed. But quite literally the next day Chernomyrdin overturned the decision, and these empty commitments were extended.

It was all extraordinarily difficult. Truly, it was like cleaning the Augean stable. Documents long ago prepared, long needed, now late by a good six months—documents on liberalizing foreign trade, on cutting the list of goods subject to quota, on lowering export fees, on protecting the rights of shareholders, on housing reform—lay gathering dust on official desks. Time and again I was persuaded that the government apparatus, which had in the past year changed and swelled out of all proportion, had become utterly amorphous and incapable of action. Only if you dealt personally with every single normative act proposed, and only if you never let it out of your sight when conferring with the prime minister, would you get any sort of results. Otherwise everything was written in sand and washed away without a trace.

There was a noticeable change in working style. The pomposity, the monumentality of years past seemed to take over once again. In 1992, I was firmly convinced that the government was obliged to shoulder the crisis along with the rest of the nation and could not permit itself any sort of excess. Only then would it have the moral right to enact harsh or socially controversial measures. I was always willing to let anyone check the Ministry of Finance's books and suggest what we could, and therefore should, do without.

Of course, frugality is one thing, and stupidity is another. A prime minister who takes a streetcar to work—well, that may play well for political campaigns, but it's a luxury a country can't afford. The whole thing comes down to common sense, and so when I heard proposals from time to time about purchasing a fleet of Mercedes, or commissioning a new line of luxury cars for the leadership, I categorically waved them away. When in 1992 the secret service proposed purchasing a fleet of Mercedes automobiles for use by members of the government, I answered that we had only one President, and that anything that he needed for his security was fine. But that I myself used a Volga to get to work, and there was nothing preventing other cabinet members from doing the same.[1] Gradually I began to notice that my stance was annoying some people. I'll grant that much of this might have been done not because of anyone's penchant for luxury or conspicuous display, but because Russian tradition held that such things would promote "respect" for authority. But it didn't sit right with me. The same sort of overkill, by the way, came up in the White House remodeling story and in the plan for a new parliament building. Modesty in government was no longer the norm.

It was obvious, too, how much the atmosphere around Boris Yeltsin had changed. In 1992, when I headed his government, it was unthinkable that some Korzhakov or Barsukov should intervene in economic policy.[2] They were security men, nothing more. Now the fact of their drastically increased influence was an open secret.

Instead of a clear-cut and consistent line on rules and fair play, instead of a unified tax and customs system, after October 1993 we had a stream of rather strange decisions on individual tax breaks. There was a definite tilt in the direction of corrupt bureaucratic capitalism, with its intertwining of property and government. And my influence and resources were clearly insufficient to stop any of it.

And so, as it turned out, soon after the October rumbling of tank fire fell silent, and the political situation stabilized, I began to wonder just how long-lasting or useful my second "call-up" for government work would really be.

Meanwhile, efforts to reduce unbacked government obligations and to control the budget crisis began to yield results. Average monthly rates of growth in the money supply for October through December were around 10 percent. That meant that by spring of 1994, rates of inflation should drop to the same level. Of course, by the standards of stable market economies this figure was too high; the threat of hyperinflation was, however, behind us.

But here's the thing. What was a success in terms of the country's economic future could, in an election campaign, lead to a major defeat. Custom has it that politicians in power have to answer for other people's mistakes; no one remembers, or wants to remember, that these empty promises were handed out in the spring and summer, when you yourself had no part whatsoever in running the government. The first sprouts of financial stability take a long time to grow and mature, and meanwhile unpopular decisions like the abolition of grain subsidies or low-interest loans come back at you, and come back in very painful fashion. And so we end up having to pursue an economic line that could turn out to be a political boomerang. By that I mean the approaching election deadline.

By the end of 1992, and my dismissal, the democratic movement in Russia had become a rather sorry spectacle. It still had fairly powerful public support, and Yeltsin's popularity remained high. Democratic rallies, when well planned, drew tens of thousands of people. But the organizational weakness and fragmentation of the democratic camp were becoming more noticeable all the time. The most powerful group on our end of the political spectrum, Democratic Russia, was in a state of near collapse. One new political faction after another kept emerging from it, while DemRossiya itself was quite amorphous, with no fixed membership, no publications of its own, no working public-relations system, no money, no leaders of any stature. Some of the structures that had come out of DemRossiya—among others, the Republican party, which was based on the former democratic platform within the Communist Party—were better organized, but very small in numbers and had little clout. Tiny new democratic groups representative of little but their leaders' own ambitions were constantly popping up.

Understanding the reasons underlying the democracy movement's weakness is hardly a complicated task. The intelligentsia, which had been the engine of democratic change, was by its very nature alien to organized political activity. Its dislike had been honed to particular sharpness by decades spent under the yoke of a well-organized Communist Party. But the fact that it was all understandable didn't make things any easier.

For me, the need for reformers to be actively involved in political work was an issue posed during my visit to Prague in spring of 1992, by Vaclav Klaus, then minister of finance for Czechoslovakia. At the time it was important to me to demonstrate that Eastern and Central Europe remained one of Russia's highest economic and political priorities, and that we had no intention of pulling out, but instead had a real interest in creating new market mechanisms to foster cooperation.

Many of those who had occasion to carry out reforms in postsocialist nations were terrifically envious of Klaus. He'd drawn two valuable trump cards. The Czech Communists had left the country in relative financial order, with a low level of foreign debt and limited financial distortions. Traditional Czech financial discretion had outweighed the destructive tendencies of late, crumbling socialism. National character, including the Czechs' stalwart "petit-bourgeois" tendencies so detested by Lenin, also played a role.

Klaus was remarkably successful in playing his trumps. Of course, Czechoslovakia too saw a sharp drop in industrial production during the first three years of reform, an increase in social inequity, and a jump in prices as soon as they were freed. But here the creation of a base for market growth was far less controversial, and support for the changes undertaken was far greater. It's no accident that Klaus was the only reformer to remain at the helm throughout five difficult years.

As a very young man Klaus had taken part in the short-lived Czech reform efforts of 1967–68 and had served as deputy chairman of the National Bank; he then sat on the sidelines for many years, working as an accountant. It was only in the late eighties, when the Czech regime, influenced by Soviet perestroika, became slightly more liberal, that he was allowed to do scholarly work at the Institute for [Financial] Forecasting, known at the time in Prague as the "dissidents' institute." Life's vicissitudes had left their mark on his character, making Klaus rather harsh and stubborn—a man sometimes inclined to say things for their shock value.

Our conversation in the spring of 1992 turned out to be both surprising and important for me. At the time, I was totally involved in the transformations, and my head was full of numbers and graphs, inflation indices and growth percentages. Klaus and I discussed all that, and then he abruptly turned the conversation to politics. The overall sense of his words was this: "I told Balcerowicz and he didn't listen, and now I'm telling you—all these economic subtleties are interesting, and we can all understand them in the long run, but if you can't create a political base of support for market reforms, you'll forever be hostage to whatever unexpected moves the people who brought you into the government in the first place are going to make. And that can easily cancel out anything you're now doing or planning to do. Your most crucial task is to consolidate the political forces capable of providing a support base for the reforms. How often do you appear in public, in front of audiences, to explain your views, to convince people that you're right? Not all that often? Well, I don't begrudge the time I spend doing that; I go out several times a week."

Of course, the easiest thing would have been to brush off what he said, to object that proving the necessity of liberal reforms was, in Czechoslovakia, a country that was bourgeois through and through, hardly the same as creating such a base of support in Russia. Yet this conversation forced me to give some serious thought to the question of political backing for the transformations we had begun.

As prime minister I had well realized how serious were the problems brought on by the democratic movement's organizational weakness and helplessness. For all the democrats' sincere and selfless willingness to support the tough policies of 1992, fragmentation and weakness in the democratic camp drastically reduced the effectiveness of such support.

Democratic leaders competing among themselves for influence had suggested often enough that I join the political fray, and asked for my help. I turned down all such offers on the grounds that this wasn't really my field of expertise. But I was ready to provide help for any group that could unite as broad a range of democrats as possible. There was a growing need for such a union, especially in the spring of 1993, when preparations for the referendum began. It was crucial that democratic forces win it.

We met fairly often—sometimes at Gennady Burbulis's, sometimes at Arkady Murashov's, and sometimes at my office. The makeup of the group varied, but it included Aleksandr Yakovlev, Gavriil Popov, Sergei Shakhrai, Gleb Yakunin, Lev Ponomaryov, Vladimir Lysenko, Sergei Kovalyov, Boris Zolotukhin, Anatoly Sobchak, Sergei Yushenkov, and Mikhail Poltoranin. We discussed recent developments, and worked out agreements on joint action. And every time the same question arose— what about after the referendum? It was widely understood that the most probable result of the power crisis would be early elections in the fall of 1993 or, at the latest, the spring of 1994. To go into the elections in a weak and organizationally fragmented state was exceedingly risky. Hence the constant discussions of how to get the democrats to unite, how to form a democratic organization capable of real action.

The crux of the problem was this. Given the complex tangle of relations already formed within them, existing democratic structures—first and foremost DemRossiya—were hardly likely to serve as a base for unification. At the same time, any attempt to build a new organization would inevitably mean a crisis in the existing one, and new and unneeded conflict. Gradually two alternatives crystallized: the creation of either a broad preelection bloc without any internal organizational structure, which would unite existing groups, or a new organization intended to replace existing ones. The most vigorous supporters of the first option were the leaders of DemRossiya—Lev Ponomaryov, Gleb Yakunin, and Ilya Zaslavsky. Support for the second came from Gennady Burbulis, Arkady Murashov, and Aleksei Golovkov—people whose relationship with the leadership of DemRossiya had not been particularly smooth.

In late spring and early summer my role in these negotiations was more as mediator than anything else. I tried to reconcile the broadest possible range of like-minded people, who might share the same overall stance on strategy and platform, but were alienated from one another by what in my view were petty, tactical, or sometimes merely ambition-driven concerns. I tried to reconcile everyone with everybody, work out compromise proposals, deflect ultimatums. Only gradually did I begin to understand that the logic of events was dragging me into a role I was utterly unaccustomed to playing. I was becoming a leader of the Russian democracy movement.

Among the factors at work here were my previous lack of involvement in politics and the absence of any history of longstanding mutual grievances or grudges from years past. The democrats had supported our policy in 1992. In the referendum of April 1993 they had supported the President, which included casting a "yes" vote on that most complicated second question on the ballot: do you support the government's economic policy? I, the person most closely identified with that policy, unexpectedly turned out to be one of the least controversial figures on the democratic end of the political spectrum.

The role of a democracy movement leader was remarkably uncomfortable for me; it didn't feel right. I was well aware of my weaknesses as a public politician, a person called upon to campaign, to explain, to win elections. At the same time, I recognized how fragmented and weak democratic organizations were. The people who supported us in 1992 had a moral right to expect something from me in return. Right now what they needed from me was my name, which might help them unite. I mulled over all this for quite a long time, and in the end I couldn't bring myself to refuse. It might be a serious mistake; after all, making a democracy movement leader out of a person whose name, for most people, was associated with loss and hardship, was probably dangerous.

We were trying to reconcile democrats by the fall of 1993. Our guiding principle was this: bring together all those who agree on major issues. We ruled out anyone setting ultimatums or insisting that this, that, or the other democracy group be excluded from the alliance. What emerged was Russia's Choice, a broad-based electoral bloc made up of scores of democratic organizations. On the whole, it was a remarkably amorphous structure with no organizational integrity whatsoever. Conflicts in the "center" were complemented by fierce squabbles on the periphery. The campaign staff had to deal with the claims of any number of candidates from each district, each convinced that he and he alone truly represented Russia's Choice. The tragic events of October 1993 only complicated the situation.

For all that, many democratically oriented politicians seemed to be in an incomprehensible state of euphoria, probably the effect of April's referendum victory. The prevailing feeling was that the upcoming elections were already won. The only question was which one of the democratic leaders would end up in first place. Along with Russia's Choice, Sergei Shakhrai's PRES (Party of Unity and Accord), Anatoly Sobchak's RDDR (Democratic Reform Movement), and Grigory Yavlinsky's Yabloko party would be on the ballot. My calls for democratic unity in the face of a possible Communist comeback were taken skeptically: "What's Gaidar panicking about? What Communists? They're done for!"

What was happening was dangerous. Particularly absurd was that members of one and the same government were campaigning under two different banners, for two different and rival blocs—Russia's Choice and PRES. I tried to talk Shakhrai into withdrawing his list of candidates, and offered him the top slot as leader of the Russia's Choice slate; I myself hardly cherished the job and would have loved handing all the preelection fuss over to one of the politicians. All the more because as first deputy prime minister of the government I was dealing with some extremely difficult stabilization issues. Miners were about to go on strike. Grain prices had just been liberalized. We were fighting a tough battle with the agrarian lobby over the funding commitments they had managed to extract, but which never had any resources to back them.

Sergei, however, turned down my offer. Perhaps because there were several people in Russia's Choice whose radical-democratic past might hurt his chances. A lot of people still had it in for Gaidar, after all. Later, one month before the elections, the Moscow city government in the person of Yury Mikhailovich Luzhkov organized coalition talks among leading democratic blocs. Representatives of Russia's Choice, Yabloko, PRES, and RDDR were working out a preliminary document. We met at Luzhkov's office—Yavlinsky, Shakhrai, Popov, Burbulis, and I. Luzhkov insisted that this had to be a joint effort. Then each of us articulated his position. It became clear that neither Yavlinsky, nor Shakhrai, nor Popov was ready to sign a unification agreement. I stood alone, in far from splendid isolation.

Up to my ears in official concerns, I became increasingly convinced that as one of the founders of Russia's Choice, I could more or less manage the role of mediator in reconciling numerous democratic organizations, but certainly not the role of campaign organizer. Moreover, there were any number of experienced and talented politicians in Russia's Choice, all of whom had a far better feeling for rough-and-tumble campaigning than I did. There was Gennady Burbulis, for example, who headed our campaign staff. Or Mikhail Poltoranin, who ran public relations, or Aleksei Golovkov, the executive secretary. I was willing to follow their orders, to go where I was told, to take part in television debates, but certainly not to be a strategist or organizer for the whole thing.

A key question for us was Yeltsin's stance. Russia's Choice came together as a bloc of people who supported and continued to support his policies. He was, in fact, our natural political leader. In late fall of 1993 he still had tremendous public support. This meant that if there was a clearly designated Yeltsin bloc on the ballot, the choice for voters was rather simple and clear—either yes or no to the policy he undertook in 1991. And so there was a real chance of success, of markedly strengthening the democrats' position in newly elected governmental bodies. On October 10 the President and I flew to Japan. On the way we discussed the political situation, and we agreed that on the 17th he would attend the Russia's Choice convention.

After our return, I learned that the President had changed his mind, that he would not come after all. Apparently some of his closest aides persuaded him that he should act the role of father of the nation, and refuse to intervene in the ongoing political struggle and parliamentary elections. I think that this was a political mistake. His departure from the preelection fray, under a democratic banner, prompted a certain amount of confusion among his supporters, and played into the hands of the Communists and nationalists.

The election campaign was not going well. The democrats' confidence in an easy win, instilled by the October victory and bolstered by the press and by public opinion polls, was backfiring. A certain flippancy and carelessness on their part was demobilizing the democratic electorate. Meanwhile the country's economic situation was hardly a simple one. We were straining mightily to deal with the consequences of the summer's economic and political mistakes, of demagoguery and empty promises. We were passing one unpopular resolution after another. And naturally, Russia's Choice would have to bear the responsibility for all these government measures.

It was also natural that, for tactical reasons, PRES and the other democratic parties and groups were striving to distance themselves from the government and from Russia's Choice. But what was unnatural was that by criticizing us they were willy-nilly aligning themselves with the Communists and nationalists-patriots. And the President remained silent, above the fray.

Personal problems arose as well. Ratings of various politicians' level of influence, regularly published in the newspapers, showed that I was just behind the President, pushing Viktor Chernomyrdin back into third place, and later Yeltsin himself into second. It was the sort of nonsense that smacked of provocation. After all, many people remembered Chernomyrdin's appointment in December 1992 as a sort of forced compromise, a concession by Yeltsin to the opposition. And so rumors were spreading that a democratic win would bring a change of leadership in the government and that the evil Gaidar would again be at its head! None of this, to put it bluntly, made for good relations in the upper echelons of Russian government, or in the campaign.

Boris Nikolaevich said nothing, but nonetheless, for the first time in all these months, I felt a little chill, a distance. Viktor Stepanovich, for his part, regularly brought the conversation around to postelection prospects. The prospects were complicated ones, but I tried to reassure him, and promised to support him as prime minister. I had the impression he wanted firmer guarantees.

The final week before the 1993 elections brought alarming news. According to surveys done by the central polling office, support for Vladimir Zhirinovsky was growing rapidly and was now at practically the same level as support for Russia's Choice. If that tendency continued, his Liberal-Democratic Party of Russia might garner more votes than we would. Analyses done by my adviser Leonid Gozman confirmed those disagreeable shifts. What was particularly absurd was that by law, results of polls could not be made public. A significant number of democratic voters remained certain that since a Russia's Choice victory was guaranteed, they needn't bother to vote.

December 14. The election results are announced. Our bloc will be the largest faction in the State Duma, with 75 people. The second most numerous faction is LDPR, with 59 deputies. Two other democratic blocs, PRES and Yabloko, make it to the Duma along with Russia's Choice. Each of them has a contingent of just under 30. The alignment of forces between Communists and democrats is slightly better than it was at the last Congress of People's Deputies. So it would seem nothing terrible has happened. Still, the enormous gap between the expectations born of the April referendum and the reality today is perceived as a defeat for the democrats.

Now, with the experience of the past five years behind me, I think that this fall and early winter of 1993 was a turning point, when the mistakes of the democratic government were to have their most serious impact on further developments. I cannot agree with such perspicacious Western observers as Anders Åslund or Michael McFaul that Boris Yeltsin made his most serious mistake in the fall of 1991 when he failed to dissolve the congress and conduct new elections. At the time, there was simply no such opportunity. In September and October of 1991, the Supreme Soviet had just vigorously supported Yeltsin in his standoff with the GKChP; it remained a credible, democratically elected body. Soviet administrative organs, while having lost their real influence and authority, still legally existed. Their Russian counterparts were extremely weak, and Yeltsin had no constitutional right to dissolve a Congress of People's Deputies. In that situation any move to hold early elections would have made no sense at all to the public, and would therefore have been doomed to failure.

In analyzing Yeltsin's actions from autumn of 1991 to autumn of 1993, people often forget that throughout that time he was acting in the context of *dvoevlastie*, of constantly conflicting resolutions by the executive and legislative branches, of a battle that had spread from Moscow out to other regions of Russia. The real-life part of all this was that key Russian government structures—the prosecutor's office, the Central Bank, the Pension Fund—were utterly dependent on a politicized Supreme Soviet majority, which had, since late 1992, consciously striven to weaken the President's position, to destabilize the country.

On October 4, 1993, the situation changed radically. After the dangerous events in Moscow, the *dvoevlastie* crisis was resolved, unequivocally, and enormous power was put into the President's hands. Now the question was how well he would use it. On October 5, 1993, there came an opportunity to radically accelerate change in Russia without rolling back democratic freedoms and safeguards. Previous events had shown just which leaders, both in Moscow and on the local level, stood for what. We might swiftly, without fear of organized opposition, have begun a reform of the armed forces, reduced the size of the standing army, making it more compact but also more manageable and better armed. We should have seized the levers of control at the KGB, which, for all its name changes, had not been working for Russian democracy. And we should have made radical personnel changes on the local level, promoting people who had proved their dedication to reform and democracy; should have taken on agrarian reform and reforms in the social support system, put the tax system in order, and banned fascist and Communist propaganda and activity by groups bent on fanning the flames of social and ethnic conflict.

That autumn of 1993 we had paid dearly enough for our absolutely vital stabilization measures, but we had also built up a certain momentum toward a decisive break in the whole economic situation. If movement in that same direction were to continue and intensify, it would be possible, as early as 1994, to force a radical drop in rates of inflation, stabilize the exchange rate for the Russian ruble, and lower the prime interest rate.

We would pay the inevitable political price for all of this, but go into 1995 with stable finances and the requisite preconditions for economic growth on a free market base. This would allow us to set the machinery in motion for increasing prosperity, and so approach the next parliamentary and presidential elections with a working market whose effects were both visible and tangible.

I spoke to the President about this fairly often at the time, trying to sway him toward vigorous action in all these directions. He listened, agreed with me, but made no decisions; he was clearly putting them off until after the elections and the adoption of a new constitution. He was acting in character—abrupt changes in mood, rapid shifts from vigorous action to passivity. True, some of his behavior was understandable enough. When I had returned to government in September 1993, Chernomyrdin had told me at our first meeting that the prolonged standoff of the last few months had been hard on the President. I soon became convinced of this myself. I got the sense that the President was worn out from the constant tension, from the weight on his shoulders; he had lost much of his energy, was slower to grasp the essence, the point of a conversation. Hence, I think, his tactical missteps in the resolution of the crisis of September-October of 1993, and the streak of political passivity, the wait-and-see period that immediately followed the October crisis.

Andrei Kozyrev later told me that, in his view, the President was ready to force a political breakthrough should democratic forces take the elections. But they did not. For the President, the December election results were a very unpleasant surprise. When the first preliminary tallies came in, he telephoned me and asked whether our data confirmed what was coming out through Central Election Committee channels. His mood was subdued, much as it had been the night of October 3.

But even after the election results became known, I was convinced that the only reasonable strategy was to speed up reform. No, we would not have a majority in the newly constituted Federal Assembly. But Russia's Choice was now the largest faction in parliament, and the constitution delegated very broad powers to the President and gave a significant measure of autonomy to the government. Besides, the President had both the right of veto, which was very hard to override, and broad regulatory powers.

On the whole, our political base for implementing a consistent reform policy had improved immensely since 1991–92. Once again I tried to convince Yeltsin of that. I soon saw that for the moment this was impossible: he saw our election setback as a signal to retreat, maneuver, reorient ourselves. Since I would be unable to implement a policy that I was convinced was the only right one, what was the sense of remaining in the government? To be a symbol, a sign to the West and to Russian democrats that reforms were continuing? That wasn't for me.

After the elections there was some reshuffling in the government. The President proposed that I continue to serve as first deputy prime minister. However, by late December and early January, I was convinced that the government as currently constituted was not ready to pursue another round of serious reforms. Once again, ideas about finding nonmonetary methods of combating inflation and about giving up on "economic romanticism" prevailed. My attempts to see through resolutions I considered crucial were blocked at almost every turn. For months I couldn't even manage to publish a resolution on long overdue staff reductions in my own Ministry of Economics.

The last straw was the shocking story of the plan to construct a lavish new administration building for the parliament, which I briefly mentioned earlier. I telephoned Vladimir Kvasov, then head of the apparatus, only to hear his assurances that the government had made no such decision. Then two days later the papers, already drawn up, were handed to me.

This time I didn't think too long. I sat down at my desk and took out a pen.

Dear Boris Nikolaevich!
More than two years ago you placed enormous trust in me and my colleagues in assigning us to implement the radical economic reforms being enacted under your leadership. In my work as deputy prime minister, first

deputy prime minister and acting prime minister of the government of the Russian Federation, I have tried to do everything possible to put Russia's economy on its feet, to ensure that this transition period, so painful and difficult for every Russian citizen, passed as quickly as possible. Thanks to the courage and patience of our fellow Russians, thanks to your resolve and consistent support, we have been able not only to avoid the social and economic cataclysms now rocking many former USSR republics, but also to lay the foundations of the country's rebirth.

Our working conditions were never ideal. You know full well how much we were unable to implement, less because of objective circumstances than because of the unremitting pressure applied by various conservative political circles. In September 1993, when I agreed to rejoin your government, I was aware that since in the eyes of the public I bore chief responsiblity for the economic reform, I would have only a limited amount of leverage on the economic situation. But I hoped that a sense of shared responsibility for the nation would permit the government, even one comprised of people of differing views, to rally round the President and pursue the course necessary to stabilize the economy and avert a disaster.

To my regret, more and more resolutions which I have neither helped prepare nor with which I can in any way agree are being adopted. Let me give you just two recent examples.

An interbank agreement on the unification of Russian and Belarusian monetary systems has just been signed. Such a union is possible if scrupulously prepared, and if all the supervisory mechanisms protecting Russian national interests are properly worked out. But the provisions in this already-signed document are merely a reiteration of the chaos already current in the monetary sphere, at the expense of Russian citizens' real income. Implementation of this decision will result in a minimum wage and pension in Belarus that substantially exceeds the minimum wage and pension in Russia. We are not so wealthy that we can throw the well-being of Russian citizens out the window of political opportunity. I repeatedly objected to this decision, but my protests went unheard.

It is equally difficult to understand the decision to construct a new parliament building (at an estimated cost of 500 million dollars). This sum significantly exceeds what we, with such difficulty, managed to put into the budget for conversion. It is five times the federal budget allocation for culture and art, and one-fifth of the total funding for social programs for last year. This decision, which will have such destructive consequences, was drafted without my knowledge, and adopted despite my determined objections. Under these circumstances, it is hard for me personally to justify economic austerity in science and scholarship, culture, education, and ecology. There are serious but unavoidable losses involved in necessary change; these, however, should not be confused with losses due to hasty and poorly thought out decisions.

Dear Boris Nikolaevich! I cannot simultaneously remain in the government, and in opposition to it. I cannot answer for reform without having the opportunity to forestall acts such as those I have described here, without having the levers of control necessary to pursue a consistent economic policy, one that I am convinced is right.

Therefore, to my deepest regret, I am compelled to refuse your offer of the post of first deputy prime minister of the RF. At the same time, be assured that I continue to support you and your reform policy.

Respectfully yours,

Yegor Gaidar

I stopped in at Boris Nikolaevich's office and explained my motives to him. He said that he understood. I asked him to rescind the crazy decision on the "parliament center" and to be extremely careful about expanding the ruble zone; in 1992 we had paid far too dearly for the initial lack of a Russian domestic ruble to now put the ruble at risk. Boris Nikolaevich promised. American president Bill Clinton was in Moscow at the time, on an official visit, and so we agreed that my resignation would not be made public until after his departure.

The decision to construct a new parliament building was rescinded, as the President promised. The issue of a unified ruble zone bogged down in negotiations over presidential elections in Belarus, and was later relegated to consideration at some unspecified future date.

Meanwhile, beginning in February 1994 (as was expected) the policy of economic restraint pursued in the fall and winter of 1993–94 began to yield visible results. Rates of inflation fell to less than 10 percent per month. Subsequently, especially after the gains in stabilization efforts in the fall of 1994, after Black Tuesday[3] and an abrupt jump in inflation that wiped out any hopes for stabilization and economic growth in 1995, I often wondered whether the decision I had made back then, in January 1994, was the right one. A political commentator and analyst whom I respect, Nikolai Karlovich Svanidze, argued that I was wrong, that the ruling principle in Russia is "you leave, you lose." In some sense he's probably right.

Had I remained in government, I might have had some chance to influence the situation, to oppose the "pumping-up" of the economy begun in April 1994, to speak out more about the inevitable, destructive consequences of such a move. Perhaps even before Black Tuesday, I might have been able to persuade the President, the prime minister, and the leadership of the Central Bank of the need to make a course correction and avert the January 1995 crisis in foreign currency resources.

But even today these arguments seem extremely abstract and hypothetical. In January 1994 my ability to influence the decision-making process on fundamental economic and political issues was practically nil. This was a striking contrast to May 1992, when I also gave serious thought to resigning. Back then, difficult as it was, I still had powerful tools in hand; now it was all for show. Had I agreed to remain in government in this purely decorative role, I would simply have been demonstrating my willingness to join the cohort of people for whom being in power, or near it, was an end in itself. And if you join those ranks, don't be miffed if nobody listens to you. Boris Nikolaevich knew full well that I didn't care that much about holding high office. To agree to a decorative role in implementing policy I clearly didn't support would not preserve but rather undermine any influence I might still have on the President.

At the same time I realized that even after leaving government I would still bear, in the eyes of the public, a significant part of the responsibility for everything going on in the country. And that responsibility would extend to Russia's Choice as a whole and to its delegation in the Duma.

Immediately after the elections, the results of which left many of our supporters disillusioned, the internal weaknesses of the coalition constituting the Russia's Choice bloc emerged quite distinctly. The very breadth of this election-campaign alliance, the ideological amorphousness I mentioned earlier, the presence of a significant number of people who were focused less on democratic values than on the power associated with ruling party status, caused some rather complicated problems. They surfaced early, in the process of choosing a chairman for our Duma delegation.

I had proposed Sergei Adamovich Kovalyov as a candidate; he had been one of the Russian democracy movement's most highly regarded leaders ever since the days of dissidents and human rights campaigns, and had been a friend and close ally to Andrei Dmitrievich Sakharov. I was convinced that his moral authority was crucial to the creation of a political identity for the liberal bloc in the State Duma. Kovalyov had been listed second on the Russia's Choice ballot roster, and it seemed to me that our constituents would find him a perfectly natural and understandable choice. I suddenly learned that Burbulis, campaign manager for Russia's Choice, had laid claim to the same role. This complicated the situation. For all Burbulis's obvious qualities as an analyst, a generator of ideas, a strategist, the public attitude toward him even among democratically inclined voters was mixed, and often negative. He was ill-suited to the role of public politician. Mainly, I was convinced that many people who had voted for us would simply feel betrayed if Gennady Burbulis were to become the parliamentary leader of Russia's Choice.

Ever since autumn of 1991, when we had first worked together in the government, I had always felt a profound respect for him. And therefore I tried to explain that absolutely any post in Russia's Choice, the very highest, was his for the asking—except that of chairman of the Duma delegation, our party's public face. Unfortunately I was again persuaded that, as so often happens, even the most subtle of analysts lose their perspective on a situation when it has to do with them personally, with their role, their abilities.

Within the delegation, debate over leadership was becoming pointed and sometimes even uncivil. There was danger of a split. And this even before the parliament had begun its work! At the height of the debate, for the sake of compromise, I was forced to do what I had always categorically refused to do—consent to act as leader of the parliamentary delegation. So, having once consented for the sake of compromise to take on the role of leader of the democratic forces, I was forced once again to face the consequences of another such move, which would identify democracy even more closely with a person—me—toward whom the public had decidedly mixed feelings.

Our bloc had entered the campaign with a well-worked-out legislative program, the centerpiece of which was the protection of private ownership and creation of a legal base for the stable operation of free-market institutions. It is important to understand how complicated a task this was, especially after seven decades of a regime for which private enterprise was not merely a dirty word but a criminal act. Hostility toward private property permeated all of Soviet legislation and law enforcement. We could not simply ratify articles safeguarding private property by executive order or decree. Here we needed powerful grass-roots support, which, in turn, would not appear until the need to protect the interests of the property owner were recognized, and indeed demanded, by a qualitatively new public consciousness and by influential social groups.

In the beginning the private sector was like a newborn infant, still tied to its mother by an umbilical cord. It had to be separated from the past in order to breathe on its own. It ever more insistently demanded oxygen. Conflicts between private owners and enterprise managers, the need to safeguard shareholders' rights, massive financial speculation ending in confiscation of investors' property—all these were the realities of life in late 1993 and early 1994. Hence the perfectly understandable priorities in our lawmaking efforts: a civil code, a law on corporations, a law on securities, development of a new criminal code, attempts at passage of legislation legalizing private purchase and sale of land, and much else as well.

Several highly regarded jurists in our faction—Mikhail Mityukov and Boris Zolotukhin, plus Viktor Pokhmelkin, Grigory Tomchin, Valentin Tatarchuk, Aleksandr Pochinok, and many other deputies—soon put Russia's Choice in the forefront of lawmaking activity. On the whole, in summing up two years' work by our faction in the State Duma, I can say that the results we achieved exceeded our most optimistic expectations. The very fact that a Civil Code, this "constitution" of private property, was passed despite vigorous opposition by the Communists was an undeniable victory.

Our most serious defeat was in the area of land reform legislation. Here any attempt at legislation attaching private property rights to land faced powerful opposition from the Communists and agrarian interests. Not only were we unsuccessful in passing our proposed land reform law, but we also had to agree to delay enactment of both sections of the Civil Code pertaining to land, and also the mortgage law. This whole sphere was virtually excised from market legislation. However, this was the most serious exception. On the whole, the results of our legislative activity in the Fifth State Duma in the area of protecting private ownership proved that, despite all the pessimistic prognoses of early 1994, our forceful and energetic effort, and the effective use of the presidential veto, had allowed us to achieve a good deal.

Unfortunately, the same cannot be said of the political results. Here, a fundamental problem quickly emerged—the complexity and lack of definition in the faction's relationship to the government. Resignation or no, it was on me, and thus on my colleagues as well, that the responsibility for the consequences of Russian economic transformation lay. One way or another, we still answered for every misstep or miscalculation that Yeltsin and Chernomyrdin made. And so naturally we wanted to gain some influence over actual current policy. Throughout the entire legislative session we discussed all the issues pertaining to market-oriented legislation and protection of property rights with the government, we supported any reasonable financial initiatives it took, and we criticized populist initiatives in the Duma, which emanated for the most part from the Communist Party of the Russian Federation, the agrarians, and the LDPR.

One standard feature of LDPR's tactics was to loudly revile the government while trying to strike a deal behind the scenes, to wring out a variety of concessions in exchange for supporting the government on key votes. I know from friends in the government that the LDPR had no monopoly on this sort of approach. So Russia's Choice usually ended up the loser. We openly supported any reasonable, even unpopular, government measures, yet at the same time never haggled with the government for support. Nor did we shy away from criticizing it when necessary.

We welcomed every reasonable reform measure undertaken by Yeltsin and Chernomyrdin, but were the first to oppose them when they did anything irresponsible—as we did when the war in Chechnya began. But again, as soon as Chernomyrdin entered negotiations over Budyonnovsk, our faction was the first to take his side.[4] Throughout this time, we pursued a single line—support of democracy and private property, stability and peace. Unfortunately, the government's position on these issues was changing radically. Many voters took our consistency in overall policy for a lack of consistency in action.

In the spring of 1994, having learned our lesson in the 1993 elections, we concluded that we had to create a more rigorous and ordered structure at the liberal end of the political spectrum. However severe our allergy to the word "party" might be, we realized that we truly needed an organized party to represent the liberal-democrat movement, one capable of doing both public relations and political work outside Moscow. Its natural base was the movement encompassing Russia's Choice and Democratic Russia, plus those individual political groups left over from the broad coalition that in its time had assured Yeltsin his victory.

In the summer of 1994 such an organization emerged. We named it Russia's Democratic Choice. At the time, we had no idea how severe were the trials that awaited it in the months ahead.

Chapter 13

Democracy and Chechnya

- The bone in Russia's throat
- Negotiations with the Chechen delegation
- A historical digression
- Dangerous government illusions
- The bombing of Grozny
- Andrei Kozyrev leaves
- Yeltsin's popularity drops
- Negotiations on unity
- Grigory Yavlinsky's about-face
- Budyonnovsk
- A vote of no confidence
- Parliamentary elections
- Pervomaisk
- Presidential elections

I've already written that my first entry into government in 1991 coincided with an attempt to declare a state of emergency in Chechnya. Ever since that time, developments in that republic had been closely intertwined with the fate of reforms and democracy in Russia. At first, when Chechnya was still only on the periphery of public attention, this link was less obvious, but later it became ever more visible and alarming.

As I mentioned earlier, the accepted custom in the tsarist empire was to have the minister of defense report directly to the tsar. Of course he worked with the Council of Ministers on financial and economic issues, but he was not authorized to report at council meetings on mobilization plans, garrisoning of troops, et cetera. It was unimaginable that a prime minister—say, Stolypin or Kokovtsev—might give direct orders to the minister of defense on what to do with his weaponry or how to deploy his forces. That was simply out of the prime minister's jurisdiction.

This sort of government structure had outlived both the tsar and the

Soviets, and was inherited by a democratic Russia. And therefore the essentially military issues around Chechnya had never been within the purview of our reform government. The first Chechen problem we had to deal with was the Grozny oil refinery, on whose output the petroleum products supply for the North Caucasus depended. The government's general disposition on this issue was extremely simple: apply economic pressure, restricting and reducing delivery of Volga and Siberian oil to the Grozny refinery. The Ministry of Fuel and Energy maintained, however, that for purely technical reasons any sharp reduction in deliveries to Chechnya was fraught with potentially serious problems. There were arguments citing the lack of analogous capacity in other refineries, the difficulty involved in reorganizing shipping to the North Caucasus, and the impossibility of halting the supply of paraffinic oil from Stavropol without catastrophic damage to the pipelines and the wells themselves. On the whole, the supply of oil to the Grozny refinery was being reduced, but only moderately: in 1992 it was down from 1991 levels by roughly 4 million tons.

The second problem involving Chechnya became more acute in the late spring and early summer of 1992. This was the matter of the so-called Chechen promissory notes, a major financial scam involving an unsanctioned currency emission. The whole business was tangled up with the overall problem of restructuring the payments system and of relations within the ruble zone. From an economic standpoint, there was no difference between Chechen, Kazakh, Ukrainian, or Uzbek promissory notes. All were vestiges of the continuing fictive existence of a Soviet ruble zone, with no administrative or political supervision over any element in the structure. We were working at top speed to shift the central banks of the former republics over to a system of correspondent accounts. This was an absolutely necessary prerequisite for establishing order and setting up stringent controls on monetary circulation in Russia. It was the only sure way to shut off the flow of Chechen promissory notes.

It was in the summer of 1992, when it became clear that people would not go hungry, that Russian federal structures had acquired some modicum of stability, and that the most crucial problems stemming from the collapse of the empire had been resolved without catastrophic consequences, that the question of working out a strategy for resolving the issue of Chechnya began looming large on the agenda.

On one of those summer days, I received a Chechen government delegation. The general sense of their remarks was, "Chechnya has its political problems, but we're men of action, economic planners, and we think it's time to establish serious economic ties." I answered that they were doubtless men of action and economic planners, but at the same time, as economic planners they should be urging their leadership to recognize the need for political movement in a more reasonable direction and along less harsh a line.

I was quite aware of the dangers of attempting to solve the problem by force. Chechnya is unlike other parts of Russia. It lives with a painful legacy left by tsarism and aggravated by Stalinist deportations. It was no surprise when the tectonic processes that led to the breakup of the Soviet Union also gave new momentum to Chechnya's desire to break away from Russia. Time would be needed, no small amount of time, for the natural logic of economics and common interests to give rise to integration processes, to make Chechnya see its need to exist within a Russian economic and political framework. The long history of wars waged by Russia in the Caucasus in the nineteenth century also testified to the futility of trying to resolve the issue by force. Everything suggested that another such war would be very costly, painful, and prolonged.

The problem of choosing what tactics Russian authorities in the region should apply came to a head in late autumn of 1992, when the bloody Ossetia-Ingushetia conflict broke out. Troops had to be sent in immediately; they entered Ossetia first, then Ingushetia. Against this backdrop, an idea came to certain military leaders: If we have troops in the area anyway, why not go ahead and solve the Chechnya problem while we're at it? One paratrooper regiment, two hours. Besides, the border between Ingushetia and Chechnya has never been precisely defined. It's not clear where troops in Ingushetia should stop their advance. So why not seize the chance to get rid of this thorn in the side of the whole North Caucasus?

The question was clearly outside the cabinet's jurisdiction; it was a presidential matter, but I decided to get involved anyway. I personally had no sympathy with the Dudaev regime, but I didn't quite believe all the jingoist bravado, the claims that it would crumble in a minute. That didn't jibe with the history of the North Caucasus, which I knew rather well. After visiting Nazran and Vladikavkaz, talking with officers, with generals, and after looking at the situation firsthand, I was convinced that "two hours and a paratroop regiment" was not going to happen. What would happen was a long, drawn-out, bloody guerrilla war from which we would not soon escape. I summoned Dzhokhar Dudaev's representatives to Nazran. A delegation arrived, headed by First Deputy Prime Minister Yaraga Mamadaev. We began negotiations and agreed on the line of demarcation between Russian troops and Chechen forces along the Ingush-Chechen border. I then flew to Moscow and with some effort managed to get the President and the military to agree to a troop pull-back and observation of the agreed-upon boundary line.

However, as I have often mentioned, 1993 was the year of *dvoevlastie*. The struggle among the various branches of government virtually wiped out any real possibility of working out or implementing clear-cut, uniform policy, including policy for the North Caucasus. Still, we maintained consistent economic sanctions against the Dudaev regime; oil supplies to the region were cut, and the oil transport system reorganized. By autumn of 1993 the flow of oil from locked-in Stavropol oil fields was halted. Restructuring the payments system had now eliminated any possibility of further financial machinations with Chechen promissory notes. The Grozny oil fields were in a steep decline; oil output in the republic was falling rapidly. The massive disturbances and public demonstrations within Chechnya which had driven Dudaev to the use of force testified to the fact that our not overly flashy but consistently applied tactic of economic pressure was yielding results. The idea of Chechen independence was obviously losing ground.

With the consolidation of power in Mosow, and the *dvoevlastie* crisis overcome, Russian authorities had greater opportunity to pursue an intelligent Chechnya policy. At this very time, in late 1993 and early 1994, the Dudaev regime was undergoing a major crisis. Revenues from sales of petroleum products continued to fall; the oil refinery was running at less than 20 percent of capacity. The Chechen standard of living was substantially lower than that of other republics in the region. Dudaev's watchword—prosperous independence based of oil revenues—was losing its charm. His closest comrades, Gantemirov and Labazanov, had deserted him. Not only could he not police or control areas that had historically kept their distance from him (the Nadterechny district, for one)—he could no longer control the formerly loyal Urus-Martan. Ruslan Aushev told me that Dudaev had asked him and Supreme Soviet chairman, Adzhariya Aslan Abashidze, to help set up a dialogue with Moscow.

It was clear that with things as they stood, if you didn't want a bloody war in the Caucasus, you had to use this new weakness in the Dudaev regime to begin a dialogue, to gradually build a base for the real and effective inclusion of Chechnya into the Russian state structure. This path, the only right one, promised no real political dividends. Quite the contrary—Russian government officials who took this path quickly came under fire from the demagogues: *What's this? . . . negotiations with Dudaev's outlaw regime? On what legal basis?!*

And a remarkable illusion took hold among Russian authorities. If Dudaev was so weak, if his support in Chechnya itself so insignificant, then why negotiate with him at all? For a start, we could arm the anti-Dudaev opposition and help it crush the rebels. And if that didn't work, why not use direct force—shake our fist at Dudaev, so to speak, and he'd resign himself to losing. This logic seemed particularly apropos after the December 1993 election, when it was crucial to show a triumphant Zhirinovsky, with all his imperial, pro-war rhetoric, that we were no slouches ourselves, that we could rattle swords with the best of them. Clearly, all these considerations were paving the way for a military solution in Chechnya. When my Russia's Choice cohorts and I tried to persuade its proponents of the danger of what they were planning, what we heard was this: *How can you not understand that what we need right now is a small, victorious war?* The realization that this would not be a victorious war, but a senseless and bloody one, came much later.

November 1994. The siege of Grozny failed. Anti-Dudaev forces supported by Russian tanks were routed. The Russian authorities disowned them. Planes with no identifying marks bombed Grozny; the President checked into a hospital. Soon thereafter, the decision to launch a military operation in Chechnya was made.

I tried to contact the President before the decision was announced. For the first time since 1991, I couldn't get through at all. Formerly, in such a case, he would have called back immediately. Later, in hindsight, I realized that Boris Nikolaevich had guessed what I planned to talk about and was reluctant to turn me down flat. I know that Ruslan Aushev also tried to prevent a war, to persuade Yeltsin to sit down at the bargaining table with Dudaev, to sort out the claims and counterclaims himself. He was certain that a personal meeting would help avoid a calamity. Boris Nikolaevich set up a meeting with Aushev to hear out the latter's arguments, but the morning after that promise, the mass media broadcast a statement that the President of Russia would never negotiate with Dzhokhar Dudaev.

Without waiting for the President's answer, I called Chernomyrdin and told him that what they were planning posed a terrible threat to everything we had accomplished. A war had to be prevented. He seemed to agree. Oleg Poptsov and I spoke on the phone; I told him that the decision to send troops was a tragic mistake. He sent over a camera crew, and I made a television appeal to Russian authorities to prevent this calamity.

On December 9, one day before news of the military operation in Chechnya was made public, I assembled the political advisory council of Russia's Democratic Choice. We considered two options. The first was to speak out sharply and resolutely against any military operation that might be launched, and so become an opposition party vis-à-vis Yeltsin and his government. The second was to speak out against the inept way the decision was being implemented, and so leave the door open for a dialogue with the government.

Sergei Yushenkov strongly supported the first position, while Sergei Blagovolin, chairman of RDC's Moscow organization, supported the second. The decision was a very difficult one for me. I was tied to Yeltsin by three years of painful struggle to reform Russia. For all our differences of opinion, I respected him deeply for what he had managed to accomplish. I didn't see any other candidate from moderate democratic forces who might be able to stem the rising Communist tide. Only recently, in the summer of 1994, I had tried to convince him that, like it or not, he had to run for office in 1996.

It seemed to me I was one of the few people whose opinion the President still heeded. I realized that becoming the opposition party would mean estranging myself from the President, and that I would lose any opportunity to influence him, to make a difference in the resolution of key issues. Becoming the opposition would also mean an unavoidable rift between us and a good part of the entrepreneurial elite who now backed us, with people who saw the RDC as the party of those in power. There was also the threat of a rift within our parliamentary delegation, within the party itself.

But was there any other way? War would mean Grozny in flames, tens of thousands of civilians dead, and terrorism in response. All this, against the backdrop of a fragile, still unsteady Russian democracy, would inevitably push us in the direction of a police state. How could a liberal party, whatever its form, support a policy that would lead to such results?

Had I not been in the government, had I not known Pavel Grachev, or understood what far from sterling shape the armed forces were in, or how feeble the Federal Counterespionage Service really was, I might have had some illusions that a military solution would be quick, effective, and virtually bloodless. But I knew that it was all bunk, that it wouldn't end in any two-hour paratroop raid, but in a truly painful, bloody, and drawn-out war. I came to the firm conclusion that the only way out was to strictly and consistently oppose a military resolution of the Chechnya issue.

At the same time, it was clear that we wouldn't reap any dividends for ourselves with such a stance. However loudly we might oppose this little escapade today, the very fact that responsibility for it would be laid at Yeltsin's door would be a major blow to all democrats and consequently to Russia's Choice.

Immediately after the announcement that the military operation had begun, we tried to organize mass protests. We set up a demonstration on Pushkin Square, then one on Theater Square. It was a bitter feeling, not having enough public support. True, not many people liked the idea of a war, but they didn't like Dudaev's regime either, and they had no comprehension of what an enormous calamity, what a bloodbath, it would all turn out to be. Some people sincerely believed that it would all be over in a few days. My RDC colleague Sergei Yushenkov had it exactly right: the public, too, was at fault for not opposing the war decisively enough, and this encouraged the authorities to act recklessly.

For the RDC the war in Chechnya resulted in a painful internal split. Russia's Democratic Choice was created as a liberal party with close ties to a democratic government. Many of its members were genuinely devoted to democratic ideals, but many others had joined simply to back a government that more or less suited their needs. I realized that the events in Chechnya would inevitably cause a schism. The liberals would stay with us. Those who had followed the party in power would go off in search of new political horizons. Andrei Kozyrev's departure from Russia's Choice immediately after we voiced our opposition to the Chechen war was graphic confirmation of that.

Andrei Vladimirovich and I had become acquainted in the autumn of 1991, when we worked on the action plan for the Russian republic government. He often dropped in at Dacha no. 15, interested in our work. I don't know to what extent the feeling was mutual, but I felt an immediate liking for him. He was an educated person, a smart guy. You couldn't help but sympathize; his problems were far from easy ones. His own status was absolutely undefined. No one had a clue what Russia's Ministry of Foreign Affairs was supposed to do within a formally intact Soviet Union. The country was in critical condition, was not paying its debts.

To avoid famine, we needed new loans right away. The traditional pretenses to imperial greatness stood in stark contrast to the realities of state bankruptcy.

One has to acknowledge that for all the difficulties and missteps in foreign policy between 1991 and 1993, Kozyrev was able to resolve the issues of Russian succession in relation to the USSR with amazing ease, and move Russia into the USSR's seat on the UN Security Council without anyone batting an eye. Gradually, under quite difficult circumstances, he had been able to make positive changes in relations with the West, and in October 1993 take a significant step toward normalizing relations with Japan. By the end of 1993, with a measure of internal political and economic stabilization in Russia, and the end of the *dvoevlastie* crisis, one could say that the most pressing of the problems born of the collapse of the Soviet Union had on the whole been resolved by Russian diplomacy. In three years, Kozyrev had acquired a good deal of international authority, and had for many people become a symbol of Russia's new foreign-policy strategy, which was oriented toward integration into Europe and a system of alliances with free-market democracies.

Granted, major missteps were undoubtedly made in the Balkans and in relations with states that had emerged out of the former Soviet republics. The Ministry of Foreign Affairs was very slow in adapting to this new and unfamiliar set of relations. But here, too, there was obvious progress. The chaos in relations between sovereign states, which allowed other CIS members to use old interagency connections to wring unilateral concessions out of this or that Russian agency, was gradually becoming a thing of the past.

Kozyrev's main weakness as foreign minister was, it seems to me, that he wanted so badly to be foreign minister. And this is a quality that Yeltsin can spot a mile away. As soon as he notices that one of his high-ranking officials is holding onto that chair for dear life, the official immediately forfeits Boris Nikolaevich's respect, and with it any chance to speak his own mind. And he ends up just a yes-man, a follower of someone else's orders.

Nor did Andrei Kozyrev escape that fate, as he gradually began changing his own convictions to match the changing government line. I think that it was this very series of compromises and concessions that led Kozyrev to the decision he made in December 1994, when as a sign of solidarity with the war effort just begun in Chechnya he demonstratively distanced himself from the democrats and left Russia's Choice. He thus postponed his ouster, but didn't prevent it. And he forfeited his reputation as the champion of a particular strategic path for Russia.

But let me return to the unfolding situation in Chechnya. At first it seemed there was some chance to avoid a war. Chernomyrdin received Chechen envoys, and declared his willingness to open a dialogue; there was hope that we could get away with just showing the "big fist," and constructive talks would begin. But instead came Nationalities Minister Nikolai Yegorov's unexpected ultimatum that Dudaev come to Mozdok and sign an immediate agreement to surrender his weapons.[1] The party of war was clearly convinced that force was the quickest and most effective solution. War! The military machine spinning its wheels, the terrible, bloody outcome of the New Year's Day storm of Grozny, the bombing of city squares, the deaths of thousands of absolutely innocent civilians. All just as we thought—only much more terrible.

The war in Chechnya began in the midst of a grave economic crisis. The effects of the fight against "market romanticism" and "monetarism" were staring us in the face. The government had not managed to take advantage of the preconditions for stabilization created in the autumn and winter of 1993, and it had dangerously relaxed its fiscal and monetary policy. By summer of 1994 it was clear that large-scale monetary issues and the rapid ballooning of the money supply would, by fall, blow apart whatever financial stability remained. In August the demand for hard currency rose sharply, and the Central Bank made one mistake after another. By September it became much more effective to invest in the dollar than in ruble stocks. The growth in demand for convertible currency became explosive. The Central Bank, whose hard currency reserves were exhausted, washed its hands of the whole thing and left the market. Then there was a sharp drop in the value of the ruble, and a rising new wave of inflation. All the results of our stabilization efforts in the fall of 1993 were completely wiped out. After Black Tuesday the President removed Central Bank chairman Viktor Gerashchenko, acting Minister of Finance Sergei Dubinin, and deputy chairman of the government Aleksandr Shokhin. He appointed Anatoly Chubais first deputy prime minister for economics.

Once the war began, the economic crisis deepened. Grozny in flames was hardly the best backdrop for a stabilization policy. The markets obviously did not believe that any planned stabilization line could be maintained. At the beginning of 1996 the government, which had set a goal of lowering inflation to 1 percent a month by the end of 1995, was borrowing money at a rate of 350 to 400 percent per annum.

Chubais and I met several times as the war in Chechnya progressed and thought about what to do, and whether he should remain in the government or not. We consulted with Sergei Kovalyov and discussed it with the RDC delegation. It was a tough choice: staying in the government inevitably meant bearing the moral responsibility for what was going on. Leaving in the midst of a grave financial crisis, when literally only days remained before the currency reserves were totally used up, bordered on capitulation.

I don't know what I would have done, had I been in the government at the time, had I still been acting first deputy prime minister in charge of economic policy. Probably I would have tendered my resignation, as a protest against the war in Chechnya. But Anatoly had a different role to play. By this time he was much less involved in the noneconomic aspects of government policy. His role was that of a professional specialist in charge of an important, well-defined sector of government work. After weighing all the pros and cons, together we decided that Chubais should stay in government and do everything he could to master the adverse economic situation, to protect market mechanisms, to try to pursue a meaningful economic line.

Meanwhile, in economic terms, Chechnya had presented the government with a stark set of options. It was clear that this little escapade would have to be paid for, and that the price would be high. There were two ways to go: cancel everything planned for the fall and winter of 1994, return to massive borrowing from the Central Bank and to using the printing press, and then resign ourselves to spiraling inflation, no convertible ruble, the price regulation route, and begin putting the economy on a wartime footing when the country was already at war. Or we could make drastic reductions in spending along all budget lines, pay for the war by squeezing the budget and making further reductions in what were already extremely low incomes for Russians employed in education, medicine, science and scholarship, culture. Again, the choice was between a catastrophic option and a merely bad one. The government chose the lesser of the two evils.

Later it became clear that stabilization efforts had borne fruit, that as summer approached, the inflation rate was dropping, the exchange rate was stabilizing, and currency reserves were beginning to grow. But the price of stabilization in wartime was very high. The drop in real income for the winter of 1995 was the greatest since the beginning of 1992, and the entire budgetary sphere was in a chronic state of crisis. If the failures in 1994 economic policy and autumn's inflationary spurt had substantially weakened Yeltsin's base of support, the unpopular and futile campaign in Chechnya changed the public mood even more radically.

Sociological polls, and simply conversations with voters, made it obvious that the number of people willing to support Yeltsin was shrinking. And that was not just Yeltsin's problem. This negative assessment of the President's actions extended to democrats in general, and especially to the RDC, which was so closely tied to him. In the autumn of 1995 we paid even more dearly for the rapid drop in his popularity.

As Yeltsin was becoming less popular, democratic slogans were becoming less attractive, and this was paving the way for a Communist march to power. At the next election we would clearly be swimming against the tide. This meant that it was all the more important to do all we could to unify democratic forces now. Before, this was merely an important issue for Russia; now it became a vital one.

Earlier I wrote of democratic attempts at a unified effort in the parliamentary elections of 1993. Back then, nothing particularly worthwhile had come of it. Our partners in Yabloko had laughed off our warnings of a real Communist and national-socialist threat: *So where's Gaidar found the Communists lurking this time?*

After those elections Grigory Yavlinsky asked for a meeting, but, if possible, not at the government's office building. I was planning on going to Barvikh to relax for a few days. So—without naming names, as he'd asked—I arranged a pass for him. When Grigory arrived, we walked and talked for about an hour and a half. He explained his position to me, why he had to distance himself from the government as much as possible. But at the same time he assured me that, in strategic terms, we thought alike, we were allies, and that meant we should put our heads together in the matter of reforming Russia. He talked about the tactical advantages of creating the appearance of mutual dislike; then at the opportune moment we could surprise our political opponents by agreeing to cooperate.

A couple of weeks later he called again, asked to meet, and we agreed that we would go over to my parents' and talk things out. At the time, negotiations among Duma delegations on the makeup of parliamentary committees were already under way. At our meeting, Grigory Alekseevich continued to develop his theme of working together, and urged me to support Yabloko's bid for control of a budget committee that was strategically important to him. I knew Mikhail Zadornov well; he was, in my view, the most capable member of Yavlinsky's team, and I believed I could back him as a candidate—and told Yavlinsky so. We of course kept our promise.

One difficulty for the Russia's Choice delegation in 1994–95 was the combination of parliamentary responsibility and limited opportunity to influence the government. We voted staunchly against no-confidence resolutions, and opposed populist bills likely to undermine financial stability. In short, we tried in every way we could to support any reasonable endeavors on the part of the President and his government. On many of the problems they faced they sought wide-ranging dialogue with other delegations, sometimes (why be coy about it) openly swapping resolution of this or that deputy's particular problem for his support. Support from Russia's Choice was something they could count on without making deals, except in those instances when it was a matter of resolutions that ran counter to our fundamental platform. As a result, we got none of the political advantages of real power, but paid dearly for our support of controversial government decisions on social and economic issues.

Yabloko, a rather small delegation, had taken a firm antigovernment stance and generally supported no-confidence resolutions. Unburdened by any particular obligations, it actively went after publicly unpopular government decisions, and so won itself some political points. Out of the public eye, Yavlinsky often dropped in to talk. Opposition to the war in Chechnya had brought our parties closer together. We both thought the war a dangerous and senseless folly that had no "military solution"; we spoke out in favor of a cessation of hostilities. Our deputies worked together in Chechnya for release of the wounded in action and for prisoner exchanges. In the Duma we proposed a series of joint legislative initiatives, signed them together, and supported several joint declarations. The war was alienating us both from the government and from the President. It seemed that events themselves were pushing the democrats to unite, to wage a joint campaign in the upcoming parliamentary and presidential elections.

It was clear that the key to unity was an alliance between the two major democratic forces, represented in parliament by RDC and Yabloko. If an agreement between them could be reached, the rest of the smaller democratic parties and blocs would simply have no choice but to join the larger coalition. In this connection, my RDC colleagues proposed the following solution. We make a coalition agreement with Yabloko to collaborate in majority districts, and settle on a common approach to strategy and tactics for the campaign. We also agree that the democratic bloc receiving the most votes (of all those in the coalition) has the right to designate a presidential candidate, and that we would join in support of that candidate. Yavlinsky didn't object to the idea, but thought it should go further. He frequently mentioned how important it was to name a presidential candidate, a coalition government, and a common platform now, without waiting for election results.

It was a debatable point, but not unconvincing. Translated into plain language, it sounded like this: you want unity among democrats, I want to be the democrats' candidate for president. Support me, and we'll remove any obstacles to unification. Yavlinsky had shared his idea with several members of our delegation, including my second-in-command, Boris Zolotukhin, and asked for their support. On May 9, 1995, after we had placed flowers on the Tomb of the Unknown Soldier, he approached me and suggested we have another talk.[2] We walked together, unhurriedly, as far as my institute's little courtyard on Gazetny Lane. Yavlinsky repeated his already familiar arguments in favor of such a solution and tried to convince me to agree.

For me it was not a simple matter. Democratic voters were indeed demanding that we unite. It was hard for them to sort out who was for and who was against. What *they* saw was that all the fuss and ambition among democratic leaders was keeping the democrats from joining forces to fight off the very real threat of a Communist comeback. This time nobody was asking where Gaidar had found the Communist threat lurking—it was staring them in the face. It was obvious. If we reached an agreement, our voters would feel more optimistic, more certain that Russian democracy was alive and kicking. We would have a real chance of increasing our representation in the Duma, especially if democratic candidates from majority districts managed to avoid backbiting and competition among themselves.

I realized that there could be no coalition unless I agreed to his terms, and hence no hope of victory in either the parliamentary or the presidential elections. Either we went into the elections separately and risked suffering a major defeat, or we achieved unity at the price of backing Yavlinsky for president.

I weighed all the arguments. True, Yavlinsky was vain and ambitious, but he was educated, intelligent, and had no love for either the Communists or the national socialists; he was an opponent of the war and a proponent of private property. We talked in detail about his extravagant fiscal notions, which, if implemented, I was sure could easily ruin the economy. But I understood from our conversation that he wouldn't insist on taking a hard line on that issue. We agreed to a television meeting, on the next broadcast of *Itogi*, to prepare our constituents for the possibility that we might work together.

Again I considered our options. Unless they united, the democrats could not elect a truly liberal president. The most serious threat was the Communists, and Zyuganov. Who could stand against him? Yeltsin? Chernomyrdin? By May 1995 they were too deeply mired in the war in Chechnya. So far, judging by the approval ratings, democratic voters planned to vote for neither of them. Which meant we would get Zyuganov. Hence our only chance was to create a broad democratic bloc, to bring Yabloko and RDC together. Supporting Grigory was the price we would have to pay. I headed for the TV station. Yavlinsky arrived a little later. I took him aside and told him that I was ready to accept his offer. He was literally transformed; triumph shone in his eyes. Now, with RDC's support, he was no longer just one of a raft of democratic contenders, but the designated presidential candidate. The entire political picture was changing, new opportunities were emerging. Yavlinsky suggested we emphasize this right now, on the air. I agreed. Virtually the entire political elite was watching that broadcast, which made it obvious that Yavlinsky and I had, in principle, reached an agreement on democratic unity! No direct words were said to that effect, but to anyone with even the slightest inkling of the situation it was perfectly clear. After the broadcast we went to my office at the institute and continued our conversation, talked specifically about what to do next. We discussed our options. Which would be better—one bloc, or two blocs with a shared platform and candidates in majority districts? We agreed to work it out as we went along. We talked over fundamental political problems not touched upon earlier, worked on plans for further action. My aides managed to find a bottle of Metaxa, and we raised a glass.

On the following morning I called a meeting of the RDC policy council to inform my colleagues of the progress of the negotiations and to seek their general approval. At the previous plenum of the council I had been given a general mandate to negotiate. That morning there were delighted calls and telegrams from Moscow, Petersburg, from other regions: Well, finally you've agreed to work together; you haven't let us down after all. The drastic change in the mood of the democratic electorate was obvious. Evidently we had made the right decision. The policy council meeting was held, and my colleagues unanimously supported the decision. True, there were complaints that we'd given Yavlinsky too much. But the overwhelming majority agreed that if this would indeed guarantee unity in the democratic camp for the upcoming elections, it was worth it.

Immediately after the policy council session, I was approached by a journalist who asked me to comment on Yavlinsky's statement that the two factions would not be forming a bloc. Thinking that there was some misunderstanding, I replied that I knew of no such announcement. For the rest of the day I remained convinced that there'd been some mistake; after all, any unresolved issues between us were purely technical ones. That evening I watched the news, which confirmed the worst. I telephoned Yavlinsky, and asked him to come by tomorrow so that we could figure out how to get ourselves out of this spot; I was still hoping it was a matter of some purely technical glitches. The tension in Grigory's voice, however, put me on my guard. We agreed to meet in Sergei Yushenkov's office.

The next morning Yavlinsky arrived. He wouldn't look me in the eye. I said that we needed to fix this as soon as possible, to make a joint statement reaffirming our unity and mutual understanding. He uttered something incoherent in response. Something about difficulties within the Yabloko organization, about how the decision wasn't carefully enough prepared; certain problems had arisen. The rest of it I simply didn't understand at all. Something about the Communists, who, in his opinion, could be allies in the fight against the current government.

I had a horrible feeling after we said goodbye, but somewhere in the depths of my soul some doubts still lingered: Yavlinsky had probably run into resistance within Yabloko, and had yet to bring the rest of the delegation around, but he would eventually manage to do it; he wouldn't back away from agreements the whole country had witnessed, from understandings already made public. On Tuesday evening I watched him on television and learned to my amazement that, as it turned out, there could be no coalition between Yabloko and RDC under any circumstances.

So that's the way it was. At first glance, the situation was simply back to what it had been a few days earlier. But in fact this was a tragic loss for the democrats. It was as if all the air had suddenly been let out of an ascending balloon. There was hope for unity, for a real fight, for a victory, and suddenly everything had collapsed, and democratic voters throughout the nation could feel it. They didn't understand what had happened; they didn't know the details. They simply assumed that once again democratic leaders had failed to agree. Perhaps because of personal ambitions.

I think at that very moment a democratic defeat in the parliamentary elections of 1995 became inevitable. The breakdown in the understanding reached by the RDC and Yabloko opened the door to further fragmentation of democratic forces. Any real chance of victory in the elections was gone.

June 1995. A vote of no confidence in Chernomyrdin's government was proposed in the Duma. For us, the situation was complicated: if Russia's Choice supported the no-confidence resolution, it would certainly pass. Rumors were coming my way that the hawks around the President who had pressed for a military solution in Chechnya would be extremely happy to get rid of Chernomyrdin. They had Oleg Soskovets in mind to replace him. By supporting the no-confidence resolution—that is, expressing formal opposition to the war—we might in fact be helping those involved in starting it in the first place. While we were debating what to do, we received unexpected and terrible news: a detachment under the command of Shamil Basaev had attacked Budyonnovsk; a hospital had been seized, and there were enormous numbers of hostages, including many women and children.

At first I didn't believe it. It sounded like a provocation. After all, this was exactly what the proponents of extreme use of force had been waiting for—a demonstration of how amoral the supporters of Chechen independence were, proof that talk was useless.

I had a fair idea what would happen next. A "surgical strike" wouldn't succeed in freeing the hostages, and the whole thing would turn into a bloody mess. There would be massive displays, some spontaneous, some incited, of anti-Chechen sentiment throughout the North Caucasus and other Russian regions, vigilante justice, terrorist acts in response; and as an inevitable reaction, the police would clamp down and a state of emergency would be declared. Goodbye democracy.

Sergei Adamovich Kovalyov contacted me. He was in Germany, about to fly back to Moscow. He said that there was virtually no hope it would work, but we were obligated to try to negotiate with the terrorists. He was taking RDC deputies Mikhail Molostov, Yuly Rybakov, Aleksandr Osovtsev, and Valery Borshchov from Yabloko with him. Together they would fly out to Budyonnovsk.

In the morning Kovalyov called from Budyonnovsk and laid out the situation for me. The hospital was under a disorganized siege. It was under fire, some of it from an armored personnel carrier. There was no organized operation in place to free the hostages, and it was clear that there would not be one, that they would just end up killing a lot of people. Basaev, through a freed hostage, had proposed a temporary cease-fire in exchange for releasing some of the pregnant women and women with newborns from the maternity ward. Sergei Adamovich asked me to contact someone authorized to make such a decision and try to convince them of the need to agree. Yeltsin was not in Moscow; he was on his way to Canada for a Group of Seven meeting. I called Viktor Chernomyrdin from my house, on the regular city phone line. He picked up almost instantly. From experience I knew that in such crises the prime minister's telephone sometimes suddenly goes silent; nobody wants to take the responsibility for decision making.

I relayed the content of my conversation with Kovalyov and tried to convince him of the necessity for a cease-fire. We needed to save as many people as we could. He agreed, saying that he would issue the appropriate order. That day I spoke at a RDC meeting, telling them that our position on the no-confidence issue would to some degree depend on how successful the government was in resolving the Budyonnovsk crisis with the fewest casualties. At the same time I stayed in constant phone contact with Budyonnovsk.

That afternoon there was another call from Kovalyov. He told me that he thought Basaev could be persuaded to release the hostages and drop his obviously unworkable demands for the recall of Russian troops from the North Caucasus if he were promised just one thing—that peace negotiations in Chechnya would begin at once. If Chernomyrdin was willing to authorize Sergei Adamovich to carry on such talks with Basaev, Sergei Adamovich was willing to try.

I attempted to reach Chernomyrdin and Oleg Soskovets, this time with no luck. I then asked the television station to broadcast the message that Gaidar could not get through to the government leadership to discuss an urgent matter concerning the crisis in Budyonnovsk. Exactly two minutes after the information was aired on *Vesti*, Soskovets called me back. I laid out my view of the situation to him, and told him that I thought not taking advantage of this opportunity would be simply criminal. He promised to report to Chernomyrdin at once.

A bit later Chernomyrdin contacted Kovalyov, and authorized him to conduct negotiations. Kovalyov's prediction was right; Basaev indeed agreed to release the hostages, essentially on one condition—that peace negotiations in Chechnya begin at once.

Late that night these understandings were confirmed by Chernomyrdin, who personally spoke with Basaev in front of TV cameras. I think that the idea of making this a public conversation was not merely a matter of politics. By making these events public knowledge, Chernomyrdin had drastically limited the options of those who were ready to write off any such understandings and organize a large-scale operation to storm the hospital, with consequences impossible to predict.

The next day, negotiations to free the hostages moved at a snail's pace. First there were no buses, then they couldn't get enough people to agree to travel with Basaev's unit to guarantee safe passage. The Federal Security Service demanded that the hostages who went along sign an insulting document to the effect that they were joining Basaev's "band" of their own free will and were fully aware of the consequences such a decision might entail. Toward evening tension increased perceptibly.

At midnight there was another call from Kovalyov. He had just been tricked into leaving the hospital and was not being allowed back in. He was fearful that during the next few hours there would be some attempt at a strike. This would mean terrible casualties, and after that a whole cycle of bloodletting in other regions. He asked me to do anything I could to forestall such a turn of events. At half past twelve I called Chernomyrdin. I shared my information with him, and said that if I had any understanding of the logic by which our hard-liners worked, then it would be now, late at night, that they might try something, and that the responsibility for it would land squarely at his feet. Viktor Stepanovich replied that he wouldn't allow anything of the sort, and in rather forceful and plain language told me just what he would do to anyone who tried a stunt like that.

According to information that I have every reason to trust, that night a decision was indeed made to storm the hospital, and only thanks to Chernomyrdin's extremely energetic intervention were many lives saved. I suspect I'm not the only one who has reason to feel grateful to Viktor Stepanovich for his actions during the Budyonnovsk crisis.

The paradoxical result of all this was that an awful, barbaric, and bloody act of terrorism did in fact serve as an impetus for peace talks. I know people who for that very reason justify what Basaev did. I myself am not one of them. I have a fair idea of the alignment of forces within the upper echelons of Russian government at that time and I'm convinced that what saved the lives of the overwhelming majority of hostages and paved the way for peace talks was a rare confluence of circumstances—almost as if you had tossed a coin and it landed on its edge. I believe that the Budyonnovsk crisis was one of those key moments when a threat hung not only over the lives of hundreds of people, but over Russian democracy itself.

Two days after the crisis in Budyonnovsk was resolved, as peace talks were already under way, we voted against the no-confidence resolution with a light heart; however, we voted for a different resolution demanding the resignation of the military and security ministers. Still, a broad coalition, which included everyone from the Communists to Yabloko, garnered enough support for the no-confidence resolution to pass. In stating its formal opposition to the war in Chechnya, the Duma majority voted to oust the very man whose efforts had just made peace possible. According to the existing constitution, only after a second vote of no confidence was the President obliged to choose whether to dismiss his government or dissolve the Duma. Meanwhile, since the Duma could not be dissolved during the period just prior to elections, the prospect of dissolving it lay a full three months away, which meant that the next vote could make the ouster of Chernomyrdin's government a foregone conclusion. In the meantime, this government in which no confidence had just been expressed was only semi-legitimate. Such weakness suited both the Duma majority and a good number of those around the President.

The government decided to repeat our April 1992 maneuver, and raise the stakes; it immediately proposed a draft resolution on confidence in the government, which would force both the parliament and the President to make a quick and stark choice. If the resolution expressing confidence in the government did not pass, then a decision to either dismiss the government or hold early elections to the Duma had to be made at once.

This unexpected turn of events thrust the opposition leaders into a state of near panic. Having just won a vote of no confidence in the government, to then radically change position and agree to hold a confidence vote within the space of one week would be a terrible blow to their reputation. To opt for prolonging the confrontation was dangerous. If the President were to back the prime minister and dissolve the Duma, what then? Give up all their perquisites; give up that powerful Duma base which the Communists were subsequently to use so effectively during the election campaign?

I never liked going to that building on Okhotny Row. The atmosphere was heavy, the air thick with hate. But suddenly that atmosphere had evaporated, and I found myself unexpectedly popular with the spokesmen of the people. Emissaries from the opposition, especially from undecided populist groups, approached me one after another to ask my help in finding some way out of the situation.

In all honesty, I felt tempted to punish these "politicians" and little sneaks. But I realized that I mustn't give in to it. Since the fall of socialism in Russia, not a single parliament had managed to finish its regular session. This, too, had become an unfortunate tradition. Letting it happen again was simply too dangerous. Elections had to be held exactly when they were supposed to be held.

I telephoned Viktor Stepanovich and Boris Nikolaevich, and set up a meeting, our first since the beginning of the war in Chechnya. I suggested a compromise formula: the Duma brings up another no-confidence resolution; it won't get enough votes to pass. The government settles for that, considers the incident closed, and does not insist on an additional vote expressing confidence. As a result, the parliamentary majority gets a whipping, so to speak, but not a very painful one. Both Yeltsin and Chernomyrdin agreed to this proposal.

The following day this decision was agreed upon in principle at a meeting between Yeltsin and leaders of various deputy factions and groups. The Duma, with a great sense of relief, failed to pass the second no-confidence resolution. And when I walked into the building several days later, the usual hatred was back in the air.

This small victory in the Duma could not block out our worries over our prospects in the upcoming parliamentary elections. The democrats were in a very complicated, if not almost hopeless situation. The fact that the December elections would be hard on the RDC was obvious even before Chechnya. Aside from a war that was unpopular in itself, other negative factors were at work. The split within the party between liberals and government supporters, the creation of the Our Home Is Russia movement, which would inevitably take away some of our votes; the failed attempts at building a united democratic coalition; the emergence of scores of tiny democratic groups that had no chance whatsoever of making it past the 5 percent cutoff but could still siphon off part of the democratic vote—all this taken together, according to polls by sociologists, dropped the RDC well down into the risk zone. It would all depend on which way undecided democratic voters would lean, on what carried greater weight with them—the risk of losing any voice at all if the RDC didn't make it onto the ballot, or the hope of having a consistently liberal political force in the Duma.

On the morning of December 21, Chernomyrdin called with his congratulations: we had made the 5 percent cutoff and were on the ballot. The next person to congratulate me was Georgy Satarov, the President's aide in charge of elections. The same information came over TV and radio. There were numerous calls from our supporters, from all those who had sided with us, voted for us. Literally two hours later there was a wave of alarm, and then disappointment: Ryabov and the Central Elections Committee had different information. Our party was still strong in the capitals, Moscow and Petersburg, and nine of our deputies in single-seat districts had won, but we had not made the cutoff.

This, after the earlier news, put us in an especially wretched mood. The overall election results, too, were depressing. The Communists had won a compelling victory; they would have a clear majority in parliament, and Zhirinovsky was close behind them in second place; Our Home Is Russia received less than 10 percent of the vote, and Yabloko less than 7 percent. The very most that the democrats and moderates could do in the Duma was to keep the Communists from gaining a constitutional majority. And we still had presidential elections coming up in six months. If the democrats and moderates went into those elections as fragmented as they were now, a Communist victory might become inevitable.

The postsocialist political cycle is fairly clear in nature. Socialism, as a rule, leaves a legacy of financial ruin, grave budgetary problems, and a large and difficult-to-manage foreign debt. All of that, in conjunction with the absence of any tradition of respect for private property or contract law, raises some very hard-to-solve problems for whatever government comes next.

Reforms inevitably bring radical changes in lifestyle, in relative income, in social status. Society has trouble adapting to such changes, even when they are historically inevitable and right. Yes, of course it was nice not to have to queue up anymore, or grovel to your local Party chief to get a trip to Bulgaria; it was nice to have the opportunity to start your own business or choose your job or where you want to live. But at the same time there were real hardships: you don't have the money to buy all those goods suddenly appearing on store shelves, and you have to work a lot harder than before. You yourself have to plan for your family's future. These are all real-life problems, and the reform government, many people think, is to blame for them. Hence the virtually ubiquitous defeat of reform movements in the second round of elections after the fall of socialism, and the success of those movements that appeal to a sense of nostalgia for the old order.

Those who had ridden to power on this second wave were quite capable of striking a crushing blow to fragile, barely established market mechanisms. This is what happened in Bulgaria, where the socialist comeback in the spring of 1996 produced breadlines, a gasoline crisis, a sharp reduction in currency reserves, and a precipitous drop in the value of the national currency. But that is probably the exception. Within several years of the onset of reforms, in the vast majority of cases, post-Communist parties had been fully integrated into the structure of civil society. Riding to power on their criticism of the reforms, the leaders, as a rule, continued to pursue roughly these same policies. Poland, where the harshest critics of the liberal Balcerowicz continued his policies once they came to power, is a graphic example.

But such examples give rise to dangerous illusions. Many Russians believed that since nothing terrible had happened in Eastern Europe with the rise of post-Communist parties, then nothing terrible would happen here either. In my view that was a dangerous mistake. This is where the fundamental difference between the Eastern European (vassal) and Russian (imperial) Communist parties would make itself felt. The Eastern European Communist parties—say the Polish, the Hungarian, the Bulgarian—were never independent in any real sense. In essence they were branch offices of the Soviet Communist Party charged with administering their respective satellite nations. For that reason their own people always saw them as symbols of national humiliation. And after the fall of the Communist empire and the discrediting of the Communist ideology, they evolved along social democratic lines.

The situation in Russia was quite different. Here, Communist ideology had long ago come more to resemble tinsel, the trappings of empire. The collapse of socialism in Russia concided with the collapse of the empire. Communism here became intertwined with radical nationalism, and the Communist Party of the Russian Federation was evolving not toward social democracy, but national socialism. All the Nazi rhetoric of the twenties and early thirties was wonderfully adaptable to post-Soviet realities: the passages from Hitler echoing through the pages of Russian Communist leader Gennady Zyuganov's books are hardly an accident. Of course, all analogies are relative, and the roots of the CPRF are substantially different from those of the German Nazi party, yet the overall tendencies in its evolution between 1991 and 1996 were obvious. This was a party of aggressive revanchism, one that did not acknowledge the rules of the game in a democratic society. A Communist victory in presidential elections would be fraught with potential risk of a major crisis in free-market and democratic institutions.

Given current conditions—a young market economy with developed financial markets—it would be easy enough to construct a model of what might follow a Communist victory: the crash of the Russian stock market, the attempt to dump shares in Russian enterprises and change the funds paid out into convertible currency as quickly as possible, a major crisis in the government loan market, individual savings converted from rubles into foreign currency, similar actions by banks and enterprises.

As early as autumn 1995 the approach of presidential elections and the threat of a Communist return to power began to affect financial markets. The percentage of individual foreign currency savings was again growing.

The young, still unstable Russian tax system is hardly a well-oiled machine. It needs to be adjusted constantly. All the loopholes opening up in it need to be plugged, including the outright refusal by major enterprises to pay their taxes. This was what Chubais was working on so vigorously in 1995. His dismissal in January 1996 for reasons linked to the campaign sent a powerful signal to the market. Enterprise directors got it; now they could take their time with taxes, the government wasn't going to be overly zealous. Hence the sharp drop in state revenues, and the rise in defaults. Beginning in March, there was a growing crisis in the government loan market. The interest rate on government treasury bonds that would come to maturity before the first round of presidential elections was three times higher than that for bonds that would mature after the first of June.

One hardly had to be a great economist to understand that in the event of a Zyuganov victory, even before he set foot in a Kremlin office, lines would form at currency exchange offices, and there would be massive capital flight—Russian and foreign both. Rapid exhaustion of foreign currency reserves, a sharp drop in the exchange value of the ruble, the loss of the convertible ruble—all these things were virtually unavoidable stages in the development of the crisis that would unfold as a result of a Communist victory. Relinquishing a convertible ruble would mark the beginning of the collapse of all those market mechanisms that had taken such effort to create. Competition in imports would disappear, price growth would accelerate, and there would again be shortages in a variety of markets. The natural reaction of the populace to a nonconvertible ruble and the reappearance of shortages would be panic buying, hoarding of essential items, even faster-rising prices, and increasing poverty. Add to that the virtually inevitable attempts to introduce price controls for the most crucial commodities. And price controls combined with financial and consumer panic were a direct route to the reappearance of shortages across the board.

Where would cities get their grain if the ruble no longer functioned? How would they get it from farmers and agricultural enterprises? Send troops to the villages to requisition it?

In short, economic analysis showed that a Communist victory would automatically destroy market regulators, and the country would end up in the same economic chaos that it experienced in 1991, when neither money nor commands were working. It was easy enough to imagine how the populace would react—growing discontent, an unpopular regime, a feverish hunt for enemies of the people. Nor would any sort of stable totalitarianism come out of it either; there was neither the social, nor the ideological, nor the financial foundation for it. And Russia's prospects for development in the twenty-first century would be dealt a terrific blow.

At the same time, the possibility of a Communist victory was no anomaly, no accident of history. They had simply ridden the same wave that had brought a multitude of post-Communist parties to power in Eastern Europe. The question was whether in Russia they could be stopped, and if so, how.

The main hope was that society did in fact see the risks inherent in a Communist victory in Russia, that its instinct for self-preservation would be aroused. After all, it is one thing to express your dissatisfaction with the government during parliamentary elections, all the while knowing that your life won't radically change, and quite another to cast your vote for a radical "counterreformation" in Russia.

We democrats—and all those who favored continuing liberal reforms, strengthening private property rights, fair play, acceleration of agrarian and military reforms, and reform of the Russian machinery of government—certainly didn't need a Communist victory. But neither did the party in power need it, nor did those who were focused on maintaining the status quo, for whom our newly formed and far from attractive nomenclature capitalism was just fine. They didn't need any major upheavals either.

Much had changed in Russia over the last five years. What were once theoretical constructs, projects, ideas—a developed system of markets, a nonshortage economy, a convertible ruble, freedom of foreign trade, a massive private sector, auctions, joint-stock companies—had become a reality, a way of life, for millions of people. Even that part of the elite who

in the beginning of 1992 considered our free-market ideas purely theoretical now took them for granted and had no intention of rejecting the
market mechanisms already created.

Granted, we didn't see eye to eye with the party in power on what direction further development in Russia should take, but today, by force
of circumstance, we were strategic allies. Back in the spring of 1995 it
might have been possible for a unified coalition of democrats to provide a counterweight to the Communists. In early 1996, after the crushing defeat in the parliamentary elections, that possibility was no longer
real. This meant that a strategic alliance between democrats and the party
in power was a necessary condition for preventing a Communist
comeback.

Necessary, yes, but sufficient? Yeltsin was the only one who could lay
claim to the role of coalition leader. He personified the existing government, and at the same time, for all his retreats and missteps, remained
the chief initiator of Russian reform. In recent months, however, he had
been strikingly passive, and gave the impression of a tired and ailing
man; his characteristic energy was gone. One got the impression that he
was simply being manipulated by those around him. His public support
had dropped close to the zero mark. Pinning our hopes of averting a
Communist comeback on him seemed simply suicidal. What could a
layabout Ilya Muromets do against a Tatar invasion?

The crisis in Yeltsin's goverment came to a head in Pervomaisk.

I had already left for my dacha before any of the events there took
place. I had decided to get some work done and asked my secretary,
Lenochka, not to call unless it was urgent. But there was a call from the
office, and Lenochka's frightened voice telling me she had just heard a report on TV that terrorists in Pervomaisk claimed they would free their
hostages if either Gaidar, Yavlinsky, or Lebed would offer himself in their
place. Journalists were asking for comment. By this time it was clear to
me that the plan was to destroy Salman Raduev (Dudaev's son-in-law)
and his detachment, no matter what the cost. Nonetheless, if there was
any chance of limiting the number of casualties, of saving civilians, we
had to take advantage of it. I grabbed my things and dashed to the office.

I tried to telephone Barsukov, but couldn't reach him in person; I asked that he be told that I thought the Chechens' offer should be accepted contingent on what they planned to do next. I called the leadership of the General Staff and key officials in the President's administration. I sensed from their reaction that they had already more or less buried the hostages.

The operation was being commanded by Mikhail Barsukov, director of the Federal Security Service. Government actions so far made it fairly clear that the mission was to destroy the terrorists without care for the lives of the hostages. They had already been declared killed. But the strike failed, and Dudaev's fighters retreated, taking their hostages with them. It was an odd mix of cruelty and ineptitude. At the press conference afterward, Barsukov, with his characteristic tact, declared that all Chechens were either murderers or thugs or, at best, thieves. The President went before television cameras to talk about a wonderfully planned operation involving thirty-eight snipers, then about the creation of a fortified area within Pervomaisk. He looked totally out of touch with reality. It was impossible, painful, embarrassing, to watch.

I came out with an extremely sharply worded statement condemning the government's actions and said that the President was becoming no more than a puppet in the hands of some very dangerous people; I then dispatched a letter to Boris Nikolaevich, in which I resigned from his Presidential Council.

I received a letter from the President.

To Ye. T. Gaidar

Yegor Timurovich!

Fate brought us together at a most critical and dangerous moment for the country. It is in no small degree thanks to your courage that we were able to embark on economic reform and political transformation. Whatever anyone may say, I remain true to that course.

I know that you are not engaged in politics for personal gain. I very much hope that in working to resolve this year's exceedingly complex political problems, you, as you always have in the past, will put not emotions, but Russia's interests paramount, and that when the critical moment comes you will demonstrate clear strategic vision.

I thank you for all the work we accomplished together. I wish you all the best.

B. N. Yeltsin

My reply:

Dear Boris Nikolaevich!

Thank you for your letter of 2 February. Whatever turn events may take in the future, I will always remember the courage you showed in 1991, when you took on the responsibility of beginning reforms so vital to the nation, yet so politically dangerous. I am convinced that this is precisely what allowed us to avert the threat of real catastrophe in the winter and spring of 1992. We knew in 1991 that the task of reforming Russian society after 75 years of Communist rule would be very difficult; probably, though, we did not understand how painful it would be. For that very reason — that I well realize what a burden was placed on your shoulders — I will always have the greatest of respect for what you have done to bring democracy and a market economy to Russia. This is precisely why it is so painful for me to watch the people in whom you now place your trust compromise you with their lies and ineptitude — as in the hostage crisis in Pervomaisk.

Of course, my first priority in what I do today and will do in the months ahead is to prevent the Communists from coming to power, to prevent yet another bloody experiment capable of wiping out much of what we have fought to achieve. This, not emotions, will determine where I stand. Unfortunately, my many contacts with people, with voters in various regions of Russia, have made me realize all too well that, in their eyes, the responsibility for today's far from simple problems lies with those who had the political courage to begin these transformations — which means, first and foremost, with you and me. That is why the decision to center resistance to the Communists around your candidacy seems wrong to me.

Regardless of our current political differences, you will always have my profound personal respect.

Yegor Gaidar

Well, fine, but what next? Yavlinsky dropped in several times to ask me to back his candidacy. I discussed this possibility with the RDC's policy council. The opinion of the vast majority of my colleagues was that it was out of the question. After his incredible about-face of the previous May, the majority of our cohorts wouldn't hear of backing Yavlinsky. Moreover the business in January, when the stance taken by Yabloko allowed the Communists to easily push their representative Gennady Seleznev through as chairman of the State Duma, had hardly created any additional enthusiasm for such an alliance. It was all too clear: building an anti-Communist coalition between the democracy party and the party in power around Yavlinsky was impossible. It was a losing game. Even if by some miracle I could persuade all our supporters to vote for Yavlinsky, he still had no chance of getting to the second round.

By this time I saw only two very faint possibilites for preventing a Zyuganov win: either convince Yeltsin not to run and back Chernomyrdin or, if we could not do that, try to create a democratic coalition around Nizhegorod governor Boris Nemtsov. He was young, energetic, uninvolved in Moscow squabbles, didn't arouse any objections with RDC or Yabloko voters, had a talent for politics, and knew how to talk with people, charm them, get their support. He also had some real accomplishments to his credit; he was a successful governor just coming off a landslide victory in his very complicated home region. After consulting with leaders of the various democratic parties, I was convinced that for the majority of them this was an acceptable option. In the absence of any coalition between the party in power and the democrats, Nemtsov seemed to be the only democratic political figure with any chance at all of getting to the second round of elections, let alone winning.

I was soon persuaded that neither option would do. Yeltsin had decided to run, and Chernomyrdin would never go up against him. And besides, that would be foolish anyway—the last thing the government party needed was a schism in its own ranks. I tried to persuade Yavlinsky of the expediency of jointly backing Nemtsov; otherwise his candidacy made no sense and would simply split the democratic vote. Yavlinsky refused. By the end of February 1996 all the options that had offered at least some faint hope had been explored and had led nowhere.

A good number of those surrounding Yeltsin didn't think much of his chances of winning. Talk of either canceling or postponing the elections was getting louder. I had always been categorically opposed to those options, not only on principle, but for profoundly pragmatic reasons. There were no constitutional provisions for postponing an election. This would be stepping outside the law, and unlike the 1993 decision, doing so on grounds incomprehensible to the public. In that event, Yeltsin's government would not have a shred of legitimacy left, and the fate of the nation would depend on what stance the military and security ministries chose to take. I knew enough not to overestimate their support of the current government; the army wouldn't stick its nose in politics on its own, but if it were pushed that way, the President might find himself very unpleasantly surprised. The scheme would fall through, and the history of fledgling Russian democracy would end in a GKChP style farce. Or even supposing the coup were successful, a Yeltsin illegitimately in power would be a hostage, a puppet in the hands of the coup's organizers and instigators. The blatant bungling by the President's campaign staff in February left little doubt that someone wanted to leave Yeltsin no alternative but the use of force.

My colleagues on the RDC policy council tried to talk me into letting myself be nominated for President; this, they said, was the way out. I understood perfectly well that it wasn't. Nominating me wouldn't solve anything and would only cause a good deal of unnecessary commotion in the democratic camp.

Boris Nikolaevich invited me in for a talk. I explained my position to him one more time and talked about what I thought he should do if he hoped to pull democratic votes over to his side. We talked about staffing and about the need for a serious peace effort in Chechnya.

During our conversation I caught myself thinking that the Yeltsin I saw before me was not the man who just one month earlier had stood in front of TV cameras talking some nonsense about thirty-eight snipers and a fortified stronghold in Pervomaisk. He was clear, well-prepared, energetic, quick to grasp what was said. It was as if these last five years had never been, as if we were back in October 1991, at that first meeting that opened the door to a reform government. After our conversation, for the first time in months, I felt some hope that perhaps, at this pivotal moment for Russia, Yeltsin would be able to suddenly change, to regain his old energy and reestablish contact with the voters.

And indeed, in March of 1996 the people suddenly saw before them an utterly new President, the one they had forgotten they had; this was the Yeltsin of 1991, with his unique ability to talk with people, to win them over with his energy and drive. You had the feeling that Ilya Muromets had finally shaken off his "slows." The first news on the rise in Yeltsin's popularity rating was greeted skeptically: *It can't be.* But soon the realization dawned that the public mood had indeed changed, and it was clear that in the upcoming elections it would be Yeltsin against Zyuganov.

In March, once Yeltsin had managed to make the campaign a two-way fight, our choice essentially became obvious. Given Zyuganov versus Yeltsin, we, as the party of democracy, were simply obliged to back Yeltsin. Whatever serious grievances we might have, refusing to support him would mean taking the most idiotic of adolescent stances: *Mama, I don't care if my ears freeze. I won't wear this hat.*

It was easy enough to see that Yeltsin, for all his sins, was still the chief deterrent to the Communist second coming, and this meant a great deal. It meant that private property in Russia would still be safeguarded, that the markets would not be demolished, that the newly created, fledgling institutions of Russian democratic society would have an opportunity to live and develop, gradually disciplining the regime and forcing it to reckon with them. Economic growth would create resources for the resolution of the most pressing social problems, and we would finally be able to end the hopeless business of trying to divide up an ever smaller public pie. That very middle class that serves as a potential base of support for liberal ideas, for the struggle to curtail the absolute power of the bureaucracy and thus to separate property from government, would start to flex its muscles, to recognize where its own interests lay. In short, all this meant that the infinitely complex problems of making postsocialist change in Russia irreversible would be resolved. In voting for Yeltsin, we didn't support his administration so much as private ownership, a convertible ruble, a civil society in Russia. Proceeding from these arguments, the RDC convention resolved by an overwhelming majority of votes— 157 for, 1 against—to vigorously support Yeltsin in his campaign for reelection.

Some people were quick to accuse me of acting in unprincipled fashion. Not so long ago, they said, Gaidar was asking Yeltsin to drop out of the presidential race. Last spring he declared on national television in front of the whole country that he couldn't support Yeltsin's candidacy, and suddenly, look here—over the summer he makes a 180-degree turn. But really—and I repeat this for the slow-witted—since spring the situation had itself done a 180-degree turn. And you would have to be an ass to keep repeating, out of pure obstinacy, the same old thing about "never compromising your principles."

By the eve of the elections it was clear that Yeltsin had every chance of winning. But a victory was above all a victory for reform. It was testimony that the infant was alive and breathing, that it would grow and mature. This was therefore a victory for those who had stood over its cradle—the cradle of reforms. And that meant it was a personal victory for me as well.

I hope that in time Anatoly Borisovich Chubais, who took far greater part in the presidential campaign than I did, will be able to tell the real story of the struggle in the upper echelons of power over the use of military force, of the attempt to force a declaration of a state of emergency, of the crafting of the alliance between Yeltsin and Lebed, and of the dramatic events leading up to the ouster of Korzhakov, Barsukov, and Soskovets. Meanwhile, this is all perhaps too recent and too sensitive an issue for candid conversation. For me, other things take precedence;

for the point is that Yeltsin's victory in the July 3 presidential elections marked an end of the Russian revolution of the early 1990s, and of communism in Russia overall.

In failing to seize power in 1996, despite all the pain of a society struggling to adapt to a new way of life, and in missing the first wave of the postsocialist political cycle, the CPRF lost its chance of ever again ruling Russia. Unless, of course, it radically reconstructs itself.

It seems to me that this was best for the CPRF itself. Though it lost the July elections, it remains an influential opposition force, well represented in parliament, and controls a considerable number of regions without bearing direct responsibility for the state of the nation. Most likely within the party some lines will be drawn. Forces willing to accept the institutions of a civil society as a given, willing to "social democratize" themselves, will separate out.

I once happened to say, in a private conversation with one of the Communist leaders, that a Communist victory would be more dangerous for them than for anyone else. When everything eventually fell apart—which, in the event they came to power, it certainly would— they would hardly be treated so kindly as they had been after August 1991. He didn't disagree. At times, watching Zyuganov conduct his election campaign, I had the impression that he himself was afraid of winning, that he realized he couldn't manage all the levers that now regulated Russian life. Apparently, new markets, a private sector, and property relations formed the one obstacle on the road to power that the Communists could not overleap.

Conclusion

Now a fledgling, still very unattractive and imperfect Russian capitalism, happily escaped from the threat of Communist counterreformation, faces a new strategic dilemma. Property and government power in Russia are still not clearly divorced from one another; thousands of threads keep them intertwined. The success of a bank or an enterprise depends more on its close relations with government bodies than on how efficiently it conducts its business. Tax and customs regulations are full of loopholes; the system is like a sieve through which trillions of rubles are pouring. Bureaucrats have countless opportunities to spend government funds at their own discretion. There is nothing to guarantee the game will be played by the rules. The creation and redistribution of administrative rent is a far more reliable way to get rich than is the introduction of a new product or entry into new markets. The source of many of our social and economic woes is corrupt government itself, behind which stand powerful interests involved in the redistribution of this very administrative rent, who hope that this sort of corrupt, bureaucratic capitalism will establish itself once and for all in Russia. Behind all the talk about fighting "market romanticism" and "strengthening government control over the economy" lurks, as a rule, this self-interest. We know this sort of capitalism well enough from "third world" experience. It can even ensure economic growth, but invariably a very ugly form of it, accompanied by glaring social inequities that give rise to chronic social and political instability.

It's no secret what must be done to put Russian capitalism on a different and civilized track. We must:

— Clearly separate property from government power.

— Guarantee that everyone in the economy plays by the same rules.

— Patch up the holes in the tax and customs system.

— Introduce a purchasing code—an instrument of stringent control over government spending.

— Severely restrict bureaucratic intervention in the administration of rival sectors of the economy.

— Force the government to do what it must do in a market environment: guarantee order, the stability of the national currency, contract compliance, social protections, and regulation of natural monopolies.

In other words, what is vital for Russia now is a new cycle of liberal reforms that would help make our fledgling market less criminal and corrupt, our government more capable and honest, and distribution of the fruits of economic growth more equitable. The struggle over these alternatives will define the political and economic development of Russia in the coming years.

But that's another story. And another book.

Afterword to the
English-Language Edition

I finished work on this book in July 1996, just after Boris Yeltsin's victory in the elections. What has happened since has borne out my predictions: the interrelationship between ownership and government and the struggle over what form emerging Russian capitalism would take have indeed become the focus of economic and political clashes in this new stage of Russia's development. Yeltsin's convincing win and the obvious demoralization of the Communist opposition seemed to have created a unique opportunity for beginning a new round of liberal reforms. Life, however, had other plans.

The broad anti-Communist coalition—from financial tycoons to political liberals—that guaranteed Yeltsin his victory was extremely diverse. It was united by a common enemy and a shared sense of the threat inherent in a repeat of the Communist experiment, but certainly not by any shared understanding of what to do with either the Russian economy or Russian society. For some, Yeltsin's victory meant an opportunity to say no to dangerous compromises, to go the way of clear separation of property ownership and government, to ensure transparency in the functioning of the machinery of state—to guarantee a level playing field. For others, Yeltsin's victory meant the pleasant prospect of maintaining the status quo, a setting in which ownership and government were intertwined, thus offering them a new closeness to a government they had just supported in the elections and throwing open the door to new benefits and privileges. Only Yeltsin himself could clearly define the road down which he planned to lead Russia. However, his ill health dashed any hopes for a clear answer to this strategic question. As a result, the government formed in August 1997 was perhaps the weakest in recent years.

The one trait that has guaranteed Viktor Chernomyrdin's political longevity throughout Russia's tumultuous 1990s is his ability to head such diverse governments—governments that differ radically in their composition, their avowed goals, their actual economic and political priorities. Between December 1992 and August 1996, he has led five distinctly different governments (December 1992 to September 1993, September 1993 to January 1994, January 1994 to October 1994, November 1994 to January 1996, and January 1996 to August 1996). Chernomyrdin's sixth government, formed in August 1996, which included a considerable group of highly qualified people truly striving for the good of Russia, proved to be strikingly ill-matched and failed to implement any sort of integrated economic policy. Resolutions granting new benefits or allocations were monotonously followed by other resolutions repealing those just adopted. Tax compliance, already undermined by political instability during the presidential campaign, continued to decline. The apotheosis of this government was its proposed 1997 budget, later adopted by the Duma, in which both expenditures and revenues were, according to unanimous expert opinion, inflated by a minimum of 30 percent. Commitments made but never kept resulted in months-long delays in pension payments, military pay, and teachers' and doctors' salaries.

The government's failure to fulfill its obligations in supporting the army, paying on military procurement orders, paying for fuel and electricity—all of which was inevitable, given the unrealistic budget—undermined tax compliance to an even greater degree. He who doesn't pay up can hardly count on being paid back. By January-February of 1997, federal budget monetary revenues had dropped to a critical low. The social and political atmosphere quickly heated up. The Duma majority, which had taken great satisfaction in watching the government's ineffectual attempts at action, now had its bearings; its representatives began talking about the need to prime the presses for a new currency issue. It was becoming clear that the possibilities for further postponing substantive economic decisions were exhausted.

In late 1996, I assembled my closest institute colleagues and told them that in my view the situation now developing was so unstable as to herald a new and serious turn in economic policy. We might hold out for another month or two, three at the most, and then we would have to choose: either back to the printing press, extremely high inflation, and goodbye to any hope of economic growth, or else harsh and forceful liberal reforms that would allow us to escape the fiscal crisis, stabilize the budget, eliminate delays in pension and budget payments, and create a base for stable economic growth. This meant that once again, as in autumn of 1991, creation of a realistic, methodically worked-out reform program was becoming crucial. S. Sinelnikov, A. Ulyukaev, Y. Serova, S. Shishkin, Y. Gontmakher, M. Dmitriev, S. Vasiliev, V. Mau, N. Kosareva, A. Shamuzafarov, and others were all actively involved in developing such a program. The result was a set of documents delineating and describing the direction these crucial transformations should take.

The proposals included:

—major tax reform aimed at radically simplifying the tax system, eliminating unjustified tax breaks and privileges, and lightening the burden on the honest taxpayer;

—reform of the social support system to guarantee that it will remain targeted in nature and include need as a criterion for granting benefits and compensation;

—housing and utility reform, aimed at developing competition, increasing the monitoring of price-setting by local natural monopolies, introducing targeted support for low-income families, and lowering the percentage of housing subsidies in local budgets.

In the area of military reform the main thing was to break the vicious cycle in which lack of budget resources served to justify preservation of the unwieldy and obviously inefficient military structure inherited from the Soviet Union. Therefore, the chief emphasis here was on ways to ensure that the military reform would pay for itself, thus saving money even over the short term. For example, there should be a reform in military education, elimination of the enormous and now—in a market economy—unnecessary system of payment in kind (military commerce, state farms, construction, repair plants, etc.), sale of freed property, and rationalization of administrative structures.

In order to ensure transparency in the budget and increased monitoring of government spending, the proposal was to quickly do away with authorized banks, finish work on a treasury system of budget implementation, and enact a purchasing code that would ensure open and competitive expenditure of government funds. Measures aimed at reforming medical-care and education systems and regulation of natural monopolies were also proposed, as was a reform of the relationship between federal and regional budgets.

On the whole, we were talking about a reform package that would substantially lighten the government burden on the economy, increase efficiency in the use of government funds, bring the financial obligations of the government into line with its resources, and ensure that government expenditures would be both transparent to society and subject to its control. It was clear that the proposed transformations would have a serious impact on powerful and influential interest groups and that attempts to implement them would meet with serious resistance, but the critical nature of the situation and the fact that the government's policy was going nowhere made it possible that there might be movement in the direction we proposed.

The President supported the proposed program, and its most important pieces were included in a presidential address, the President's budget address. In February 1997, when a now-healthy Yeltsin gave a highly critical assessment of the government's performance so far, it became clear that major changes were on the horizon—both in the composition and the structure of the government, and in the line it was pursuing.

In March 1997 a new government, Chernomyrdin's seventh, was formed. It was a very different group of people. Anatoly Chubais and Boris Nemtsov became first deputy prime ministers. A new page in the history of liberal reform in Russia had been turned.

The renovated government resolutely set to work. Within its first few weeks in action, the President had already signed decrees on the change-over to a treasury system of budget implementation and on the introduction of a competitive government purchasing system. A draft version of a tax code aimed at implementing major tax reform was brought before the Duma, as was a social legislation package that would allow for a substantial increase in government allocations in support of poor families. Work was begun on a housing and utilities reform. After a change in Defense Ministry leadership, there was finally a movement from words to actions in this area as well. A presidential decree outlined basic directives for reforming natural monopolies. Increased state monitoring of their activities made it possible to pay down a significant part of the budget deficit. The budget for 1998 was being worked out on the basis of realistic hypotheses about the dynamics of state revenues and the need to strictly limit budget expenditures as well as drastically reduce the principal debt.

The Russian economy's most obvious reaction to the emergence of a purposeful and strict course of government action was a substantial improvement in tax collection. There was a real possibility that the amount of money owed pensioners and other recipients of budget funds would not only stop growing, but even begin to shrink. By July 1, the government had managed to pay off any remaining money owed to the Pension Fund. Simultaneously, major operators in international financial markets had begun to radically change their assessment of Russian economic prospects. The value of Russian stocks was growing by leaps and bounds, and interest rates on government obligations were dropping. What were once rather hypothetical conversations about massive direct investment in Russia by major international firms (Fiat, Opel, British Petroleum, Royal Dutch Shell, and others) were now framed in practical terms. Summer marked the first growth in manufacturing output since 1989. The huge auction of shares in Svyazinvest held in July 1997—which was generally conceded by international experts to be both transparent and honest—would seem to acknowledge that Russia had taken the crucial step toward leveling the economic playing field.

For the team of young reformers now in government, this was a euphoric time, and it seemed that everything was possible and everything was working. Just a little more time, and they could push a tax code and a social reform package through the Duma, launch a pension reform, bring the treasury system to completion, and convince the world that the rules at work in the emerging Russian market were both fixed and fair and that a Russian economic miracle was on the horizon. Support for the government was growing. Social tensions eased. Given such results in such a short time, it seemed that nothing could stop the forward momentum. This, unfortunately, was an illusion. The next few months were to show that political realities in Russia's society-in-transition are far harsher.

In fact, just as in 1992, the reform team fell victim to its own success, to the first signs of socioeconomic stabilization. The sense of profound crisis that dominated the spring of 1997 abated. Money owed the Pension Fund had been paid off, and the amount owed for military back pay was quickly diminishing. Economic growth had begun, and foreign capital was surging into the country. But who needed all this fuss and bother, these painful reforms, these young reformers and their incomprehensible notions? Meanwhile practically every step forward—every step that brought stabilization to the country—affected the interests of major banks, financial and manufacturing structures, and natural monopolies. In order to pay pensioners and other budget recipients, money had to be taken from somebody, and in this case that somebody was the rich and the powerful. And, for some reason, the rich and the powerful didn't like that much. So by early summer of 1997, for all the outward civility, relations between the young reform team and the financial and economic elites who had supported Yeltsin in 1996 became increasingly tense. The chief reproach aimed at the government was very simple: *They won't let us make a living.* The whole thing blew up after the Svyazinvest auction, where a group of economic and political heavyweights including Boris Berezovsky and Boris Gusinsky failed to win the day. The timing was, in my view, pure chance. The conflict could have come out into the open for any reason at all. It didn't matter what. Svyazinvest itself had nothing to do with it; this was a fight over the relationship between property ownership and government in Russian society.

The split in the Yeltsin coalition of 1996, the massive propaganda war against the young reformers, the alliance of part of the financial oligarchy with the Communist majority in the Duma—all this again changed the situation radically. It became clear that under these conditions any chance of pursuing radical tax reform or reform of the social support system was minimal. In preparing the 1998 budget, the government was forced into yet another dangerous compromise; the pace of reform faltered; and international investors felt that they had underestimated the obstacles standing in the way of stable economic growth in Russia. The government was working hard, fighting to make progress in reform in certain areas (housing and utilities, military reform, health-care reform, etc.) while simultaneously holding off counteroffensives along the entire front.

Now, in January 1998, I can reiterate what I said a year and a half ago, in July 1996: what is vital for Russia is a new cycle of liberal reforms that would help make our fledgling market less criminal and corrupt, our government more capable and honest, and the distribution of the fruits of economic growth more equitable. The struggle over these alternatives will define the political and economic development of Russia in the coming years.

But now it is particularly clear just how difficult that struggle will be.

Yegor Gaidar

Notes

Annotation and references to the text have been provided by Professor Stephen Hanson, University of Washington, and translator Jane Ann Miller.

Foreword

1. For a flavor of these times, see *V avguste 91-go: Rossiya glazami ochevidtsev* (Moscow: Limbus-Press, 1993); and Victoria Bonnell, Ann Cooper, and Gregory Freidin, *Russia at the Barricades: Eyewitness Accounts of the August 1991 Coup* (New York: M. E. Sharpe, 1994).

2. Gorbachev, as quoted in *Sovetskaya Rossiya*, October 22, 1991, p. 1.

3. In earlier democratic "transitions" such as those in the United States and England, the existing exclusionary democratic institutions were opened up— expanding the franchise without changing the rules of the game.

4. On peaceful revolution as a model for understanding the Soviet/Russian transformation, see Michael McFaul, "Revolutionary Transformations in Comparative Perspective: Defining a Post-Communist Research Agenda," in *Reexamining the Soviet Experience: Essays in Honor of Alexander Dallin*, ed. David Holloway and Norman Naimark, pp. 167–96 (Boulder, Colo.: Westview Press, 1996).

5. For details see Anders Aslund, *How Russia Became a Market Economy* (Washington, D.C.: Brookings Institution Press, 1995), chap. 2.

6. Interview with Khasbulatov in *Narodnii Deputat*, no. 15 (1991), pp. 7–8; reprinted in *Yeltsin-Khasbulatov: Edinstvo, Kompromiss, Bor'ba* (Moscow: "Terra," 1994), p. 90.

7. Boris Yeltsin, *Zapiski Prezidenta* (Moscow: Ogonek, 1994), p. 163.

8. Ibid., p. 165.

9. Ibid., p. 164.

10. Yeltsin's address to the Fifth Congress, October 28, 1991; reprinted in *Yeltsin-Khasbulatov*, p. 97.

11. Yeltsin outlined the general principles of the economic reform plan on October 28, 1991, before the fifth session of the Russian Congress of People's Deputies. For a summary and analysis of the program, see Keith Bush, "El'tsin's Economic Reform Program," *Report on the USSR*, November 15, 1991, pp. 1–6.

Preface

1. The Communist Party of the Russian Federation (CPRF), led by Gennady Zyuganov, attained 22.3 percent of the party list vote and an additional 58 seats

in single-member electoral districts in the 1995 elections to the State Duma, making it by far the largest party in the parliament. Zyuganov was thus the early favorite to win the presidential elections scheduled for June 1996, but he finished second to Boris Yeltsin, who then won the runoff election for the presidency in July.

Chapter 1: Childhood

1. Arkady Gaidar's children's book *Timur and His Team*, which chronicles the adventures of Timur, a heroic young Communist who with his friends defends their village against various anti-Bolshevik villains during the Russian Civil War, was one of the most widely assigned texts for schoolchildren during the Soviet era.

2. Arzamas is a city of approximately 120,000 people about 220 miles east of Moscow.

3. Marshals Mikhail Tukhachevsky and Vasily Blyukher were executed, along with almost the entire Soviet officer corps, during Stalin's bloody purge of the military in 1937–38.

4. Koktebel is a Black Sea resort known as a center of artistic life and wine-making. Mikhail Bulgakov (1891–1940), author of *The Master and Margarita*, is one the most famous and popular Russian writers of the twentieth centry. His wife, Yelena Bulgakova, had previously been married to General Shilov, with whom she had had two sons; she married Bulgakov in 1932, and became the younger son's legal guardian.

5. Pavel Petrovich Bazhov (1879–1950) published several well-known volumes of stories based on folktales of the Urals.

6. Playa Girón is the beach on the Bay of Pigs where the United States launched its failed 1961 invasion of Cuba.

7. Mikhail Prishvin (1873–1954) was the author of numerous short stories and autobiographical sketches concerning the beauty and harmony of nature. Zvenigorod is a town about 25 miles to the west of Moscow. *Podmoskovye* refers to the region of small towns and villages around Moscow.

8. The Strugatsky brothers, Arkady Natanovich and Boris Natanovich, jointly wrote many internationally known works of science fiction during the Soviet period. The immense popularity of their books among the Soviet intelligentsia owed something to the fact that science fiction often raised politically sensitive issues—including, as Gaidar mentions below, economic problems—that could not be discussed openly elsewhere.

Chapter 2: Getting My Bearings

1. Eduard Bernstein, Roger Garaudy, and Ota Šik were all known as "revisionist" Marxists interested in reconciling socialism and the market. Bernstein was the original "revisionist" within the German Social Democratic Party at the turn of the twentieth century who advocated "evolutionary socialism" rather than a revolutionary break with capitalism. Šik was the economic theorist who originally inspired the Prague Spring reforms of 1968 in Czechoslovakia. Garaudy broke with the French Communist Party in the 1960s; he has recently become associated with French fascism and Holocaust revisionism.

2. Maksim Gorky (1868–1936) and Konstantin Trenyov (1876–1945) were two Soviet authors and playwrights whose works were approved by the Communist Party and therefore were part of the school curriculum throughout the Soviet era.

3. INION is the Russian acronym for the Institute for Information on Social Sciences of the Soviet Academy of Sciences.

4. Aleksei Kosygin was prime minister of the USSR from 1964 until his death in 1980.

5. During the Soviet era, officially for reasons of national security, there was limited access to certain cities and areas where defense research or manufacturing was concentrated. These "closed cities" were completely off limits to foreigners.

Chapter 3: Options and Forecasts

1. During the mid-1960s, Prime Minister Kosygin sponsored a limited set of economic reforms designed to decentralize the Stalinist planning apparatus and to produce goods with less waste. These "Kosygin reforms" were halted after the Soviet invasion of Czechoslovakia in 1968.

2. Mikhail Speransky drew up a comprehensive legal code for Tsar Alexander I in 1809 only to have it almost entirely rejected; Sergei Witte struggled to modernize Russia's economy under Nicholas II, but was ultimately forced out of power by 1906; and Pyotr Stolypin attempted to reform Russia's agricultural production, but was assassinated by a terrorist in 1911.

3. On January 13, 1991, fifteen Lithuanians were killed by Soviet paratroopers during a failed effort by Communist Party hard-liners to foment pro-Soviet coups in the Baltic States. Gorbachev has continued to this day to deny any responsibility for the attack. The event nonetheless severely undermined Gorbachev's credentials as a liberal reformer.

4. At a Central Committee plenum in October 1987, Yeltsin called for the ouster of the more orthodox Leninist Yegor Ligachev and the speeding up of perestroika. At the Moscow city conference in November, he was berated for over four hours by a whole series of party officials for this "betrayal" of party unity; in his response, Yeltsin meekly confessed his errors. However, by the Nineteenth Party Conference in June 1988, he had once again returned to the offensive in the struggle against Leninist hard-liners in the party leadership, calling publicly for a further radicalization of reforms.

5. GUM is the Russian acronym for the famous Generalnyi (formerly Gosudarstvennyi) Universalnyi Magazin, or "general department store," on Moscow's Red Square. During the Soviet era, special closed shops in GUM and elsewhere catered exclusively to high Party officials.

6. After his ouster from the Communist Party Politburo in 1987, Yeltsin suffered through a period of depression and political marginalization, during which he often seemed disoriented in public appearances, including those on a trip to the United States. However, his energy and popularity were largely restored by the second half of 1988. In October 1989, Yeltsin was discovered emerging from a still-unexplained late-night dip in the Moscow River; at first he said that he was pushed into the water by unnamed assailants, but he later retracted the accusation.

Chapter 4: August of Ninety-one

1. GKChP is the Russian acronym for Gosudarstvennyi Komitet dlya Chrezvychainogo Polozheniya, the State Committee for the Emergency Situation. This is the official name adopted by the short-lived government of the leaders of the August coup in 1991.

2. General Valentin Varennikov, former commander of the ground forces of the Soviet Army, and General Albert Makashov, former commander of the Volga Military District, supported the GKChP during the August 1991 coup attempt and were subsequently dismissed from their positions by Yeltsin. Makashov played a key role in organizing the military attack on the Ostankino television center during the battle between Yeltsin and the Russian Congress of People's Deputies in 1993; he was arrested and imprisoned, but was later amnestied by the State Duma in February 1994. Both Varennikov and Makashov have continued to play an active role in Russian nationalist circles.

3. Gennady Burbulis was Yeltsin's main political adviser in 1991–92. A former teacher of "scientific communism" in Sverdlovsk, Yeltsin's home base, he

became an outspoken advocate of shock therapy and an equally outspoken critic of Yeltsin's adversaries in the congress.

4. Here Gaidar refers to the fact that just eight months after the collapse of tsarism in March 1917 (the "February Revolution" by the old Julian calendar), Lenin and the Bolsheviks took power.

5. The Communist Party was hierarchically organized, with obkoms (regional committees) and kraikoms (territorial committees) directing the work of various raikoms (city and district committees) at the local level.

6. Aleksandr Kabakov's novel *Nevozvrashchenets* (*The Defector*), which predicted an apocalyptic post-Soviet Moscow under military dictatorship and filled with roving bands of delinquents, Stalinists, and ultranationalist thugs, was first published in 1989.

Chapter 5: On the Eve . . .

1. Nikolai Nekrasov (1821–1877), a contemporary of Dostoevsky's, and the leading Russian poet of the latter half of the nineteenth century, wrote both civic and folkoresque verse featuring peasant life and speech. He also edited the best-known literary review of the time. Gaidar is quoting his long poem, *Who Is Happy in Russia?*, written between 1863 and 1877.

2. Baron Munchausen was the picaresque hero of a book by Rudolph Erich Raspe (1785). Munchausen was based on a real historical character prone to fantastic exaggerations both of his own prowess and of the events in which he took part, one of which was the Russo-Turkish war of 1720–97.

3. In January 1991, Valentin Pavlov, the last Soviet prime minister, announced a sudden confiscation of 50- and 100-ruble notes that did much to end all remaining public confidence in the Soviet currency.

4. Ivan Silaev was the Russian prime minister from the First Congress of People's Deputies in June 1990 until shortly after the August coup, when he and Yeltsin split over the degree to which Russia should break away from all-Union administrative structures. Gaidar took Yeltsin's side in this dispute. Silaev resigned on September 27, 1991, after Yeltsin criticized the Silaev government in the press.

5. DemRossiya, short for Democratic Russia, was the umbrella organization uniting the Russian "democrats" during the period of Yeltsin's ascendancy. After 1993, DemRossiya became a relatively marginal force in Russian politics.

6. Russian medicine still uses a traditional remedy called "cupping": glass cups are swabbed out with alcohol, then a match is lit inside them to create a vac-

uum. They are then placed on the patient's back or chest to promote circulation and break up congestion.

Chapter 6: The First Step Is Always the Hardest

1. Gosplan is the Russian abbreviation for Gosudarstvennyi Planovyi Komitet SSSR, or State Planning Committee of the USSR. During the Soviet period, Gosplan was responsible for economic decision making in practically every sphere of production.

2. Goznak is the Russian abbreviation for Gosudarstvennoe Upravlenie po Vypusku Denezhnikh Znakov, or State Directorate for the Issuance of Currency.

3. Roskhleboprodukt is a short name for the Russian bread products monopoly.

4. Gossnab is the Russian abbreviation for the Gosudarsvennyi Komitet po Materialno-tekhnicheskogo Snabzheniya, or State Material-Technical Supply Committee. Its function—performed with only limited success—was to ensure delivery of needed supplies to enterprises trying to fulfill their official planned production targets.

5. Viktor Ilyushin has long been one of Yeltsin's closest aides.

6. Our Home Is Russia is the political party formed in April 1995, with Yeltsin's backing, to support "centrism" in Russian politics. It was led by former Prime Minister Viktor Chernomyrdin.

7. Yevgeny Primakov, a former academician and expert on Middle Eastern affairs, was the first post-Soviet director of the Russian Foreign Intelligence Service. In 1996 he was promoted to the position of Foreign Minister; and in 1998 he was named Prime Minister, only to be fired from that position by Yeltsin in 1999.

8. Ostap Bender, a character in the 1920s satirical novels of Ilya Ilf and Yevgeny Petrov, schemes his way to riches by fooling Soviet bureaucrats.

9. Minfin is short for Ministry of Finance.

10. From a letter to James Madison, dated March 15, 1789, in *The Republic of Letters: The Correspondence between Thomas Jefferson and James Madison, 1776– 1826,* ed. James Morton Smith (New York: Norton, 1995), p. 588.

11. Gaidar's joke here refers to the fact that under the Soviet system the "government" had responsibility primarily for economic and social policies; "political" issues were always referred directly to the Communist Party, directed by the Politburo.

12. Vneshekonombank stands for Foreign Economic Bank. During Soviet times it had a monopoly on the Soviet state's international financial transactions.

13. The March 1918 Treaty of Brest-Litovsk marked Russia's official with-

drawal from the First World War against Germany. Lenin, against the objections of some of his more impatient associates, gave up large areas of land formerly belonging to the Russian Empire, including much of Ukraine and Belorussia, in return for peace; the Bolsheviks later retook most of these lands after Germany's defeat by the Allies in the fall of 1918.

14. The Belovezh Forest meeting between the leaders of Russia, Belarus, and Ukraine led to the declaration of the Commonwealth of Independent States and the final breakup of the USSR.

Chapter 7: The Terrible Winter of Ninety-one

1. "Thick journals" are those published for a serious intellectual audience. With the collapse of Soviet subsidies in 1991, changing consumer tastes, and the skyrocketing prices of supplies, many such journals were threatened with imminent bankruptcy.

2. Detskii Mir, or Child's World, is the biggest toy store in downtown Moscow. It stands next to the headquarters of the former KGB.

3. Kolkhoz means collective farm; sovkhoz means state farm. In Soviet theory, the sovkhoz was supposed to be run along the same lines as industry, and therefore was considered more purely "socialist" than the kolkhoz. In practice, both types of farm were prone to inefficiency and low morale.

4. Gaidar here refers to Rutskoi's famous depiction of him and his young team of market reformers.

5. Yegor Ligachev, Gorbachev's orthodox Leninist second-in-command at the beginning of perestroika, was, in 1989, demoted to the position of Secretary of Agriculture of the Central Committee of the Communist Party of USSR. He was dismissed from the party leadership altogether in 1990.

Chapter 8: An Accurate Forecast

1. Gaidar discusses the Chechen promissory note scandal in Chapter 13.

2. Sergei Witte, Pyotr Stolypin, and Vladimir Kokovtsev each served for a time as prime minister under Tsar Nicholas II.

Chapter 9: Dismissal

1. The Civic Union, led by Arkady Volsky, was an avowedly "centrist" organization uniting various representatives of the military-industrial complex in the Russian Congress of People's Deputies.

2. The reference is to the "esteemed chairman" of the Russian Congress of People's Deputies, Ruslan Khasbulatov.

3. Ludwig Erhard was West German chancellor from 1963 to 1966 and a proponent of expanding the welfare state.

4. *A Roadside Picnic* (*Piknik na Obochine*) was originally written by the Strugatsky brothers in 1971. The novel depicts a future Earth, which has been visited by aliens who have scattered their unearthly debris in five "zones of visitation." The "witches' jelly" is the name given in the book to a strange, gooey, glowing substance left in the cellars of one such "zone"; accidentally stepping in it while exploring the area is fatal.

5. AZLK stands for Avtomobilnyi Zavod imeni Leninskogo Komsomola, or Leninist Communist Youth League Automobile Factory, the auto plant in Moscow that produced the Soviet compact known as the Moskvich.

6. Valery Zorkin was the head of the Russian Constitutional Court from 1991 through 1993. During the October clash between Yeltsin and the Russian Congress of People's Deputies he sided with the congress and was subsequently dismissed by Yeltsin after the attack on the White House.

7. *Dvoevlastie*, or dual power, is the term used by historians to describe the period between March and November 1917 in which two centers of authority, the Provisional Government and the Petrograd Soviet, issued contradictory orders and thus undermined the coherence of the Russian state.

Chapter 10: Dvoevlastie

1. In Russian the institute would be abbreviated IEPPP (Institut Ekonomicheskikh Problem Perekhodnogo Perioda).

2. The "House on the Embankment" was a building on the Berseniev Embankment, best known as an exclusive apartment house for high-level Party members and government officials.

3. The referendum of April 1993 asked the Russian population to vote "yes" or "no" on four questions: (1) "Do you have confidence in the President of the Russian Federation, Boris Yeltsin?" (2) "Do you approve of the socioeconomic policies carried out by the President of the Russian Federation since 1992?" (3) "Do you consider it necessary to hold early elections to the presidency of the Russian Federation?" and (4) "Do you consider it necessary to hold early elections of the people's deputies of the Russian Federation?" The referendum was a stunning victory for Yeltsin and his team, as majorities voted yes on every question except the third.

4. Aleksandr Rutskoi, Yeltsin's vice president, announced shortly before the April 1993 referendum that he had in his possession "eleven suitcases" full of

compromising material documenting corruption in Yeltsin's government; he named Gaidar in particular as having benefited from improper deals on foreign trade. Rutskoi never backed up these accusations with any hard evidence.

Chapter 11: The Battle

1. Russia's Choice, since renamed Russia's Democratic Choice, is the political party headed by Gaidar. He discusses the party in greater detail below.

2. The OMON are the special forces of the Ministry of Internal Affairs (MVD), also known as the "black berets."

3. The Vityaz troops are a special unit of the former elite Dzerzhinsky Division of the MVD. Such units have been considered more reliable than regular military divisions in combat situations such as the battle with the Congress of People's Deputies in 1993.

4. Vladimir Dmitrievich Nabokov (1870–1922), well-known jurist and member of the Kadet party, and father of novelist Vladimir Nabokov, served briefly as head of the Chancellery for the Provisional Government after Tsar Nicholas II's abdication in February 1917. Gaidar is quoting, with minor cuts, a passage from Nabokov's memoir *Vremennoe Pravitelstvo* (*The Provisional Government*), which appeared in the émigré historical journal *Archives of the Russian Revolution*, published in Berlin between 1921 and 1937.

5. Aleksandr Kerensky was a moderate socialist who led the Provisional Government, made up of former members of the tsar's Duma, from May 1917 until the Bolshevik takeover. General Lavr Kornilov made a halfhearted coup attempt against the Provisional Government in September 1917. General P. N. Krasnov led troops loyal to Kerensky in a battle against the Bolsheviks shortly after the fall of the Provisional Government; he later became a leading White Army commander.

6. Viktor Anpilov is the leader of the Working Russia movement, a hard-line Leninist and anti-Semitic organization that calls for a "second Bolshevik Revolution" against the Yeltsin regime. Aleksandr Barkashov is the leader of the Russian National Unity, an avowedly neo-Nazi organization.

7. F. F. Raskolnikov, *Kronshtadt i Piter v 1917 godu* (*Kronstadt and Petrograd in 1917*) (Moscow: Politizdat, 1990), p. 131. Raskolnikov is referring to events leading up to the failed Bolshevik coup of July 16–18, 1917. He adds that when Kronstadt soldiers, sailors, and workers sailed for Petrograd to take part in a demonstration on July 4, the Provisional Government not only could have forced the ships to turn back, but could have sunk them, thus ridding itself of a number of Party leaders as well as followers.

Chapter 12: Lost Opportunities

1. The Volga sedan is a Russian-made automobile designed in the Soviet era.

2. Aleksandr Korzhakov was for many years Yeltsin's personal bodyguard and one of his closest political advisers. Mikhail Barsukov was the former head of state security and an ally of Korzhakov's. Both were fired by Yeltsin amid a pre-election shakeup in June 1996.

3. "Black Tuesday" refers to October 11, 1994, when the ruble lost over 27 percent of its value in a single day's trading.

4. Budyonnovsk is a small southern Russian city where Chechen rebels under the command of Shamil Basaev took two thousand Russian citizens hostage in June 1995. Since Yeltsin was out of the country at the time, then Prime Minister Chernomyrdin opened negotiations with Basaev that ultimately led to the release of the surviving hostages and the safe return of Basaev's forces to Chechnya. Some critics felt that Chernomyrdin dealt too leniently with the Chechen rebels under the circumstances.

Chapter 13: Democracy and Chechnya

1. Mozdok is the site of a major Russian military base in the region of North Ossetia, neighboring Chechnya.

2. May 9 is Victory Day, the holiday celebrating the defeat of Nazism in World War II. It is customary in Russia to spend part of the day laying flowers at a war memorial.

Index

Yushenkov, Sergei, 106, 260, 281, 283

Zadonsky, Georgy, 106
Zadornov, Mikhail, 260
Zaslavsky, Ilya, 260
Zhirinovsky, Vladimir, 265, 299

Zhuravskaya, Yelena, 54
Zolotukhin, Boris, 106, 260, 274, 290
Zorkin, Valery, 194–95, 221–22, 328n
Zyuganov, Gennady, xxi, 301, 321–322n